D1826389

Against the Personification
of Democracy

Against the Personification
of Democracy

A Lacanian Critique of Political Subjectivity

by
Wesley C. Swedlow

continuum

NEW YORK • LONDON

2010

The Continuum International Publishing Group Inc
80 Maiden Lane, New York, NY 10038

The Continuum International Publishing Group Ltd
The Tower Building, 11 York Road, London SE1 7NX

www.continuumbooks.com

Library of Congress Cataloging-in-Publication Data
A catalog record for this book is available from the Library of Congress.

ISBN: 978-0-8264-3421-0

Typeset by Newgen Imaging Systems Pvt Ltd, Chennai, India
Printed in the United States of America

Contents

Introduction: Problems with Reality 1

Chapter 1 Desire and Ideology in the *Leviathan* 16
   1. Rational Action 19
   2. Reckoning Reason 24
   3. Passion and Power 27
   4. Hobbesian Ideological State Apparatuses 34
   5. The Politicization of Desire 39

Chapter 2 Internal Externalities 49
   1. The Spirit of the Letter 49
   2. Money or Life? 54
   3. Stateless Nature 64
   4. Universal Oblivion 67
   5. Biological Violence 72
   6. Persona Non Grata 77

Chapter 3 The Return of the Political 87
   1. Being All That You Can't Be: The Mirror Stage 92
   2. Money or Life: Alienation and Existence 95
   3. Signifying Nothing 100
   4. The Paternal Metaphor and its Phallusy 107
   5. *Che Voi?* From Separation to Desire 114
   6. Traversing the Fantasy 120
   7. The Return of the Political 124

Chapter 4 The Personification of Democracy................... 136
    1. The Gutting of the Sovereign: Lefort's Democratic Void 142
    2. Laclau and Mouffe's Hegemonic Strategy 146
    3. Lacan as Theorist of Democracy 153
    4. Only an Act Can Save Us.............................160

Conclusion: Against the Personification of Democracy 180

Index 197

Introduction: Problems with Reality

We accept reality easily, perhaps because we intuit that nothing is real.

—*Borges*

The disjunction between the real and reality is difficult to parse out, particularly because it is unnerving to think that such a distinction even exists. On first glance, both would seem to indicate what is true in existence, and yet the notion that experience is often deceptive is a proposition that shocks no one, though it pleases few. To add insult to injury, the deception of experience does not bear with it any concomitant and infallible set of criteria by which to make the distinction. As such, it indicates that perhaps there is no real at all, but rather a series of appearances that are, at best, temporarily coherent. Indeed, Borges' suggestion that reality is much easier to accept in lieu of the Real gets at the brunt of the issue, for is it not easier to take things at face value than to dwell in the thought that there is nothing behind the mask? The paradox that ensues is that while we know that the Real is not within our grasp, we cling to a reality that indicates truth nonetheless, one that is essentially reducible to a state of fantasy.

Reality thus delineated by an absence of the Real elaborates a fine etching of the logic of the subject that constitutes the main focus of this work; namely, desire. For the difference that one obtains when the Real is subtracted from experience creates reality, which can only be defined as the fantasy of the Real reinstated through inevitably failed projections of its obtainment. That is, we constantly stage moments of reality for ourselves in order to cover over the nagging suspicion that such staging is not in and of itself connected with a more basic and necessary truth. As such, desire is nonetheless productive of an altogether wonderful and distant truth. Desire thus creates its various forms of the fantasy that we can be "somewhat

1

nearer to what *is*. . . ."[1] The Real is over there, on the other side of reality. The trick of the process is therefore that the Real gets produced through our seeking it. As such, insofar as there is by definition a gap in reality, a factor that makes it incomplete and not wholly truthful, that gap is taken for the Real, something by which we can hope, however consciously, if only because of its very absence. But the logic is yet more twisted—the Real is palatable only insofar as it is filtered by its fantasies, or reality. To truly face the Real is not such a pleasant experience given that it arrives only as the very loss of reality and all of its attendant supports in fantasy.

Perhaps it was Rousseau, in his peripatetic solitude, who best understood the vicissitudes of this fantasy-driven reality, for he saw that the desire for a return could only happen in opposition to our weathered, knowing bodies, bodies ravaged by our desire and the desire of others:

> For how can the source of inequality among men be known without first knowing men themselves? And how will man ever succeed in seeing himself as Nature formed him, through all the changes which the succession of times and of things must have wrought in his original constitution . . . ? Like the statue of Glaucus which time, sea, and storms had so disfigured that it less resembled a god than a ferocious Beast, the human soul, altered in the lap of society by a thousand forever recurring causes, by the acquisition of a mass of knowledge and errors, by the changes that have taken place in the constitution of bodies, and by the continual impact of the passions, has, so to speak, changed in appearance to the point of being almost unrecognizable. . . .[2]

Wizened by time, hungry for balance in the face of a ferocious society of men, Rousseau tells us that we are compelled to return to our original design. In so doing, we are left to ponder what we were before we became who we are such that our being is almost impossible to recover, perverted as it is by the social inanities of an *amore propre*. The dream of recovered authenticity, of course, has yet to wake unchanged. This fact, though, does not prevent the "thousand forever recurring causes" from recurring nonetheless, for, as Rousseau understood, nothing has put a stop to them—a point we can derive from the fact that the original was a statue to begin with, an artificial construction of a god no less. Again, the dream of reality and its repetitions are the result of an unnerving intuition, an intuition that the dream of the Real, the unfettered and unadorned self, is false. But why, we are left to wonder, does the intuition create its own falsehood, a belief in reality nonetheless?

This work argues that the answer is to be found in the conundrum of desire. Indeed, I will argue that we must return to the seemingly hoary notion of the state of nature in order to accomplish a number of tasks. To begin with, we must reorient ourselves with the problem that is often overlooked in contemporary political philosophy—that of subjectivity. For it is one of the primary views here that the political, whatever it might be, cannot be understood severed from subjectivity. That cohabitation of a plurality, wherein the question of the authentic state of the many always reigns, cannot be answered until we know the plurality itself. Hence, the problem of the natural human, the human outside of any given political formation is our starting point. Of course, it is impossible to bluntly affirm a sort of political vacuum wherein we can analyze subjectivity in a purely ahistorical fashion. However, it is possible to seek within the excesses and failures of government the manner in which they are conditional for it, whatever form it takes. Though there are many who, like Giorgio Agamben, reject out of hand such a necessary relation, what he terms " the suggestive notion of a parallelism between external and internal neuroses . . . ,"[3] this work argues that the issue of desire points to a division in subjectivity that is indeed internal, as well, to the political. This division is found within the distinction between the public and the private, one that occurs both personally and politically. Subjectively speaking, this division has as its two factors the person and the persona, or the natural self and its public presentation. Politically speaking, it is located in the fact that 'the state of nature' is but the inverse of the equally necessary formulation 'the nature of state'. The object of desire, as Lacan pointed out, is no real object insofar as it is an object of the Real. The real object does not exist, and yet its nonexistence is productive of desire's endless crawl toward it nonetheless. This crawling is made by individuals and political formations alike, and such shared impossibility is the primary logical link between the two as an outgrowth of the fact that the former composes the later.

While there is no single object of desire, and though its proliferations are as varied as humanity, for want of a better word, itself, it shares in all of its formations a single attribute that connects us all, though, in the end, doing so only by dissolving all necessary connections. In effect, subjectivity is defined by a primal loss that, in its instantiation through language, forces it to seek an ever receding primary truth. This seeking, otherwise called desire, is always an anxious seeking given its impossible task. Thus, to use Borges' terminology, the very relationship between the reality that is accepted and the impossibility of the Real creates desire. For insofar as we sense that something most important is missing, we search through reality or, better put, invest reality with answers, with something to believe in, something to put in the place of that lost and very Real object, reality itself. And because the object is not in any verifiable or even intuitive form *there*, the relationship is doomed to an endless proliferation of metaphors for its hopeful recovery, metaphors such as a statue of Glaucus, the sun outside of a cave, an infallible and undeceiving God, a leader with vision, Man, Woman, Rights, and so on. The absence of the Real is productive of reality, and it is from this failed and lost site of productivity that all of the fantastic, fetishist forms of society emanate.

The primary result of the impossibility of desire qua definitional of the political leads to our second thesis: in the divide between the public persona qua represented and the natural person qua unadorned, stripped of all social clothing, the political must exist in and for the person, not the persona. The so-called clash of civilizations, in which Western representative democracy faces down an increasingly theocratic absolutism, obfuscates the fact that in each political case, such personas will find various ways to destroy any persons deemed unworthy of recognition. In other words, the current unifying factor (and thus contradiction) par excellence is that neither democracy nor totalitarianism outright lead anywhere but the same place—a drive toward imperialist, militarist expansion predicated on the principle of pure sovereignty. The right of any country or grouping is based on the assumption of a protected persona, or, otherwise put, a set of persons who are properly outfitted with certain socially codified protections in the name of which concrete power apparatuses will be deployed. Because, for instance, the body of the U.S. has been infringed upon, the power of the U.S. to protect itself allows it to create rules as it sees fit designating who is within the law or, more notoriously, who is not. Similarly, Islamic fundamentalist will commit serial murder in the name of destroying inauthentic persons—persons who do not fit into the proper definition of a particularly elaborated persona. Both, in other words, are defined in their ability to make, as Carl Schmitt put it, the friend/enemy distinction, and thus both achieve a similar result: the destruction of persons (enemies) in the name of personas (friends). One should note, of course, that this is a logical function at work in sovereignty and the sovereign, one that cannot be reductive to any given sovereign. Nonetheless, the fact of the sovereign decision is always at play, always possible, and often used.

As can be seen from the previous, a persona functions as a socially constructed and invested conception of what a proper self is while, conversely, a person functions as that self which has been stripped to varying degrees of social legitimacy. The former is the fantasy against which the latter will do much in overcompensation. As such, the person is a negation to the persona—it indicates to the persona that it is simultaneously constructed and subject to loss, whether we speak of an individual or a plurality. To the degree that the person negates the persona, it is antithetical to desire, which falls squarely on the side of the persona. Furthermore, desire, the incessant seeking of an object which does not exist save in fantasy, must by definition fail, and this failure requires explanation. The perfect object of this reasoning is an object that is abject and thus antithetical to the fantasies of desire, which takes, in the human form, that of the person. The practices of sovereign states have shown that the best way to clear the path to having one's way with people is to legally and socially dehumanize them, a point which Hannah Arendt made some time ago. This insight leads to another fact of the logic of desire: the Real, the perfected object of desire as impossible, has two modalities. To the extent that it is invested positively, the object is an ideal object that functions by virtue of its impossible obtainment. However, to the extent that the object shows itself as impossible, as stripped of all fantasy, the Real functions as expression of the gap in desire, a gap which is reprehensible to the continued functioning of subjectivity within its normal operations. As such, in a simplified form, the person (enemy)/persona (friend) distinction can also be formulated as: person (Real-gap)/persona (reality-fantasy).

Of course, all theories have their assumptions, though the one operating here is as old as Plato's *Republic*, if not older. I start with the presumption that the political requires, on some basic level, the commodious living of its subjects. I, in other words, reject Thrasymachus, and with him Schmitt, and concur that the political exists in and for the maximization of commodious living for all persons, not personas.[4] Given that a persona indicates, through various forms of legitimized identification (nation, ethnicity, creed, religion, sexuation, class, etc.), a *delimited* grouping by definition, the political, in its most universal sense and in the promotion of commodious living is appropriate only to the person. Hence all persons are legitimately covered by the political, and the political is illegitimate insofar as it is applied only to a subset of personas. Such is the main conclusion of this work, and we will attempt to elaborate it by beginning with a figure who was thoroughly preoccupied with desire: Thomas Hobbes. The first chapter, then, will be our starting point both numerically and theoretically. In it I will make the argument that Hobbes was neither a master rational action theorist, as Russell Hardin has claimed, nor a proto-bourgeois nihilist, as Hannah Arendt and C. B. Macpherson have argued, at least not primarily. Rather, he was a thinker entirely convinced that the cause of all social decay was desire, an unsatisfiable and unavoidable trait of the human condition, a trait that is deadly because it is thoroughly social. No less, and less noted, Hobbes was also a grand thinker of ideology, a point which functions as the bookend to his ruminations on desire. For only insofar as there is a grand master to take up the desire of subjectivity can the social body retain cohesion in the face of itself. There must be, in other words, an Other to fill the treacherous gap of desire, and this Other must actively interpellate its subjects into obedience. Hobbes, as we shall see, will have much to say about the current situation in Iraq, though it will also become evident that ideology does not necessarily ameliorate the issues of desire.

In essence, then, the first chapter will set up the problem of desire by providing a formal model that establishes its logic as one of an inherently anxious and thus impossible satisfaction, and in doing so it will allow us to ask a two-pronged question: is desire the fundamental force of humankind, and if it is, what are its political implications? The question will be extended in the second chapter, where the concept of the state of nature will be taken seriously. We will restage the debate between Hobbes and Locke in order to see who has the correct view of our natural condition. While it is clear that Hobbes will be the pyrrhic victor in the debate, in answering this question, however, a second argument will be made; namely, that the state of nature is neither an abstraction nor a theoretical pleasantry. Rather, it is to be understood as a metaphysical condition of the political, internal to its structure by virtue of its externality. As such, it is not a temporal condition, something coming before or after political formations (though that is an aspect of it). Rather, it is internal to the political as the division of the social body that always threatens its decay, what Hobbes called fractiousness. There is no such thing, in other words, as a political body that is not already fractured and subject to dissolution. This is its state of nature. On the other hand, the political is internal to the natural insofar as subjectivity always seeks out stability in the form of a grouping that attempts some form of commodious living. The state of nature, the argument goes, is an internal externality, something that cannot be avoided by producing even the best social arrangements, and the theoretical result of the metaphysical reality of the state of nature is that the converse formulation is also necessary; namely, the nature of state.

Still, the question of the fundamental disagreement between Hobbes and Locke is not resolved by arguing for the reality of the state of nature. Nor can the argument be overcome on the merits of their positions alone. As such, a third is required, and Hannah Arendt is precisely that dialectical element that indicates why Hobbes is correct in naming desire the social mortal coil and, at a higher level, indicates the manner in which such desire expresses the universal. Hence, in Arendt's discussion of the stateless in World War II, she argues that it was the absolutely generic universality of the stateless, in conjunction with certain historical conditions, that made them repugnant and caused in others a desire for their extermination. This broaches a question: why would the universality of the human ignite mass-scale murder? What is it about ourselves that makes our essential condition so undesirable? In order to answer this question, we turn to Arendt's thought on violence. In so doing, three stages of violence are uncovered: one physical, one psychological, and one biologically primordial. Arendt only explicitly distinguishes physical violence in her work, but the other two are constantly at play, especially when she attempts to articulate her concept of the social. And though Arendt essentially dismisses psychology as a pseudoscience that produces a mere check file of human horrors, in the process she ironically articulates an essentially psychoanalytic concept: the idea that the human is split between a dark interior that is only kept at bay by a public persona.

In so doing, Arendt produces an argument for why the state of nature, a state in which the *homo sapiens* becomes mere *homo* and thus repellently violent. In other words, she makes the Hobbesian case, but thoroughly complicates the notion of desire. While Hobbes' idea of desire was that we are incessantly in need of further objects of satisfaction, with no final goal, Arendt saw that there were different levels to the human. In so doing, she outlines a problem about the public self; namely, that when we attempt to make public what is most private and most dark about ourselves, we suffer from a Cartesian doubt so impossible that it tips over into a rapacious need for cleansing, thus eliciting a Superego-like faculty. At the heart of the soul is thus an irresolvable doubt by which attempting to verify it produces an anxious and murderous result. On the other hand, when others are stripped of their social wares, their image is so disgustingly unbearable that the bulk of us have a need to destroy it, as was done to the stateless. Arendt thus uncovers a dyad of psychological death and destruction. Seeking the purified self only ends in misery, a misery whose core logic is reproduced in encountering the universal self.

But Hobbes and Arendt leave us with a number of questions, questions reducible to the following: why is the universal self repugnant? What drives these reactions into reality, especially if, as both contend, they are mainly the result of fantasies? Arendt muses that there must be some profound violence both to the beginning of all societies and to the beginning of all properly beating hearts, an unthematized counterpart to her concept of natality. But what is the nature of this violence or, more correctly, what is its cause?

In the third chapter, then, I turn to Jacques Lacan to provide an answer. What we will find is less than felicitous, however, for while Lacan's theory of the subject begins to explicate the reasons that Hobbes and Arendt are led to a deadly and very public concept of desire, one that is inextricably linked with the problem of our persona, or our symbolic ego, Lacan argues that the impossibility of desire is rooted neither in a universal motion, as Hobbes thought, nor in a primordial biological voraciousness that needs to be kept in its proper realm, as Arendt proposed, but in the very formation of subjectivity in its normal socialization. As such, the problem of desire is the problem of the human condition. In the creation of a normalized subjectivity, the subject suffers the loss of the Other, but on the basis of an imagined presence that was never really there. What the subject loses, then, is something that never quite existed, though the subject fantasizes nonetheless that the loss can be recovered. The statue will be returned to its original state, the sun will shine brightly, the nation will be led clearly and divinely, and so on.

But it is not so direct as that. The loss of the subject is ameliorated by a fantasy of fulfillment, no doubt, but all subjects fantasize differently, and they do so unconsciously. Our daily certainties are mere covers for an essential uncertainty, for a basic lack that has, indeed, torn our heart in two. But the answer is not simply to keep that private realm private, as Arendt thought. For the unquenchable repetition that lies just below it is a sign of a force that will not go away. That force is none other than drive. While the notion of the conscious versus the unconscious self is nothing new, Lacan's argument concerning drive twists it into a partialized arena that produces an unbearable and surplus *jouissance*.[5] What was repressed, what was forbidden in the creation of the thinking substance that we call a self is the pleasure of the Other, the terrible, painful pleasure of a fully sensual and unbridled connection. But while subjectification will ameliorate the impossibility of this pleasure, it will not disappear; its supposed original unity is rather atomized, turned into continuously repeating unconscious excesses that always seek a return onto themselves, unto that lost unity. These are the partial drives, which are, Lacan argues, all death drives: for they circulate around an essential loss of the self via the Other, seeking constantly and, to the chagrin of our socialized selves, with an unmentionable excess of pleasure. This extra, forbidden, and unconscionable pleasure is our *jouissance*, and it is only via our fantasy laden selves that we avoid it, allowing us to see ourselves in an acceptable, socially realizable form. The problem is that this form is not our true desire. There is thus a disconnect between who we think we are and what we truly seek to be and to have (to have and to hold, we say, because the two do not necessarily go hand in hand), and this unconscious, generally inaccessible undercurrent (though in slips, mistakes, and jokes we glimpse it) is not to be taken as the true, authentic inner child. Rather, it is the turn around a loss, and what one must come to see in the therapeutic process, in the traversal of the fantasy, is that, as Gertrude Stein said upon learning that her childhood home had been demolished, "there's no there there." The phrase and its background are telling; one cannot go home again, but, in a sense, the return brings an inverted biblical message: in the beginning was the loss. To return to our previous language, the persona, the represented entity on a legitimized social stage, is a cover for the person in all of us, the stripped and unbearable, empty universal being that, at its core, is undesirable *and* conditional. It cannot be escaped while, and herein lies the deadlock of subjectivity, the persona cannot not escape it nonetheless.

Hence the reason that desire is infinite, as Hobbes thought, that there is no *summum bonum*, is because there is no first good, no real object to begin with. Desire is based on a demand for the ultimate object, for a pure and unrefined love, but it never gets it and seeks it by other fantastic means. It is a painful loss of a nonexistent object that the subject loses, what Lacan calls the *objet a*,[6] and it explains further why Arendt was correct in arguing that our split selves can withstand neither a full and public internal review nor face the other who has been universalized: seeking the purified self means facing the fact that it does not exist, and thus means seeking an impossible object directly, which can only end in revealing an internal tragedy. Conversely, in seeing the subject with no social safety, with no persona to provide, the self sees its own repulsive failure, its own internal and unbearable loss. It is not surprising, then, that the fantasy would want to maintain itself, that the persona would fight against the natural, especially by means of an Other who has an ideology ready to hand. In each case, whether it is one's own or that of another, a persona encounters a person in total recoil.

This, then, leads to our final chapter, a chapter on the political implications of subjectivity, though narrowly defined. Though the traditional question of the political implications of subjectivity often requires arguing through all political formations, a different route will be taken. Rather, with the assumption these days, for the most part, that democracy is the only plausible political alternative (which makes the notion of an alternative theoretically, though not practically, void), subjectivity as outlined in the previous chapters points to a crisis inherent to democracy. The very notion of the state of nature works on the assumption that, on some level, the nature of humankind, if we can come to understand it, will tell us what the correct political formation will be. The results of the state of nature as defined by desire thus provoke the following question: is democracy the best political formation for subjectivity given its person/persona divide? Does democracy in fact deal well with subjects to the degree that they themselves are suffering from a loss and a tendency toward fantasy-based answers?

Many in the radical democratic camp, such as Ernesto Laclau and Chantal Mouffe, Janis Stavrakakis, the early Slavoj Žižek, and Claude Lefort, almost invariably argue yes, and their arguments stem largely from considerations closely aligned with or directly derived from Lacanian theories of subjectivity. What is important about these theories of democracy is their view that because democracy, in its formal state, resembles a subject that is traversed and thus rid of fantasmatic attachments to an internal and truthful core, it is therefore the political form that is best suited to subjectivity as such. The argument stems from the understanding that subjectivity, society, and democracy all stem around an empty center, an essential impossibility. As such, while Claude Lefort's arguments are foundational insofar as he argues that the democratic adventure circulates around a void (for democracy cannot present anything other than the space of its own argument concerning the legitimate), Laclau and Mouffe show that this void extends further: the debate around legitimacy is itself a sign that there are those who have no voice. That the battle for the center is fought by some contestants who are not even recognized shows us that at the heart of democracy is an irresolvable conflict, which they call 'antagonism'. Antagonism, like Ranciere's concept of dissensus, is another name for the excluded, for the impossibility of utopia within society due to the fact that no representation is final, no description is the last, and thus no ideology is ever fully embodied. What is important about democracy, they argue, is that it provides a space for the articulation of the excommunicated, a way for the voiceless to find a place to speak.

But radical democratic theory, so defined, ought to listen more closely to Hobbes. For it does not deal with desire, nor does it even broach the underlying antagonism at the heart of subjectivity itself: the impossible, unavoidable *jouissance* that can be found quite clearly in the social body as much as our own. Thus the argument will be made that radical democratic theory does not see that in producing a realm of competing identifications with no final or ultimate answer, democracy replicates the deadlock of subjectivity itself, spurring on desire but giving it an explicit dead end of repetition (indeed, such theory repeats Locke's mistake of not taking into account the desire of demos). For this reason, rather than giving us a traversed political sphere, democracy only incites desire, leaving it anxious and all too ready for 'strong leadership', a leadership that might well be strong enough to negate democracy itself, something evidenced by the fear that all of them have of what Gramsci called an organic crisis, a total lack of identifiable reference points (which is, otherwise put, political psychosis). Another way to put this is that although it may be the case that democracy resembles a traversed subject insofar as it does not believe in any ultimate content, it does not therefore follow that the subjects of democracy stop wanting one. The radical democratic theorists have no clear response to this problem, not even a Lacanian such as Janis Stavrakakis. Though it would appear that he, in his explicitly Lacanian approach, would find a way out of this problem, such is not the case, for the issue of *jouissance* is not adequately broached. The problem of *jouissance* and, with it, drive, is that it is, as Freud argued, a constant force, a movement toward unseemly pleasure nonetheless, and only by returning to it, by coming to a new relationship with it, is a subject freed of its forbidden grip. This grip is held in place by fantasy, which is why the fantasy must be worked through (traversed) in order to reach one's core symptom. Similarly, for a society to be truly Lacanian, truly released of its fantasy, it would have to examine what is at the heart of its antagonism, what it desires most fundamentally and thus what it can afford least to admit to itself, thus forcing it to come out in a number of perverted, illegal, illicit, and, unfortunately, tacitly condoned ways. Or, it would have to restructure itself as the negation of its own fantasy-laden personification. Stavrakakis, like the radical theorists, fails to show us what such an admission or restructuring might look like or how we might endeavor toward them.

However, Slavoj Žižek does confront the problem of democracy quite directly, arguing that the call for a constant articulation by the radical democratic theorists only leaves us with a sort of bad political infinity, one that opens the way for ideological sutures to invade and provide the sort of passionate leadership that subjects desire. For him, then, the only truly liberating response is a Lacanian *act*, an attack on the fundamental fantasy of our current social configuration. This is, according to Žižek, none other than capitalism, the unquestioned presupposition of all current democratic theorists.[7] Only by negating capitalism, only by truly socializing our economy, can we destroy the fundamental fantasy that undergirds our belief that something, even if it is the market system, is giving meaning to the mad parade rolling onward. While it may be arguable whether capitalism is indeed the fundamental fantasy of the current political hegemony (perhaps, as Žižek himself seems to think sometimes, democracy itself is the unconscious assumption), the real problem with Žižek's formulation is that there is no clear way to accomplish a political act. While the therapeutic situation provides parameters for how to proceed, including, most importantly, an analyst and its desire, the political realm does not; the closest we have to an analyst would be a leader, but most leaders do not desire to be anything like an *objet a* qua impossible. Leaders are not elected by promising a painful and constant return to our social symptoms, a tearing apart of our social identity—such people are called terrorists. And if the alternative is a broad social movement, its arrival is rendered random. Indeed, the act, though it is arguably the highest moment of freedom, is something that just seems to happen to people, taking them by utter and necessary surprise. As a model of political praxis, the psychoanalytic act is lacking, thereby pointing to a fundamental problem with the combination of Lacanian psychoanalysis and political formations. As a theory of subjectivity, it is insightful, and as a critique of ideological tendencies in politics and society, it is disturbingly perceptive, but as an actual praxis, even in the guise of democracy, it is, interestingly enough, nothing. That is, there is no necessary psychoanalytic redemption in democracy, though there may be some serious implications between the two. There is, furthermore, no clear psychoanalytic political mode of action, at least in its democratic and act-driven forms, though there are definite uses of psychoanalysis for critiquing political acts and institutions. What radical democratic theory suffers, then, is the trap that, according to Russell Hardin, most traditional theory falls into, a fallacy of composition. What applies to the psychoanalytic subject does not necessarily also apply to its political formation. A psychoanalytic cure, in other words, may work on the couch, but it does not necessarily do so in the polis.

What psychoanalysis does tell us, however, is that between the person and its persona, between the *homo* and the *sapiens*, there is an irretrievable gap that, when things go awry, begins to explain why we unwittingly and, unfortunately, quite willingly succumb to various forms of reactive and active ideology, along with it exclusion, oppression, and violence. As such, because democracy can only ever circulate publicly around an empty center, there is no democracy as such, only personifications of democracy, indicating that democracy always drives, on the basis of its subjective conditions, toward some elaboration of one persona or another. Democracy is thus always the personification of democracy. In the process of personification, however, the natural, driven person does not go away, and it is the failure of dealing with this relationship proper, with no universal God or

Nature to fall back upon, that has left us with what Arendt called our "predicament of common responsibility." Democracy alone will not provide the answer to this predicament, for what subjects desire is something true, something universal, a knowledge that there is an Other to the Other, that society is grounded beyond itself in an unflinching realm of meaning. Democracy tells us that there is no such thing, but only through the sleight of hand that says, nonetheless, here it is. The more inclusive, the more radical, and thus more formal democracy becomes, particularly in its represented or parliamentarian modality, the more desire anxiously demands a reason to believe in it, to less and less avail.

To be for the political proper is therefore to be against the personification of democracy. For this reason, the notion of the empty center of democracy must be rethought and the political must be reconceived. Indeed, rather than a proliferation of sovereignties kept in check, the political must be eradicated from the space of fantasy and the play of representations. It cannot, in other words, be a realm of Arendtian freedom or, no less, a Lacanian act. This returns us again to our person/persona distinction—the universal human is represented by the unrepresentable, by persons, and protection, according to Arendt, is only to be found in the intensification of protection for the personas in the public space. While Arendt's notion of the universal human is central to the argument here, at the point of the political there is a divergence—the political is defined not so much by the division maintained between the dark interior of the person and the maintenance of a public space, but rather by the increased protection of the person on a universal scale. The universal human, in other words, achieves its political expression in the universalization of the political. The political functions then as anti-sovereignty and anti-persona and, more importantly, as not radically democratic. Radical democratic theory assumes a logic of 'yet one more'—yet one more subjectivity outside of legitimacy, yet one more issue that requires a political act to shake up the police state, to antagonize personas. As such, radical democracy is a kind of political bad infinity, a universalization without end, or, in the case of the act (and the same goes for the Badiouian event), it is reduced to a passive waiting, in which case agency remains either on the horizon or the specific privilege of a select few militants. Rather, the political must be already universal and, therefore, must identify with that which is most universal in the human condition, the person. Therefore, the logic of the political is the 'everyone already'; that is, the political in its most universal form must assume that every person is expressed by it, that no sharply delineated or narrowly defined grouping (set of personas) is somehow the legitimate heir of the political, however temporal the change of command. The results are as clear as they are counterintuitive; sovereignty is antipolitical for it, at best, can only ever promise the 'yet one more', and thus the sovereignty of nations functions, universally speaking, as an anti-person enterprise.

In the conclusion, we will see that the thinker who located the logic of the person in its universality, Hannah Arendt, also found its universally local space of appearance in the commune and the call for a world government. Nonetheless, she pulled back from the implications of her thinking, putting in their place a fear of world government and a space of appearance that is to be occupied only by those personas who enjoy public appearance. As such, Arendt's greatness is to be located in the level to which she understood the core political implications of the person, but she did not tarry with it to the end and fell into the trap of the sovereign persona. Rather, the truly political formulation would eradicate sovereignty from its registers and place in its stead the many localized voices of persons. As such, a political body must be total to the persons inhabiting the earth and is, in that sense, totalitarian. But to the extent that persons are only ever locatable in their given situation, that totality can only be composed of the localities of persons insofar as they are explicitly speaking to one another (and therefore existing within the social and material conditions of such a gathering). Thus, to the degree that no political formulation in the name of a chosen set of personas is valid, the political is antitotalitarian in the classic sense. The personification of democracy indicates the ever expanding proliferation of personas as they inhabit the empty center of the represented demos, drawing in the process a structural line of relation between democracy and totalitarianism. On the other hand, universal localization of the person requires the practice of the commodious living and speaking of all persons as composing the political body, thus indicating that political agency is always in the name of the continued presence, the 'everyone already', of persons qua universal and thus inhabiting the entirety of the planet. It is the task of this work to lay the foundations for making such an argument.

Notes

1 Plato, *The Republic*, trans. Allan Bloom (New York: Basic Books, 1991): 515d.

2 Jean-Jacques Rousseau, *The First and Second Discourses*, trans. Victor Gourevitch (New York: Harper & Row, 1990): 129.

3 Giorgio Agamben, *Homo Sacer: Sovereign Power and Bare Life*, trans. Daniel Heller-Roazen (California: Stanford University Press, 1998): 6.

4 Clearly, Plato was not averse to the personification of the political, and thus the philosopher king becomes the ultimate expression of 'one who knows'. Nonetheless, it is this early staging in the *Republic*, wherein Thrasymachus accosts Socrates and promotes a neo-Darwinian mode of justice, that encapsulates the raw aggression of personification. That they are on their way home on an open road could be said to represent the very rubric of the state of nature which we will be examining. It may be the case that Socrates' incessant publicity is to be opposed to Plato's radical systematicity. Ranciere thus argues that Plato had a "resolute hatred of democracy," although one that gave him insight into the essence of democracy nonetheless. Jacques Ranciere, *Dis-agreement: Politics and Philosophy*, trans. Julie Rose (Minneapolis: University of Minnesota Press, 1999): 10, hereafter referred to as *Dis-agreement*. See also chapter 4 of the same text. My work could be said to be somewhere between Plato and Ranciere, seeking as it does a totalitarian system that discounts none, but predicated on the very person, or, to use Ranciere's phrase, 'part that has no part' that he believes such systems negate.

5 *Jouissance* is left untranslated given that there is no equivalent in English that encapsulates the simultaneous pleasure and pain the term indicates. *Jouissance* thus points to the fact that even before alienation, a subject suffers its pleasure in the loss, the uncertainty, of its relation to the Other.

6 Rendered in English, the phrase would be object o, or object of the other. However, in order to maintain consistency throughout this work, I will use the French *objet a* formulation.

7 This disposition was expressed clearly at the beginning of the occupation of Iraq when L. Paul Bremer III declared the following: "A free economy and a free people go hand in hand. . . . History tells us that substantial and broadly held resources, protected by private property, private rights, are the best protection of political freedom. Building such prosperity in Iraq will be a key measure of our success here." *Washington Post*, 27, May 2003. Of course, in a sense Bremer was partially correct insofar as protection is an essential component of prosperity, though the Bush administration tellingly proceeded to protect only the oil fields.

1

Desire and Ideology in the *Leviathan*

Hobbes wrote his *Leviathan* to a large degree as a response to the civil wars that had, in his view, forced him out of his homeland. Of course, Hobbes, never one to be easily slotted, did not even get along all that well with the entirety of his own kind, for, ironically enough, it was in part fear of fellow royalist exiles which caused him to leave Paris and return to a more accommodating though parliamentarian England.[1] Of course, the irony is partial given that Hobbes was not an entirely traditional royalist, believing, for instance, that one had a right to self-preservation even against the sovereign.[2] Nonetheless, Hobbes obviously was no parliamentarian and argued rigorously and infamously that the Sovereign was a "mortal god" to whom one transfers, in essence, control over one's life in exchange for well-being.[3] Given the endless and tortured public wordplay on the subject of civil war and stability in Iraq, it is more than merely interesting to turn to the two questions that Hobbes brings to the fore: what is the human subject, and what, more importantly, motivates it in the face of other human subjects when none clearly hold power? In other words, does Hobbes have something to tell us not only about the causes and motivations of opposing forces in war but as well about all political institutions, democracy and totalitarianism included?

The short answer is yes, indeed, for Hobbes' ruminations on human anxiety and desire indicate that what is at stake in any social schism is ultimately a function of the relation between desire and ideology, not brute power. Hobbes' primary political concern is the level to which desire leads to fractiousness, destroying any possibility of a relatively structured life. In *Origins of Totalitarianism*, Hannah Arendt figured that it was this same fractiousness, internalized in the utilitarian individual, that paves the way for imperialism and, finally, an imploded subject that clings to powerful, unifying ideologies.[4] Indeed, four years previous to C. B. Macpherson's well-known version of the argument, Arendt proposes in her masterful work that it is to Hobbes that we owe our thanks for producing a prototypical bourgeois individual, an impressive accomplishment not least due to the fact that Hobbes knew only a mercantilist form of economic configuration. Nonetheless, Arendt's main point has less to do with issues in economy than what is missing in the Hobbesian subject; namely, humanity. For without a conception of humanity internal to the political, according to Arendt, we are doomed, either in the short or the long run. To this, Hobbes would reply that it is the lack of a powerfully unifying ideology united in a singular individual that truly dooms us to an inhumane existence.

Indeed, it is precisely this ideological Hobbes that is missing in so much theory about him, a lacuna that becomes especially apparent when talk turns to outlining a prototype of the market-driven, utility-oriented, and, broadly considered, value-free individual perfectly molded for the sort of economy that will form itself in the following centuries.[5] By ideology, I refer not merely to a system of ideas that attempts to describe the nature of reality from an arguably biased or reductive slant, but, more importantly, a system whereby juridical, cultural, pedagogical, and repressive institutions coalesce to create and inform subjects that are not merely receptive, but consciously aligned with the system of thought promoted. Such ideologically aligned subjects express something like what Antonio Gramsci called "spontaneous consent," a consent that does not need to be forced precisely because subjects' wills are already predisposed to agree.[6] It is to such an ideological mode of thinking that Hobbes will turn as the direct result of his fear of desire, of his sense that our subjective, natural constitution is so fractious, irrational, and isolated in its core that we have no other reasonable recourse than a full-fledged control of not simply the actions of individuals, but their very conscience. The Leviathan, in other words, must be artificially constructed against the nature of humankind, not in order to release its natural tendencies, as some think that democracy and market-driven economies do (a claim at which Hobbes would no doubt smile wryly), but in order to quell and then remold them.

The Hobbesian natural subject is thus structured in a faulty way, and only through a reasonable cultivation and unification of nature's impossible desire does it realize, via the Sovereign, a stable if artificial form. It is precisely this fearful subjectivity that we need to maintain as politically relevant, particularly now within the so-called democratic consensus of the current age. Hobbes, in other words, was right to fear subjectivity in its natural state, though I will also argue that he was nonetheless wrong to conclude that the heaviest possible weight of the political must therefore rest on the represented person, what he called a persona. Whatever degree of artificial staging the Sovereign may achieve, and whatever advanced theoretical ideological edifice Hobbes had constructed, both can only ever be formulated as an overcompensation that will always eventually face, to put it in Freudian terms, the return of the repressed. Insofar as the political is used to repress one of its internal definitions, such as subjectivity voided of its persona, or desire without its stabilized object, it negates part of its own definition, leading to intractable contradictions, which are nothing less than political symptoms. To eradicate the natural within the artificial is impossible, however powerful the sovereign state is. Indeed, the increase in its strength over its natural, fractious conditions will only ever be expressed in an increasing anxiety over the return of what has been so artfully excised. This is why Locke will turn out to be correct about the problem of monarchies—but not, as he had it, because one ought not trust in singular sovereigns who may be bad, but because, as Hobbes knew all too well, any given human will always succumb to the anxious projections in the name of its persona that motors our very being, otherwise called desire. But this means, pace Locke, that what applies to sovereigns also applies to democratic subjects.

I thus begin this work with Hobbes because he provides the greatest and most succinct model of a human and political subjectivity predicated on desire. While Leo Strauss is no doubt correct that the basis of the Hobbesian political science is fear,[7] the issue of the cause of this fear is of the greatest import in the establishment of the primary thesis of this text. Insofar as desire is paramount in the Hobbesian state of nature, a state of nature which will be, particularly in the second chapter, affirmed as necessary to thinking through the political, the kind of death that motivates the Hobbesian subject cannot be reduced to a physical end. Indeed, it is precisely because the end of life in Hobbes is defined as the end of desire that there is a second kind of death that is the functional ground to the war of all against all—this second death is an entirely social death, or a death of the persona. Because personas proliferate in ever exaggerated modalities of eminence in the state of nature, modalities whose uneven hubris can only serve to mutually assure a life of its destruction, thereby producing a state of abjection (which, by definition, teeters the subject between a brute personhood and the establishment of a more stable persona), an absolute Persona must be established in order to structure a well-ordered set of personas; i.e., the commonwealth. Or so Hobbes thought, as do we, though now we call it democracy, which is not to say that there is therefore no distinction between monarchy and democracy. Rather, it is to propose that what they ultimately share is personifications of the political, or imaginary instantiations predicated on the logic of the persona and, to a greater or lesser degree, the denial of persons.

In the first section of the following, then, I will produce a rational straw man of sorts, outlining the sort of utilitarian chooser that has become dear to political scientists and their model, the economist. We start with this subjectivity because it provides a clear counterpoint to the Hobbesian subject, despite the fact that many rational choice theorists find Hobbes to be thoroughly amenable to their arguments. In the second section, and in contradistinction to the free and rational chooser, I outline how Hobbes' concept of reason is the improbable and external result of the passions, thereby indicating that our passions are not in themselves reasonable, not even on a macro-level. In the third section, we will see how these passions are constituted by an impossible desire whose ultimate outcome in human agency is anxiety. In other words, the natural subject, the mere person that teeters in its desire for a stabilized persona, in the Hobbesian state of nature is an anxious and desirous one, and it is precisely from this anxious desire that Hobbes derived the need for an external Other, a unifying entity otherwise known as the Sovereign. In section four, I will turn to Arendt's persuasive view that, by virtue of this disconnected and desire-filled natural subject, Hobbes established the blueprint for the bourgeois individual in advance of its bloody arrival on new continents. However, my reading of Hobbes indicates that he was appalled by the voracious nature of the atomized subject, so much so that he understands that politics meant its eradication via a full throttled indoctrination of the subject, a view that is not so different from how Althusser, through a Gramscian lens, saw ideology and its loci, ideological state apparatuses.[8] Lastly, we will return to the fallacious aspect of the Hobbesian conclusion concerning the Other, at least to the degree that it will pose so many questions as to force a new discussion in the second chapter about this state of nature. There, we will turn to Locke and, again, Arendt, to attempt to further settle the issue of both the nature of this natural subject and its proper political modality. At this point, however, I will now outline the vicissitudes of the liberal choice maker.

1. Rational Action

With the fall of the Berlin Wall in 1989 went the legitimacy of Marxism. It is currently nothing more or less than obvious that the failure of the USSR has entailed the failure of any socialist agenda.[9] Such socialist countries such as Cuba and China are of no account, though the South American swing to the Left does seem to be causing trepidation. Nonetheless, the entire calculation takes place singularly in terms of those countries that fall within the category of 'superpower'. With only one left standing, the fact that it is both democratic and capitalist seems to indicate not only the historical, but the ideological inevitability of capitalism, as Hobbes might put it, as democracy's true life blood.[10] This could be seen in the equation found on the signs put up by shops everywhere soon after 9/11: 'America, Open for Business'. "They" may have destroyed the twin world trade towers, went the subtext, but they failed to destroy our way of life, or our ability to buy and sell. The signs' counterpunch was clear recognition that the surface meaning of the twin towers was understood by all, even if the idea that their destruction may have a historical causality remained patriotically unthinkable.

These two events strike at the heart of the present Western condition and its oft-professed liberal democratic project. There are, of course, a number of theories and vehement debates on what constitutes liberalism, a notion whose history of development stems back to a radical critique of authoritarian aristocratic society.[11] However, a certain set of basic categories have entrenched themselves, many of which hold forth from the twin notions of utility (Bentham) and individual self-possession (Locke). Internal to traditional liberal theory is the stencil of a free subject that is autonomous and thereby able to make choices that maximize utility. As John Gray puts it, "A free man is one who possesses the rights and privileges needed for him to think and act autonomously—to rule himself, and not be ruled by another."[12] Gray goes on to note that this viewpoint tends to presuppose a liberal state with its protection of certain rights as well as an emphasis on contract and property law. Similarly, Milton Friedman proposes in *Capitalism and Freedom* that freedom is a function of individual choice, an act which highly individuates ethical concerns: "The 'really' important ethical problems are those that face an individual in a free society—what he should do with his freedom."[13] We can note a couple of important aspects of this generalized liberal view, indicating the core of what Michael Sandel calls the "procedural republic."[14] On the one hand, autonomy is both primary and negative. Under liberalism, freedom does not indicate, as Rousseau, Hegel, or Marx might argue, a necessary, even if unrealized, and responsible connectivity to others. Rather, it indicates the limits of what we can do for ourselves without regard to others. As Oliver Wendell Holmes famously said, "the right to swing my fist ends where the other man's nose begins." Freedom so understood takes on a primarily localizing persona, and the functionality of the subject is defined by where it is disconnected from the Other. Personal freedom terminates where it negates another's freedom, and the rest is an island of free play. As Locke succinctly stated, "To understand Political Power right, and derive it from its Original, we must consider what State all Men are naturally in, and this, a State of perfect Freedom to order their Actions, and Persons as they think fit, within the bounds of the Law of Nature, without asking leave, or depending upon the Will of any other Man."[15] Finally, it is the state's job to keep this negative space open, to act, as Friedman had it, as umpire but *never* father (thus placing the lineage from Lockian anti-paternalism along a clearly theoretical line, for the paternalism of leadership, the name, as Lacan had it of the father, has never stopped being written into any leadership that has dared to enter into the democratic void).

The individual is thus a self-deciding and reasonable unit within a general aggregate. Liberalism has to take into account those who fall outside the range of normalcy, for instance what Locke called 'Children, Lunaticks and Ideots', and what the ever dwindling coalition of the willing call 'the terrorists'. But they are easily reckoned out of the account as either in the process of becoming rational, or statistical anomalies separable from the smooth flow of the state and its free, particulate subjects. The political realm that is thereby envisioned, broadly speaking, presupposes that most do as they will without harming other people. While it is true that positions vary with respect to the issues of freedom, equality, and utility, liberal theorists qua liberal theorists take them as their starting points. Furthermore, that this conception is alive and well today can be seen in rational action theory, a prevalent concept of political analysis and agency which sees subjects, more or less, as *homo economicus*.[16] One of the earliest proponents of rational action theory, David Easton, puts the general concept of agency in rational modeling as follows:

> He or she was not just a subject reacting to external circumstances but was proactive—choosing, selecting, rejecting in terms of his or her own preferences or utility-maximizing behavior. The focus shifted decisively from the structure or constraints surrounding behavior (what became for rational modeling exogenous variables) to the actor and his or her strategies of choice in pursuit of individual utilities. The reasoning human being driven by intentions and goals was brought back into politics.[17]

The move by rational choice theory from an intention-free behaviorist model to an intention-sensitive modeling theory was lauded for returning agency to political theory and science according to Easton. Contra behaviorism, no longer were individuals mere units subsumed by a general system of activities—they were now choosing beings that had ideas and goals, and these goals and ideas could be shown to affect the general structure of political events in a various of ways. For Russell Hardin, this places rational action (or choice) theory firmly in the traditional realm of political theory a la Hobbes and Locke: "Though rational choice is inherently addressed to the individual level, it reaches conclusions at the collective level. In this it is not different from the bulk of tradition political argument."[18] Hardin continues with the view that rational choice theory is able to show how strategic interactions of individuals produce general events and is not limited to mere theorizing from a narrowed view of human actions. It is in this way that rational choice theory applies the "laws" of economics to the realm of the political. The *politikon zōon* is subject to that good which is parceled out in goods, each to be weighed by a cost-benefit analysis relative to an individual perspective.

It is thus proposed that failure of traditional theory is located in its assumption an overly generic conception of human activity and, therefore, subjectivity. To some degree, rational choice theory thereby comes close to much of what is called postmodernism. While postmodernism is notoriously inexact, one of its verboten concepts is the notion of a singular willing agent grounded in some sort of objective truth. As the early Foucault has been misquoted *ad infinitum*, the subject is dead, if by that is meant the Cartesian subject acting on the basis of self-conscious intention.[19] But rational choice theory did not hear this proclamation, save with dismissive annoyance. As Easton's quote above showed us, there is a choosing subject that acts according to utilitarian or teleological patterns; all goals may not be the same, but most subjects have certain goals or goods they seek, and locate rational ways of maximizing them. The theory's name alone is clear—it is a theory of rational choice, not a theory of describable though irrational power relations, as a Foucaultian argument might produce. However localized and specified the individual agent is, it is still thoroughly structured in its choosing. Insofar, then, as the choice is in and of itself undifferentiated in its utility, the agent remains generic.

But political empirical theorists are not unaware of the issue of irrationality and unpredictability, and rational choice theory has undergone a process of self-questioning because of it. Indeed, Easton is fully clear about the attacks that are made against the theory: "The rational actor approach . . . leaves the impression of a world made up of atomized actors interested only in their own well-being, a view that fits in well with free-market philosophies of the 1980s. The existence, in theories, of ideological predispositions such as these should not be news to social scientists" (33). Easton's response to this dilemma is to tell us to wait; the process of interdisciplinary recalculation should eventually balance out the ideological predispositions of such theory. A theory, after all, is only as good as its predictability. Real world events, critiques, and reformulation will eventually rid the theory, as far as this is possible, of its bourgeois assumptions (34). Such a response only causes the problem to redouble upon itself. The idea that new events and views will alter a theory that is being criticized for merely reflecting its ideological origins in old events expresses the general definition of madness as the expectation that a repetition of the problem will be its cure. There is thus nothing in such a method that overcomes the probability that those new events and theories will not be the introduction of yet another ideological foundation to what is supposed to be an objective scientific study.

Similarly, it does not deal well with the problem of values. It has been assumed in recent rational choice theory that values cannot be fully divorced from facts nor from the theories that set about analyzing them. But as we have just seen, each theory requires a current series of human values that help to motor its very process of analysis. The assumption of a certain set of values brings us fully into the problem of theoretical grounds. If a set of values will in each case be assumed when conducting analysis, is there, one wonders, anything more to the notion of subjectivity in rational choice theory than a container of values? Do we not need a sense of what we mean by an actor when we theorize it?

As we saw earlier, Hardin argues that such questions merely stick us with the old overgeneralized philosophical approach to theory. But Hardin makes another interesting argument; namely, that Hobbes was indeed the first rational action theorist given that he was the first to avoid the fallacy of composition, or the idea that individual interests will be reflected in general movements:

> The fundamental turn, however, is with Hobbes and his recognition of the need to avoid the fallacy of composition that arises from the focus on individuals. Hobbes' program was about how to found a government on individuals, and in that program he rigorously avoided arguments by analogy from the individual to the social level.[20]

Hardin does not spell out just how Hobbes avoided this move, but perhaps the assumption is that individual preferences, which in Hobbes tend toward the increase in personal power, result in the need for a government that in fact denies those preferences. In this way, collective preference does not resemble individual preference. Even more intriguing is that Hobbes is invoked as "a master at rational choice theory" (203), an argument that, consciously or not, reproduces the view that Hobbes was the progenitor of the liberal bourgeois subject, whatever his monarchical professions. As Deborah Baumgold puts it, "These days, more attention is being paid to his account of rational action than to his observations about the passions. It is now more fashionable to reconstruct Hobbesism around the problem of generating cooperation among rational egoists than to accent his concern with controlling men's appetite for power."[21] While his primary goal was the protection and promotion of commodious living for human beings, certain assumed human traits were at the center of his theory. It is these traits that place him in the liberal category for some who wish to focus on his supposed rational egoism. Hobbes, however, makes no real sense if we avoid those aspects in his theory which emphasize the passionate and fundamentally irrational elements of human nature. From this perspective, one will see a Hobbes which is indeed prescient, but not for those who seek reason.

Still, one aspect of Hardin must be maintained and fully dealt with; namely, the idea that there can be a fallacy of composition within a political assumption. Insofar as Hobbes clearly saw the political realm as negating, in its proper instance, the base nature of subjectivity (we must, after all, give up our desire to an Other who shall desire for us, though, it must be admitted that we desire this as well), there will be consequences for democracy no less than monarchy. In other words, and this will be examined in the final chapter, democracy does not necessarily give us what we want to the extent that it most closely fits our subjectivity. Why this is the case can locate an initial answer in Hobbesian passion as the outgrowth of our essential irrationality, to which we now turn.

2. Reckoning Reason

Let us begin, then, with reason. While reason is clearly at the heart of Hobbes' thinking on the nature of subjectivity, it depends on a basic human irrationality and hence functions by virtue of a sort of natural ruse; in essence, humans achieve reason by failing at it. So what is reason for Hobbes? While reason receives a truncated description in the *Leviathan*, five years later it obtains a modicum of depth in *De Corpore*, wherein the simple definition of reason is found to be a series of reckonings:

> By Ratiocination, I mean *computation*. Now to compute is either to collect the sum of many things that are added together, or to know

what remains when one thing is taken out of another. *Ratiocination*, therefore, is the same with *addition* and *substraction*. . . . So that all ratiocination is comprehended in these two operations of the mind, addition and substraction.[22]

Reason thus entails distinguishing the connections of things by a process of addition and subtraction. Later in the text Hobbes will indicate that these things are in fact names grounded in definitions, a move made in all three of his systems. Hobbes thus creates a mathematic definition of reason—one sees the relations of meanings to one another by marking their possible combinations and subtractions.

We are not, however, working here with a simplistic correspondence theory of meaning due to the fact that definitions, the core parcels of reckoning, are somewhat arbitrarily grounded. In fact, definitions find their stability in the tricky entanglements of a public discourse:

Seeing then that truth consisteth in the right ordering of names in our affirmations, a man that seeketh precise truth had need to remember what every name he uses stands for, and to place it accordingly, or else he will find himself entangled in words; as a bird in lime twigs, the more he struggles the more belimed. And therefore in geometry (which is the only science that it hath pleased God hitherto to bestow on mankind) men begin at settling the significations of their words; which settling of significations they call definitions, and place them in the beginning of their reckoning.[23]

Hobbes continues this line by arguing that true science requires the sifting of all possible definitions for veracity. While Hobbes consistently argues that all thoughts begin with sensation, science clearly takes a socially constructed turn here, though we speak here of a society that admits only the learned. As one starts out with definitions and continues to build, erroneous foundations can only lead to increasingly absurd ends.

Though it might be argued that in a Hobbesian system, which submits fully to causation and materialism, the commonwealth is but the manifestation of what *is*, or the logical result of the motion of things, the problem of definition produces an epistemological gap between what is and how it is known. Words are objects too, and thus for Hobbes they have their good and bad forms of causality. Those words that are denotationaly incorrect, such as metaphor, or suffer a confused order, lead the listener or reader into a false conception of reality.[24] Thus the description of definition, which is at the heart of any possible science of philosophy, begs a fundamental question: how do we know if our definitions are correct? Hobbes' answer is to call for a community of judges who shall cultivate proper definitions.[25] But this answer only provides another regressive step within the problem of criteria; by what, that is, shall they judge? Hobbes' response is rather complicated.

As we just saw, for Hobbes definitions are established by agreement. In this sense, Hobbes could be said to provide a precursor to Wittgenstein's notion of language as use in his later writings, particularly *On Certainty*.[26] In those writings, Wittgenstein is famous for arguing that there is no measure for the meaning of words other than what is given by the community of users themselves. That we share a language depends on our active and yet tacit agreement that those words have the meanings they do. Indeed, in *On Certainty*, to the question of whether one is correct in the use of a term, the proper response is that one ought to go to one who knows, which means any normal language user. Such appears to be mirrored in the following remarks by Hobbes, though in fact they indicate a radically different conception of linguistic authority:

> And therefore, as when there is a controversy in an account, the parties must by their own accord set up for right reason the reason of some arbitrator or judge to whose sentence they will both stand, or their controversy must either come to blows or be undecided, for want of right reason constituted by nature, so is it also in all debates of what kind soever. And when men that think themselves wiser than all others clamour and demand right reason for judge, yet seek no more but that things should be determined by no other men's reason but their own, it is as intolerable in society of men as it is in play, after trump is turned, to use for trump on every occasion that suit whereof they have most in their hand. . . .[27]

Hobbes foreshadows here the very nature of the commonwealth he will later articulate, for the nature of definition and science is mirrored in the nature of the structure of the sovereign's relation to his subjects. While it is true that Hobbes was a materialist, he understood that the material called language is a slippery customer and thus figured that the community of scientists needed recourse to a person of authority to settle the possible rancor of their passions. In this sense, the person of authority in Wittgenstein's realm differs fundamentally from that found in Hobbes'— in Wittgenstein's realm we turn to anyone who is a normal language user. In Hobbes' we turn to someone who has been given a specific and overriding authority, an authority which is fundamentally not shared. Hobbes has a quite specific reason for making this argument. At the heart of human interaction beats a base compulsion; namely, the desire for power, a decidedly non-Wittgensteinian concept.

When the search for power is ruled by the passions, it tends toward the ruination of society and all its accomplishments. For as the end of the above quote indicates, when the passions are the final arbiter of any debate, each individual's quest for dominance overtakes the fruits of reason, resulting in a constant attempt to trump others in order not to be right so much as to win. The question that now arises is what constitutes the nature of these passions that can lead to something as comical as brawling scientists.

3. Passion and Power

Hobbes' analysis of the passions led him to conclude that without a sovereign, the state of humankind is the state of nature, and this state tends to nothing other than war. Indeed, after his famous proclamation concerning the shortness and brutishness of life in the state of nature, Hobbes explains that his whole argument is an "inference made from the passions."[28] And, as we shall see in the following, it is within the passions that we can delineate what is reasonable and unreasonable within Hobbes' political theory.

According to Hobbes, the animal suffers two distinct types of motion: voluntary and involuntary. Involuntary motions are processes such as respiration, the beating of the heart, and excretion, while voluntary motions have an ideational root.[29] Such voluntary movements Hobbes calls endeavors, which, as in Freud's early works, function according to a love/hate dichotomy—we love those objects which give us pleasure, and hate those which afford us pain.[30] Indeed, for Hobbes, in the state of nature the only true manifestations of good and evil result from such a love/hate dichotomy. Furthermore, Hobbes argues that we never voluntarily act upon anything of which we have never had a previous idea, and hence all endeavors are a function of mental objects which we desire, are indifferent to, or aver.[31] Accordingly, voluntary motion responds to six modes of conceiving an object or end: "So that of good there be three kinds: good in the promise, that is *pulchrum*; good in effect, as the end desired, which is called *jocundum*, delightful; and good as the means, which is called utile, profitable; and as many of evil; for evil in promise is that they call *turpe*; evil in effect and end is *molestum*, unpleasant, troublesome; and evil in means inutile, unprofitable, hurtful."[32] Each of Hobbes' terms for the passions accord to one of these six conceptions, and each informs how desire for power tends to rule all passion, no matter what one's social station. Such is the result of the fact that humans are not actually solitary but in constant communication for good and ill, leading to the following conclusion:

> Continual success in obtaining those things which a man from time to time desireth, that is to say, continual prospering, is that men call Felicity; I mean the felicity of this life. For there is no such thing as perpetual tranquillity of mind, while we live here; because *life itself is but motion*, and can never be without desire, nor without fear, no more than without sense.[33]

Hobbes repeats these points in chapters VIII and XI, and his argument is dual. On the one hand, there is a mechanical facet; namely, that lack of motion is death itself. Life (and all of matter) simply *is* motion, a motion that has no formal teleological goal.[34] Though derived from Galileo, the addition of an endless satisfaction of desire leads to the conclusion that Hobbes' concept of motion is akin to the Freudian and Lacanian notions of drive, whereby our adventures in the world are based on an energy that ever circulates around impossible objects of desire, objects which are impossible precisely because they can only ever be stand-ins for desire itself.[35] On the other hand, the only reason we act on our desires at all is because we have the *idea* of an object of desire. As Samantha Frost puts it, any action toward on an object of desired amounts to "a response that is textured by the entire complex history of the organism's experiences and responses."[36] Desire is thus representational in Hobbes, and it is the distinction between our ideas of satisfaction, which places them squarely in the realm of the imaginary, and any given particular satisfaction that leads to the impossibility of full satisfaction.

Thus the bridge between our mechanized movement from object to object and a particular satisfaction is an ideational content that motivates a subject to act. The fantasmatic factor in this motivation is predicated on the logic of desire itself; it can only ever be a projection of satisfaction, and idea of what it ought to be. Desire is thus divided between what goes on in the mind of the desirer and what it obtains. And yet, due to the constant tension and push of motion itself, a given object is only a placeholder for desire. No less, the six modalities of the object produce a continuous futural projection that can only negate a given object. Worry about the future, depressed over the present and past, and glory in inabilities, achievements, and possibilities overtake any given concrete fact of achievement.

This leads to a comparative condition that Hobbes places under the general banner of virtue. Virtue, therefore, "is somewhat that is valued for eminence, and consisteth in comparison. For if all things were equally in all men, nothing would be prized."[37] This differential process of prizing leads then to Hobbes' deliberations on power—for eminence is not just the manifestation of a variety of abilities and differences in obtaining desired objects, but as well an indication of our ability to obtain those objects in relation to others who may desire the same: "The power of a man (to take it universally) is his poreent means to obtain some future apparent good, and is either original or instrumental."[38] Though Hobbes argues here that power takes on two different forms, natural and instrumental, both powers fundamentally function under the category of eminence, or the comparative, for while instrumental powers include such things as friends and rank, our natural powers (strength, intelligence, eloquence, liberality, nobility, etc.) are what we show off to others to establish our rank.[39] It is thus clear that for Hobbes, the main source of our power depends on our ability persuasively display ourselves.[40]

Power is thus a social imaginary force. As Richard Tuck puts it, "[t]he primal source of the conflict of the state of nature, for Hobbes, is thus epistemic in character. . . ."[41] It is our ability in the eyes of others, and vice versa, that decides our felicity in life, our capacity not to fulfill this or that desire or endeavor, but to respond yet again to desire's endless demand. Such logic is indicated most clearly in the fact that Hobbes notoriously disavows any Kantian notion of humanity as an end in itself: "The value or Worth of a man is, as of all other things, his price, that is to say, so much as would be given for the use of his power; and therefore is not absolute, but a thing dependent on the need and judgment of another."[42] We are public commodities, vying to reach the highest price on the market of eminence. To put this point in contemporary terms, we achieve our success in the eyes of the Other, or the social body that delivers judgments of success or failure. Disavowed is any idea of achievement that is sought for its own virtuous sake: all of our success depends on our feelings of having been seen, of recognition.[43] Such desire let loose and unbounded will dutifully dissolve into a generally constant and voracious need for ever more. Propped up within a social matrix that promotes would provide for its absolutely imaginary intensification. It would, as we now know well, make all too summary Warhol's fifteen minutes—it is now typical to be 'plugged-in' to a multitude of devices that provide a twenty-four hour feed of connectivity, providing up-to-date information on the world and on the most mundane activities perpetrated by the individual.

This point is necessary for understanding Hobbes' concept of rationality. Since our notions of eminence are based on our view of what others can do, and since our desires in motion are dependent on the way we imagine things to be (*pulchrum, jocundum, turpe*, etc.), we have no direct understanding of the world and our position in it. Our concepts of reality are entirely mediated by what we think others are capable of in relation to our comparative advantage. And because said concepts are themselves further mediated by language, the ability for us to be swayed by badly organized or falsely constructed viewpoints is an inherent danger. As Hobbes argued early on in the *Leviathan*, only language can turn us into extraordinary fools.[44] Therefore, we all suffer not from reality, but from self-serving *Weltanshaungen*, worldviews fueled by received opinion and yet fully malleable according to personal need. True, Hobbes thought that a measured, syllogistic method of reason can take us away from our confused dispositions, but it is the wont of desire to be swayed by a passionate attachment to received, self-gratifying, and self-affirming beliefs.

At this point one could comfortably pause and argue that Hobbes provides the perfect model of a utilitarian market-oriented conception of human agency. We measure our abilities and thus our worth against that of others and thereby make our decisions and transactions, acting in a congenitally if not congenially capitalistic fashion. For Hobbes, however, our excesses of competitive eminence lead us to the Monarch, not the market. Hobbes focused neither on the subject as such nor on the presuppositions of the ruling class. Rather, the very relation between the two disturbed Hobbes since reason indicated that only a unified power produces a reasonable human state, particularly given that all noncentralized fragmentation leads to irrational excess. Reason, that is, arrives as a savior to our natural condition, and only by tightly knitting our individual powers up into a singular being.

This point is clarified by a close reading of paragraph four of chapter thirteen, which establishes the erratic nature of the passions. The paragraph starts out indicating that our diffidence points out the reasonableness of staying in a state of war against all others by overpowering them. However, it continues with the following: "Also, because there be some that taking pleasure in contemplating their own power in the acts of conquest, which they pursue farther than their security requires, if others (that otherwise would be glad to be at ease within modest bounds) should not by invasion increase their power, they would not be able . . . to subsist." The unreasonable and excessive, the vain-glorious and competitive, those who go beyond what is needed and thereby produce a violent domino effect in every subject who is to remain true to his or her natural fear of death, *define* the state of nature as war.

And who shall win? Hobbes makes it clear that since the entirety of the war of all against all is an "inference made from the passions," what differentiates the abilities of different humans in Hobbes are the varying levels or their desire: "The passions that most of all cause the difference of wit are principally: the more or less desire of power, of riches, of knowledge, and of honour. All which may be reduced to the first, that is, desire of power. For riches, knowledge, and honour are but several sorts of power."[45] More importantly, in chapter eleven, paragraph twenty-four, Hobbes notes that what causes us to seek ways to overtake others and be in a position of relative safety is anxiety: "Anxiety for the future time disposeth men to inquire into the causes of things, because the knowledge of them maketh men the better able to order the present to their best advantage." Power is a nervous thing, and hence a stronger desire for power will lead to a higher level of anxiety inducing wit with which one can find the proper motivation to dominate. Knowledge, then, is anxiety, and anxiety, to alter the popular equation, is power.

Here we must pause and note that the foundation of the Hobbesian system is desire in the form of anxiety. The idea that Hobbes has produced a classical outline of the rational actor is not correct given the fact that, as we can see, the actor that best represents the core of subjectivity is essentially neurotically irrational. Desire leads subjectivity astray in its natural form, a form which is unnatural because it is subject to the beliming of language and, with it, eminence. No less, the relational nature of subjectivity is not even. Desire is not distributed justly among the species, and the maldistribution produces an unfortunate relation. Those who will seek power the most will force the logic of power on the rest. Hence, anxiety can take various forms, and its discussion with desire is not uniformly malevolent or self-centered. Rather, the fact of the neighbor, whom one may or may not love, produces the fact of war because, at some point in the neighborhood, the avarice of a given subjectivity or group of subjectivities will cause the dissolution of commodious living. In this way, Strauss is incorrect in naming Hobbesian human nature as evil; rather, the relation of moderate and excessive desiring subjects leads to an evil condition when there is no unification over and above.[46]

The inherent irrationality in the Hobbesian subject, broadly speaking, is worsened further still by its ability to believe in the nonmaterial. As has been mentioned, Hobbes is a materialist, arguing that no conception comes from something not sensed. However, due to the abstracted nature of language and the ingrained assumptions of custom, we are able to believe in that which is not seen nor heard, to follow the rule of opinion rather than reason:

> Ignorance of the causes and original constitution of right, equity, law, and justice disposeth a man to make custom and example the rule of his actions, in such manner as to think that unjust which it hath been the custom to punish, and that just, of the impunity and approbation whereof they can produce an example. . . , like little children, that have no other rule of good and evil manners but the correction they receive from their parents and masters; save that children are constant to their rule, whereas men are not so, because, grown strong and stubborn, they appeal from custom to reason and from reason to custom, as it serves their turn, receding from custom when their interest requires it, and setting themselves against reason as oft as reason is against them; which is the cause that the doctrine of right and wrong is perpetually disputed, both by the pen and the sword. . . .[47]

Because we tend to follow our own self-interest, overriding custom or reason when it is convenient, we are prone to coming into conflict with one another, just like brawling scientists. The fundamental problem Hobbes is trying to grapple with is the fact that our natural condition of desire leads us into a series of self-serving calamities that are entirely avoidable if we would just consult reason steadfastly. But we don't: ". . . for the passions of men are commonly more potent than their reason. From whence it follows that where the public and private interest are most closely united, there is the public most advanced."[48] Here Hobbes makes his basic move—a fractious body politic must overcome its individuated and relational desire by the identification of its constituent selves with the self of the sovereign. Hence, the image at the beginning of the Leviathan is a sovereign in composition, a unity constructed out of all of the individuals that provide it with substance.

But the relation is bi-directional. To the degree that political subjects must identify with the sovereign, the sovereign must in return instruct the people in their laws and duties. The inherent danger in not teaching them is that they will be persuaded by rebellious factions, thereby leading to the downfall of the Leviathan and their lives.[49] Clearly, then, the Hobbesian view is that humans left to their own devices will tend either in part or whole to irrational and ultimately self-destructive states of want. Even if it is only some who tend toward the excessive, they have the ability by virtue of acts of violence, damage, injury, and persuasion to cause others to pursue their own irrational endeavors leading to society's fractious end.

We can thus conclude that the passions in themselves are not rational. Rather, reason itself comes into being because the effects of the passions are detrimental to our continued existence. Here one can note a tension in Hobbes' thinking, for on the one hand, reason appears to be but another aspect of the passions, as when Hobbes argues that thoughts are like the scouts of desire, being sent out to accomplish its various tasks.[50] In this metaphor, reason is the result of passion, its realization. But on the other hand, as noted in the previous paragraph, passion is reason's nemesis. However, this tension is resolved if we note that Hobbes thought that reason resulted only from the special application of the mind to what the passions are doing to us: "By this it appears that reason is not, as sense and memory, born with us, nor gotten by experience only, as prudence is, but attained by industry. . . ."[51] Hobbes sees reason as both caused by passion and separate from it. Though some may have the sort of disposition that leads them to be able to reason better, this in itself is not the accomplishment of reason. One needs to work one's wit: ". . . the difference of passions proceedeth, partly from the different constitution of the body, and partly from different education."[52] Accordingly education, as we shall see in the next section, is essential for Hobbes. A misdirected wit can lead not only to all sorts of fractious thinking, but to the kind of pathetic leadership that causes rebellions and civil wars.

Thus while it is true that we generally seek our own goods, or our own utility, our means and methods are anti-utilitarian in that, sans a unifying power, they cause a continuous war. Unmitigated self-preservation, uncontrolled desire, and ignorance of causality produce self-destruction. The Leviathan must be artificially constructed against the nature of humankind, not in order to release its natural tendencies, as some think that democracy and capitalism do (an idea at which Hobbes would no doubt smile wryly), but in order to quell and then remold them.

We can thus not agree fully with the likes of Macpherson and Arendt when they argue that Hobbes was the theorist of irrational, greedy, and ultimately solipsistic bourgeois individuals. On the contrary, such an argument misses not only the thoroughly anti-utilitarian nature of the self-destructive natural subject, but also the rather complicated manner in which Hobbes constructs as necessary a state of ideological training of and against our fractious desire, a point which will now be fully elaborated.

4. Hobbesian Ideological State Apparatuses

Arendt is not commonly noted in Hobbes studies, but her argument predicts C. B. Macpherson's by some four years.[53] In her early work *Imperialism*, Arendt analyzes the manner in which the bourgeoisie came to political power during the Imperialist era, replacing a national community with a privatized and commercial conception of political existence:

> When in the era of imperialism, businessmen became politicians and were acclaimed as statesmen, while statesmen were taken seriously only if they talk the language of successful businessmen and "thought in continents," these private practices and devices were gradually transformed into rules and principles for the conduct of public affairs. The significant fact about this process of revaluation, which began at the end of the last century and is still in effect, is that it began with the application of bourgeois convictions to foreign affairs and only slowly was extended to domestic affairs. Therefore, the nations concerned were hardly aware that the recklessness that had prevailed in private life, and against which the public body always had to defend itself and its individual citizens, was about to be elevated to the one publicly honored political principle.[54]

Arendt goes on immediately to point to Hobbes as the "only great thinker" who saw public good as a manifestation of private interest, thus nailing the bourgeois sense of power as endless, ruthless, and utterly individualized accumulation.[55] Arendt correctly explains that Hobbes thought of reason as a form of reckoning, eschewed the notion of free will (thereby seeing humans as merely thoughtless functionaries of society), and argued that we are all ultimately reducible to our bargaining price. She further notes that Hobbes viewed us as equal murderers in the struggle for power, thus reducing the political state to a reactionary safe-guard against the inherent insecurities of such a situation. Indeed, the Hobbesian state is such a flimsy response that outsiders have no obligation to it, nor do those who are members really hold anything more than a passing commitment to it.[56]

Compressing Macpherson's later insights into a few lines, Arendt arrives at the following conclusion: "This new body politic was conceived for the benefit of the new bourgeois sketch for the new type of Man who would fit into it. The Commonwealth is based on the delegation of power, and not of rights. It acquires a monopoly on killing and provides in exchange a conditional guarantee against being killed."[57] For Arendt, Hobbes was not attempting to create a psychological realism or even a philosophical truth,[58] but rather sought the right political outfit for a new class of powerful men, men who needed a structure of power to facilitate an endless and purely privatized process of accumulation.[59]

However, there are some difficulties in her analysis, which is, no doubt, highly condensed and speculative. To begin with, it is unclear why Hobbes would be fitting his theory of man to the political structure if that structure itself is primarily monarchical. If the bourgeois individual is at heart individualistic and seeks to avoid any limit on the accumulation of power, why would so much power be placed into the hands of the sovereign, who is simultaneously legislator and executor, not to mention the holder of all rights save the right to self-defense for an individual in the common-wealth? Even if we are speaking of a power-elite here, Hobbes generally avers any sort of aristocratic intentions, placing all hope of true stability into a unitary holder of power.[60] However, Arendt has another argument; namely, that man is so individualized in Hobbes that even if there is a sovereign at the helm, each individual is left to do his or her bidding according to a law of atomistic competition:

> Excluded from participation in the management of public affairs that involve all citizens, the individual loses his rightful place in society and his natural connection with his fellow men. He can now judge his individual private life only by comparing it with that of others, and his relations with his fellow men inside society take the form of competition.[61]

The general thrust of this argument is that Hobbes' theory of political structure relies on atomized accumulation of power. Given that power accumulation can, as with imperialism and finance capitalism, only main-tain itself by its constant increase, it has no internal stabilizing factor and eventually will fall like a house of cards. With no check and no principles of stability other than power itself, a Hobbesian state will always reach a critical mass and explode, leaving the average subject by the wayside as a mere casualty of the war of all against all.

No doubt it is true that the accumulative process that Arendt speaks of sounds like the desirous drive at the heart of the Hobbesian subject out-lined above. However, the details of the Hobbesian theory indicate a more elaborate state apparatus. Indeed, a better starting point would take its cue from Russell Hardin's point that Hobbes saw that the political state was the antithesis of the natural state.[62] The development of his notion of power with regard to the duties of the sovereign indicates that the production of stability must structurally control subjects' hearts and minds, must, in essence, negate their private interest. While it is true that the sovereign can leave subjects free to seek their fortune to some extent,[63] Hobbes is clear that property, contra Locke, begins with the sovereign. In fact, it is the sovereign's duty to make sure that a distribution of wealth is properly organized within the commonwealth: "In this distribution, the first law is for division of the land itself, wherein the sovereign assigneth to every man a proportion according as he (and not according as any subject, or any number of them) shall judge agreeable to equity and the common good."[64] Hobbes even maintains that a commonwealth must, in some basic sense, function as a welfare state.[65] Indeed, he warns against the dissolution of the government by placing too much wealth in the hands of the people, either as a group, or in the form of individuals with monopolies.[66] It is fairly clear that Hobbes does not instate his war of all against all within the commonwealth, much less does he leave a competitive relationship to deal with or even discard the weak.

Subjects in a Hobbesian commonwealth are therefore not reduced to an isolated atomization. On the contrary, he was at pains to argue that a commonwealth dissolves as soon as it is individualized, that individualization leads to discord in the form of a private opinion churning into public passion and with it the ruination of the sovereign. Indeed, while Hobbes famously said that "covenants without the sword are but words . . . ," as one moves through the Hobbesian systems one can see that his thinking veers close to the construction of what Althusser termed 'Ideological State Apparatuses', which require a fundamentally ideological rather than merely repressive approach to control: "To my knowledge, *no class can hold State power over a long period without at the same time exercising its hegemony over and in the State Ideological Apparatuses.*"[67] The apparatuses of which Althusser speaks, including the church, the educational system, the family, and the media, are precisely what Hobbes thought the sovereign must use in order to educate his or her subjects not only in the letter of the law, but its active spirit *in forno* as well. No doubt, while Althusser's science is the revealed truth, knowledge, and "property" of the proletariat,[68] Hobbes' science is intended for the universities and, above all, "[h]e that is to govern a whole nation. . . ."[69] While it is clearly the case that Hobbes, in his assumption that both he himself and the sovereign can control the ideological process, is not as radical as Althusser, nonetheless, one of the main goals of the sovereign is an ideological process of indoctrination such that members of the state are not merely subjects, but believers.

Hobbes establishes this point on a double plane. To begin with, he is clear that civil law establishes sin and crime. Where there is no law, there is no crime given that everyone has a right to everything in the state of nature. However, where there is law, not only does the manifest breaking of that law count as a crime or sin, so does the intention to commit it: "A sin is not only a transgression of a law, but also any contempt of the legislator. For such contempt is a breach of all his laws at once. And therefore may consist, not only in the commission of a fact, or in the speaking of words by the laws forbidden, or in the omission of what the law commandeth, but also in the intention or purpose to transgress."[70] Noting that intention is fundamental to the law, Hobbes later goes on to argue both that the law is the "public conscience"[71] and that the sovereign must instill in his or her subjects a moral understanding of this conscience: ". . . they are to be taught that, not only the unjust facts, but the designs and intentions to do them . . . are injustice, which consisteth in the pravity of the will as well as in the irregularity of the act."[72] While Hobbes does not go so far as to create a structure as thorough as Althusser's 'interpellation' (in which a subject formation occurs on the level of the minutiae of everyday life, occurs, in fact, before one is born[73]), he comes quite close: ". . . common people's minds, unless they be tainted with dependence on the potent, or scribbled over with the opinions of their doctors, are like clean paper, fit to receive whatsoever by public authority shall be imprinted on them."[74] While it is true that Hobbes is worried about the loss of power that a sovereign might suffer and hence places power as central to the establishment of the commonwealth, the logical outgrowth of this insight for him is that subjects must be unified not simply into obedience, but as well into a fully internalized sense of civic duty. Once the subject relinquishes its right to everything, it must be invested with a thorough identification with the Other, the Sovereign. Subjectivity is thus by necessity an internalization, a moral, legal, and notional interpellation in which its very sense of self must be anchored in the sovereignty that will, so the guarantee goes, serve to protect it (even if this is at the cost of the subject's very life).

Thus the Hobbesian subject is not the object of alienation that Arendt paints, though some sovereigns may achieve such a state through failure. Indeed, since Hobbes thought that subjects are already naturally alienated due to their inherent anxiety, any political system will have to structurally resist alienation. The good sovereign de-individualizes humans, gathers them into a conception of themselves as duty-bound citizens rather than limited power scavengers. Such de-individualization, moreover, is not the function of an arbitrary or capricious ideology. Hobbes calls for a strong publicity of the laws so the very grounds of the sovereign's duties and the authority of the laws are made clear: ". . . it is against his duty to let the people be ignorant or misinformed of the grounds and reasons of those his essential rights, because thereby men are easy to be seduced and drawn to resist him, when the commonwealth shall require their use and exercise."[75] Hobbes continues in the next paragraph to state that merely decreeing laws and punishing those who disobey won't work. As long as subjects don't understand the reasons for the laws they are under, they will merely act as they do in the state of nature, fighting the sovereign for power when they think they can. Only by understanding the necessity of the commonwealth and what it provides can subjects truly understand the necessity of the laws that govern them, and in the process come to have a conscience that is self-ruled. In essence, Hobbes knew that the Sovereign had to create what Foucault called docile bodies, bodies that would not internalize the law and thus merely submit to it, but live and breathe it on a daily basis.[76] Hobbes therefore created a quite deep concept not only of the power of the sovereign, but of the need for a public existentially immersed, as it were, in the very grounds of the institutions of the sovereign.

This last point is important given that Arendt's entire discourse on Hobbes and bourgeois thinking tends to circle around it. For Arendt, when we are isolated from one another our agency is depleted, thereby creating a vacuum between us that is left to be taken up by an all-consuming power. The double loss of will and interconnectivity become the fundamental loss of what Arendt calls humanity. Such vacuums then are not simply to be filled by power, but any doctrine that can motivate lost souls into belief, violent, racist, or otherwise:

> Hobbes at least provided political thought with the prerequisite for all race doctrines, that is, the exclusion in principle of the idea of humanity which constitutes the sole regulating idea of international law. With the assumption that foreign politics is necessarily outside of the human contract, engaged in the perpetual war of all against all which is the law of the "state of nature," Hobbes affords the best possible theoretical foundation for those naturalistic ideologies which hold nations to be tribes, separated from each other by nature, without any connection whatever, unconscious of the solidarity of mankind and having in common only the instinct for self-preservation which man shares with the animal world.[77]

What is at stake in this critique is the obliterating loss of any grounding notion of humanity. When freedom is reducible to accumulation and private choice, any ethical principle of cohabitation fades and an ominous portal to the infusion of doctrines of completeness, from racial to totalitarian, swings wide open.

Of course, this is also Hobbes' concern, though it is true that he did not call for a return to humanism, in the current sense, nor did he bother with the problem of international relations. Like many theorists of his time, he considered rulers to be in a state of nature with regard to one another, placing their relations squarely within the framework of war. All the same, Hobbes' account of the duties of the sovereign toward her or his subjects should strike one as rather profound given the usual concept one has of the brutal Hobbesian subject. From education to welfare distribution, Hobbes conceived of the sovereign's public duties in a comprehensive way. The sovereign *has* to be preoccupied with her or his subjects' understanding of ethics, with the formation of their conscience, and with their commodious living. As Hobbes points out, justice and injustice "are qualities that relate to men in society, not in solitude."[78]

5. The Politicization of Desire

Hobbes was preoccupied neither with the natural rationality of subjects nor with the commonwealth as a container for alienated self-obsessed individuals. Hobbes viewed the state of nature as consumed and defined by an interrelational sort of being that ended up negating itself for want of right reason. It is only reason in its opposition to the general trend of unorganized, natural passions that leads us out of the state of nature and into the commodious living and industry of the commonwealth. Ironically, once we get there we find that the sovereign's duties have only just begun. The sovereign, in order to continue with what reason dictates, must begin educating her or his subjects not only about the content of the commonwealth's laws, but about their necessity as well. Indeed, the sovereign must educate these subjects even in the grounds of sovereign power. The most obvious text for such a classroom is the *Leviathan* itself, as Hobbes so selflessly understood.[79]

It is with the latter that we find the prime difference from Arendt and other proponents of humanity and individual rights. Hobbes was clearly not taken with the power of the individual given that, as far as he could tell, individual power is almost always subsumed under the dictates of desire, which leads directly to the question of the current place of the Hobbesian subject, particularly given that both capitalism and democracy have achieved, as far as the West is concerned, an orthodox status in this post-welfare state, post-9/11 age. Much, unfortunately.

One of Arendt's main intentions in charting the path toward totalitarianism is to provide warning signs should we begin to walk it again. Insofar as there is little to argue against in seeking such an end, Hobbes becomes prescient and, more than ever, important due to his emphasis on desire and anxiety. For what Hobbes tells us is that there is something inherently irrational in human subjectivity, and this irrationality ought to make us think not only about markets and freedom, but about the limits of their ability to provide a true stability. Hobbes had the bulk of his systematic thinking in place before the outbreak of the English Civil War, but that political fracture did nothing to diminish his views. And, indeed, Hobbes would no doubt have much to say now about recent wars, civil or otherwise. Nonetheless, what would cause Hobbes no surprise whatsoever is how, to use a relatively recent historical example, the following list only exacerbated the divisions in Iraq: a complete lack of any post-invasion plan (under the assumption that we would be greeted, as in World War II, with flowers rather than looting); a virtual give-away of large weapons caches; the loss of large numbers of necessary technocrats through 'debaathification'; Abu Ghraib; a weak and imposed leadership and, most importantly, a complete lack of understanding of both local issues and those in the regional Middle East at large (not to mention a dearth of interpreters), thus providing nary a meeting point or context on an ideological plane.

If Iraq looked like a bloody game of catch-up Hobbes would argue that it is because there was no concept of just what a stable, relevant, and integrated government looks like, not to mention what a fully interpellated subject requires. Or, possibly, the ideological assumptions carried in with the invasion were so presupposed that it was forgotten that ideology is an always enacted process—that without interpellation, the subject is left in an ontological condition of wanting. The civil war in Iraq, in other words, provides another example of that very anxious desire, no doubt led by a certain number of exceptionally power hungry individuals, that leads to the dissolution of society. It appears, then, that Hobbes' argument that most subjects are as blank sheets of paper was taken entirely to heart in the Iraq invasion, but the fact that they must be intensely and continuously indoctrinated into their new political self-understanding was not.

Such ideological work indicates a corollary; namely, that the mere instantiation of democracy and capitalism do not, in and of themselves, produce a coherent social organization. Perhaps the thinking behind the removal of Saddam Hussein and the concurrent debaathification was that a market-driven and representative republic would flourish in their place. Indeed, L. Paul Bremer III argued in the early days of the occupation of Iraq that "[a] free economy and a free people go hand in hand. . . . History tells us that substantial and broadly held resources, protected by private property, private rights, are the best protection of political freedom. Building such prosperity in Iraq will be a key measure of our success here."[80] Such a view was behind the removal of the Baathists, and it is the logical companion to the lack of a post-invasion plan. Both were premised on the idea that capitalism and democracy are, in a sense, systems that arise *ex nihilo* from any lack of authoritarian power. Clearly they are not, and we thus see vividly that when subjectivity has no clarified and *explained* context, no delineated paths of authority, limit, and definition, then, as Hobbes tells us, the only way to forestall a full decline into fractious, civil war is to put in place, alongside the sword, a thoroughgoing set of ideological apparatuses that create a new kind of desire *in forno*.

No political system arrives without its heralds, ideologues, enforces, and institutions. For given human anxiety, an utter lack of relevant and continuous explanation dissolves the subject into a constant uncertainty, one only exacerbated by chronic violence, and this is precisely that which opens up Pandora's box insofar as subjects will repeatedly go looking for this lost authority, whether in themselves or some other who would be king. Does such a theoretical truth indicate, then, that only a Sovereign, be it democratic or otherwise, can save us from our desire and provide for what is the essential goal of all political formations, some modality of commodious living?

To answer in the affirmative is to only repeat the impasse of desire. Desire, as Hobbes so clearly shows us, is defined by its impossible satisfaction, by its bad infinity that can only be described as a 'yet one more': 'yet one more' object to bolster my position, 'yet one more' accomplishment to establish my eminence, my virtue, 'yet one more' that must be obtained after this one. Desire is thereby an exponential division, one that increases its need on the basis of the intensification of its previous achievement. To provide desire with the object, the Other, who shall be its fulfillment, who shall even desire for it is surely to unburden desire. What a relief, after all, that there is another who will take up the long slog of obtaining object after object. And what a relief that there is a One who will destroy any other that negates my instantiation, now established through a contract of the self, in the Other. And yet this Other, because I must continue to live, can never really provide the final it (*Es*) of desire, or my death is imminent.

It is true, I am relieved of the second death, the social death, the one in which my self is banished to an abject seesaw of indetermination which places me firmly in a realm that may eradicate me at any given moment (and which, no less, makes me expendable). Indeed, I can only desire through the other by virtue of a basic repression of my own desire, by transferring my want to the singularity of the Sovereign, by replacing my basic ignorance of the *summum bonum* with the fantasy that someone else has it. For this is the trick of ideology and therefore all modalities of sovereignty: in the absence of any final object of fulfillment and, therefore, in the space between objects, it is promised that there is fulfillment. Hence, the apparatuses of ideology (school, church, economy, government, media) are there to repeat the message, which is: "you have it." Of course, you don't, and the fantasy can only eventually provide within its cracks a space for a symptomal return. The classic argument that democracy escapes this trap of desire by emptying the center of any given ideological formation (save for democracy itself) does not, in fact, escape the problem, for the question of what ends up in the center of democracy is one that is all too often not broached, save for those moments in which its contradictions begin to appear. For instance, insofar as democracy was one of the *expressed* goal of the American occupation of Iraq, to the degree that there would be a democracy producing a Shiite majority, the U.S. administration understood that what it did not want was precisely what it got: democracy (the same can be said of Hamas' election victory in Palestein). This means that the content and structure of democracy is not unitary. Democracy has its ideological formulations, and the peculiarity of a given democratic structure, not to mention the motivations of those who are attempting to run it, will indicate the ideological underpinnings that motivate its policing of subjects.

In other words, democracies have their sovereigns too, a point that we will return to in detail in Chapter 4. At this point, it must be pointed out that the rubric of the Hobbesian is found in the vicissitudes of desire, and that it thereby indicates our starting point. Subjectivity is shot through with desire, and this desire, to the degree that it is defined by its impossible fulfillment, is the political issue *par excellence*. But not everyone agrees, of course, that desire is so gravely political, and we can obviously go beyond the rational choice theorists to a more philosophical debate on the issue. For that reason, we turn now to what is taken as the eminent anti-Hobbesian position; namely, Locke's arguments in the name of freedom and property, two intertwined aspects of subjectivity that, political speaking, are considered codependent in within the democratic consensus. It is in the debate between Hobbes and Locke that we will locate, however, the manner in which Hannah Arendt will ultimately define the terms of what is at stake in subjectivity, politically and otherwise, for she will provide its universal definition, one which takes that empty place holder that rational choice theorists reject (while producing it nonetheless), and indicates why the state of nature is definitional to the political. As such, Arendt will explicate why it is the case that the political can exist only in the name of the abject person, not the proliferation of desirous personas to which Sovereignty throws its ideological line.

Notes

1 See A. P. Martinich, *Hobbes: A Biography* (Cambridge: Cambridge University Press, 1999): 214–15, hereafter referred to as *Hobbes*.

2 Thomas Hobbes, *Leviathan*, ed. Edwin Curley (Indianapolis: Hackett Publishing Company, Inc., 1994): chapter XXI, paragraphs 11–13, hereafter referred to as *Leviathan* followed by chapter and paragraph number. For an historical account of attitudes toward self-preservation in medieval and early modern periods, see Johann P. Sommerville, *Thomas Hobbes: Political Ideas in Historical Context* (New York: St. Martin's Press, 1992): 33–7, hereafter referred to as *Political Ideas*.

3 *Leviathan*, XIII, 9. Even here, it should be noted, Hobbes parted ways from many of the royalists given the absolute degree that he placed religious authority in the hands of the sovereign. See *Political Ideas*, 119–27.

4 Hannah Arendt, *The Origins of Totalitarianism* (New York: Harcourt Brace & Company, 1973): 140, hereafter referred to as *Origins*.

5 Rational choice and game theorists, who seek different aims given that they are political scientists, are nonetheless quite fond of Hobbes. Russell Hardin goes so far as to deem Hobbes a "master at rational choice theory." See *Contemporary Empirical Political Theory*, ed. Kristen Renwick Monroe (Berkeley, California: University of California Press, 1997): 203. One of the main reasons that rational choice and game theorists turn to Hobbes is the fact that his version of the state of nature seems to outline the prisoner's dilemma. See, for instance, Pasquale Pasquino, "Hobbes, Religion, and Rational Choice Theory: Hobbes's Two Leviathans and the Fool," *Pacific Philosophical Quarterly*, 82 (2001): 406–19. However, at one point Pasquino notes that "an element of irrationality in human behavior" is probably at the root of civil war (411). It is precisely the philosophical ramifications of

this irrationality for subjectivity, and not rational choice, that interests me here insofar as I believe Hobbes saw it as the prime reason the sovereign needed an ideological answer to our ever present natural anxiety.

6 Antonio Gramsci, *Selections from the Prison Notebooks*, eds. and trans. Quintin Hoare and Geoffrey Nowell Smith (New York: International Publishers, 1997): 12.

7 See, in particular, chapter VII of Leo Strauss, *The Political Philosophy of Hobbes*, trans. Elsa M. Sinclair (Chicago: The University of Chicago Press, 1963), hereafter referred to as PPH.

8 Louis Althusser, "Ideology and Ideological State Apparatuses," in *Lenin and Philosophy*, trans. Ben Brewster (New York: Monthly Review Press, 1971). Hereafter referred to as *Lenin*. Of course, Althusser saw in his reading of ideology a total and complete interpellation of subjectivity, including that of the sovereign, a point which Hobbes classically excludes from his worries. Still, one could argue that Hobbes and Althusser, as authors of the structure of political consciousness, both inhabit the same extra-ideological position, each, in their own way, laying claim to the elaboration of a *science*.

9 As Nancy Fraser puts it, we are in a "Post-Socialist" age, one whereby "the culture-blindness of a materialist paradigm [was] rightfully discredited by the collapse of Soviet Communism[.]" Of course, in the title of her article, "From Redistribution to Recognition? Dilemmas of Justice in a 'Post-Socialist' Age," the use of scare quotes around post-socialist alerts us to the fact that she is going to be engaging in some socialist redistribution shenanigans. See *Theorizing Multiculturalism: A Guide to the Current Debate*, ed. Cynthia Willett (Massachusetts: Blackwell Publishers Inc., 1998): 18–49. All the same, the assumption of the death of communism is quite clear, while the distinction between the latter and socialism is something that evades many in the U.S.

10 According to Hobbes, the life-blood of the commonwealth is money, foreshadowing the modern democratic tendency toward reducing most political problems to economic modes of distribution. See *Leviathan*, xxiv, 11–12.

11 Will Kymlicka, *Contemporary Political Philosophy* (New York: Oxford University Press, 1990): 45. Kymlicka is speaking there of the early utilitarians.

12 John Gray, *Liberalism* (Minneapolis: University of Minnesota Press, 1995): 59.

13 Milton Friedman, *Capitalism and Freedom* (Chicago: University of Chicago Press, 1982): 12. On p. 27 of the same text, Friedman goes on to more or less repeat Gray's view: "In summary, the organization of economic activity through voluntary exchange presumes that we have provided, through government, for the maintenance of law and order to prevent coercion of one individual by another, the enforcement of contracts voluntarily entered into, the definition of the meaning of property rights, the interpretation and enforcement of such rights, and the provision of a monetary framework."

14 "The political philosophy by which we live is a certain version of liberal political theory. Its central idea is that government should be neutral toward the moral and religious views its citizens espouse. Since people disagree about the best way to live, government should not affirm in law any particular vision of the good life. Instead, it should provide a framework of rights that respects persons as free and independent selves. . . ."

Michael J. Sandel, *Democracy's Discontent: America in Search of a Public Philosophy* (Cambridge: The Belknap Press of Harvard University Press, 1996): 4.

15 John Locke, *Two Treatises of Government* (Cambridge: Cambridge University Press, 1988): paragraph 4, hereafter referred to as *Second Treatise* followed by paragraph number.

16 It should be noted that rational action, or choice, theory is a part of political science, and therefore in many ways conceives of humans as *homo oeconomicus*, thereby foregoing in many ways questions of rationality. Part of the reason I analyze rational action theory is that it succinctly expounds a prevalent view of politics in which humans are seen as equal and free utility maximizers who rationally go about their way. As such, rational action theory succumbs to the fault of not questioning what reason might be in the first place.

17 CEPT, 21–2.

18 Ibid., 203.

19 What Foucault actually says in the final pages of *The Order of Things* is the following: "As the archaeology of our thought easily shows, man is an invention of recent date. And one perhaps nearing its end," Michel Foucault, *The Order of Things: An Archaeology of the Human Sciences*, trans. Alan Sheridan (New York: Vintage, 1973): 387. Thus given that no historical configuration is necessary, man, qua recent historical emanation cannot be counted on to last. But, and here is where the exaggeration carries a truth; there is little doubt that Foucault carried little regard for the Cartesian subject, save in its moment of doubt.

20 CEPT, 214.

21 Deborah Baumgold, "Hobbes's Political Sensibility: The Menace of Political Ambition," in *Thomas Hobbes and Political Theory*, ed. Mary G. Dietz (Kansas: University Press of Kansas, 1990): 74.

22 Thomas Hobbes, *The English Works*, vol. 1 (Germany: Scientia Verlag Aalen, 1966): chapter 1, paragraph 2, hereafter referred to as *De Corpore*, followed by chapter and paragraph number.

23 *Leviathan*, IV, 12.

24 See *Leviathan*, IV, 4.

25 Ibid., IV, 13.

26 "Giving grounds, however, justifying the evidence, comes to an end;—but the end is not certain propositions striking us immediately as true, i.e. it is not a kind of *seeing* on our part; it is our acting, which lies at the bottom of the language-game," Ludwig Wittgenstein, *On Certainty*, eds. G. E. M. Anscombe and G. H. von Wright, trans. D. Paul and G. E. M. Anscombe (New York: Harper Torchbook, 1972): 204.

27 *Leviathan*, V, 3.

28 Ibid., XIII, 10.

29 Ibid., VI, 1.

30 See Sigmund Freud, *The Origins of Psycho-Analysis*, trans. James Strachey (New York: Basic Books, 1977).

31 *Leviathan*, VI, 3.

32 Ibid., VI, 8–9.

33 Ibid., VI, 58 (emphasis mine).

34. Hobbes followed in the path of anti-teleological Galileo here, whom he most likely met in 1636. See *Hobbes*, 91.

35 See, in particular, Jacques Lacan, *The Four Fundamental Concepts of Psychoanalysis: The Seminar of Jacques Lacan, Book XI*, trans. Alan Sheridan (New York: W. W. Norton & Company, 1998). As Lacan puts it on page 180, "The object petit a [which, according to Lacan, is nothing but the representation of desire itself] is not the origin of the oral drive. It is not introduced as the original food, it is introduced from the fact that no food will ever satisfy the oral drive, except by circumventing the eternally lacking object." Indeed, the impossibility of ultimate satisfaction in Lacan, which constitutes the basis of anxiety in the subject, provides an important parallel to Hobbesian anxiety that we will examine later on.

36 Samantha Frost, "Hobbes and the Matter of Self-Consciousness," *Political Theory*, 33, no. 4 (2005): 502.

37 *Leviathan*, VIII, 1.

38. Ibid., X, 1. According to Hobbes, what is the same in all of us is our desire for objects, but what often differentiates us, besides our natural and learned capabilities, is the objects we desire. See VIII, 3.

39 *Leviathan*, X, 2.

40 Hobbes clearly saw the state of nature as one of congregation, even if a doomed one: ". . . that in a condition of war wherein every man to every man (for want of a common power to keep them all in awe) is an enemy, there is no man can hope by his own strength or wit to defend himself from destruction without the help of confederates (where everyone expects the same defense by the confederation that anyone else does); and therefore, he which declares he thinks it reason to deceive those that help him can in reason expect no other means of safety than what can be had from his own singular power." *Leviathan*, XV, 5.

41 Richard Tuck, *The Rights of War and Peace: Political Thought and the International Order from Grotius to Kant* (New York: Oxford University Press, 2001): 131.

42 *Leviathan*, X,16.

43 This argument applies to our fundamental equality. Hobbes does not argue that our equality is absolute, but rather relative.

44 "Nor is it possible without letters for any man to become either excellently wise, or (unless his memory be hurt by disease or ill constitution of organs) excellently foolish. For words are wise men's counters, they do but reckon by them; but they are the money of fools, that value them by the authority of an Aristotle, a Cicero, or a Thomas, or any other doctor whatsoever, if but a man." *Leviathan*, IV, 13.

45 *Leviathan*, VIII, 15.

46 See PPH, p. 3.

47 *Leviathan*, XI, 21.

48 Ibid., XIX, 4. Hobbes then argues that it is in monarchy, despite its obvious problems, that we find an absolute union of public and private interest. Contra Locke, a monarch's

interest is clearly self-preservative, and thus he or she will do all that is possible, generally, to preserve the commonwealth.

49 *Leviathan*, XXX, 6. Hobbes goes on later in the Latin edition to say that for this reason universities need to be reformed (see footnote 7, p. 225).

50 *Leviathan*, XI, 15–16.

51 Ibid., V, 17. See also VIII, 13.

52 Ibid., VIII, 14.

53 See C. B. Macpherson, *Political Theory of Possessive Individualism: Hobbes to Locke* (New York: Oxford University Press, 1964), hereafter referred to as *Possessive*.

54 *Origins*, 138–9.

55 Arendt thus reverses Hardin's point that Hobbes saw the public good as a negation of the private.

56 *Origins*, 139–40.

57 Ibid., 141.

58 Ibid., 140.

59 As Macpherson puts it: "We have here the essential characteristics of the competitive market. Every man's value, manifested by the honour given him by others, is both determined by and determines the other's opinion of his power, manifested by what they would give for the use of his power . . ." *Possessive*, 38.

60 Hobbes, of course, often speaks of democracy and aristocracy as legitimate political forms, but his arguments about the unification of power make it clear where his preference lies. See, for instance, L, XIX, and XVII, 13.

61 *Origins*, 141.

62 CEPT, 214.

63 "The liberty of a subject lieth, therefore, only in those things which, in regulating their actions, the sovereign hath praetermitted (such as is the liberty to buy, and sell, and otherwise contract with one another; to choose their own abode, their own diet, their own trade of life, and institute their children as they themselves think fit; and the like)" L, XXI, 6.

64 *Leviathan*, 160.

65 Ibid., 228.

66 Ibid., 217–18.

67 *Lenin*, 146.

68 Ibid., 7.

69 *Leviathan*, 4–5.

70 Ibid., 190.

71 Ibid., 212.

72 Ibid., 224.

73 "I shall then suggest that ideology 'acts' or 'functions' in such a way that it 'recruits' subjects among the individuals (it recruits them all), or 'transforms' the individuals into subjects (it transforms them all) by that very precise operation which I have called interpellation or hailing, and which can be imagined along the lines of the most commonplace everyday police (or other) hailing: 'Hey, you there!'" *Lenin*, p. 174. A few pages later,

Althusser argues that the subject is already essentially hailed before they are born, in terms of all of the expectations that surround an unborn child.

74 *Leviathan*, XXX, 6.

75 Ibid., XXX, 3.

76 See Michel Foucault, *Discipline and Punish: The Birth of the Prison*, trans. Alan Sheridan (New York: Vintage Books, 1979): 135–70.

77 *Origins*, 157.

78 *Leviathan*, XIII, 13.

79 Ibid., A Review and Conclusion, 16.

80 *Washington Post*, 5/27/03.

2

Internal Externalities

Clothes make the man. Naked people have little or no influence on society.

—*Mark Twain*

1. The Spirit of the Letter

In the first chapter, in contradistinction to the usual models of cynical theorist of realpolitik and master of rationality, Hobbes was presented as the thinker of desire, a human fact neither avoidable nor curable. For him, noncausal entities of the imagination, futural projections of loss of power and discomfort, false doctrines on the nature of reality and the common-wealth, and an imbalanced distribution of passions across the human plane converge in creating a natural condition of shared calamity. Such is what leads Hobbes to his thoroughly ideological conclusions—conclusions that bring him closer to Althusser than Friedman. Hobbes abhorred a vacuum, and hence divisions of power, which define both democracy and capitalism, were anathema. As such, the state of nature indicates a distinct realm only to the degree that an artificial sovereignty within which ideology forces its root can successfully mould the consciousness of subjects. But all that we have established thus far is that Hobbes was inordinately preoccupied with desire and that, as a result, the Leviathan must serve to control it.

A number of fundamental questions therefore remain unanswered. For example, is desire so fundamental to subjectivity that it is the lens through which we must think the political? And even if it is, does it make sense to speak of a state of nature in a time when even nature appears to be a mutating and mutable entity (when, for instance, even our genes are subject to copyright)? Ought we to not stand with Macpherson when he calls out the state of nature as a mere projection rooted firmly in our social historical location? Hence, "[a] more decisive evidence that the state of nature is a statement of the behavior to which specifically civilized men would be led if even the present imperfect sovereign were removed, is that the full state of nature is in fact reached by successive degrees of abstraction from civilized society."[1] Of course, Macpherson is no doubt right. A state of nature conceived as a fully apolitical realm is an abstraction. There was and is no place that lacks entirely for the political, but this does not therefore mean, however, that the state of nature does not exist. Whether or not all the world was, to begin with, America, is irrelevant to the arguments here. The state of nature refers less to prepolitical time than the very condition of the political. As such, to ask the question of the state of nature is to broach the problem of subjectivity and the manner in which it determines any given political formation.

The thesis of the present chapter takes up Hobbesian desire in order to establish that the state of nature is to be retained as an entirely valid and necessary concept. I maintain that the state of nature is both real and only understandable within the logic of desire as Hobbes has established it, but with the further addition that the distinction between a person and its persona, or between our selves denied their social codifications and their personifications within established realms of mutual recognition, is where we can locate the truly political factor of desire (not, as Hobbes had it, in motion). Insofar as political formations tend to the maintenance of the persona in the name of sovereignty (for instance, my nationality protects my identity, provides me with papers, numbers, and legal institutions, educates me from an early age, describes the conditions of my death, and so on), the person, to the degree that it is not outfitted with such identifications, indicates the state of nature insofar as one is outside of sovereignty, is without a persona. Hence, as Arendt has argued, the stateless in World War II had no place within any national structure, allowing them to be liquidated. Similarly, prisoners sent to so-called dark sites, or at Guantanamo Bay, are designated as extralegal beings, placing them entirely outside of national and international law, allowing interrogators to do as they will, stepping across the thresholds of what is discussable in polite conversation. Or, to arrive at a grander example, the effect of occupation in Iraq led to a division so fraught that its result was civil war, one whose internal fracture is such that it is unclear where sovereignty exists, what identities are stable, and who shall ultimately prevail. Within this list, the stateless and our prisoners are within the state of nature, but at the mercy of personas whose desire is monstrous in its ability to use power against those who have no power (to, as Schmitt would have it, take the reins within the state of exception), while in Iraq we see a broader crisis of personas, or, otherwise put, an entire country seesawing on the two sides of abjection, with no party establishing a stable persona and all parties fighting against their reduction to mere persons who are expendable.

Here, Giorgio Agamben will argue that this is the definition of the Sovereign as such, that part of its very biopolitical definition is the banning of *homo sacer*: ". . . the inclusion of bare life in the political realm constitutes the original—if concealed—nucleus of sovereign power. *It can even be said that the production of a biopolitical body is the original activity of sovereign power.*"[2] But Agamben leaves us with the question of why any Sovereign would want to ban in the first place. For within the froth of political desire, a factor that Agamben ignores as merely psychological, the realm of human rights, that most venerable liberal institution, is rendered mute as to its legitimacy and, more importantly, reach.

Indeed, the concept of human rights only seems to weaken with age. While its roots in medieval Christian theory have a lengthy and detailed outgrowth, perhaps the primary obstacle that human rights face today is thought itself. For within current doxa, whatever the forces of absolutist theology have produced, the quandary of secular relativism cannot, thus far, disappear. Indeed, it is one of democracy's weaknesses that to the degree that it professes freedom it cannot profess any singular or specific ground for that freedom. It may, for instance, pay head to a god of some sort, but it cannot discount those who discount the same god. This is not merely an issue of historicism or relativism. It is, more than anything, an issue of a theoretical concern made painfully practical. Indeed, one can see how such thinking has produced a straightjacket of sorts in President Ahmadinejad's letter to President Bush sent in May of 2006—its basic premise was that as a Christian, Bush was not being very Christian while, simultaneously, as a representative of freedom, he was not producing much freedom. All this from the president of a strictly theological and autocratic regime. Such contradiction is definitional to our current time, indicating as it does that rights, insofar as they have any true anchor, find only the negative foundation of the person qua rightless and mute as their source. Of course, the grounding moment of this negative foundation, at least in terms of our collective memory, is the Nazi Holocaust, an as yet unparalleled instance of mechanized, abject murder born within an ideology of completeness that necessitated its emptied Other. To return again to Arendt, it is to her credit that she noted in reference to the stateless in World War II that only insofar as humanity was made absolutely universal by being utterly stripped of any social signifier whatsoever (name, nationality, legal designation), could it then be decimated guiltlessly and, in some cases, with pleasure.

It is this universal human being that functions as the key to unlocking the relevance of the state of nature, and it is only from the vantage point of the repugnance of our universality that we can begin to speak about things like human rights, though we are precluded from establishing, as Arendt desperately called for, a right to have rights. In essence, the distinction between a person and its persona, or a stripped and discarded human and its more dreamlike instantiation within a protected social order, results in the conclusion that the particular will have to be the ground of the universal in regard to the political. This will mean, then, an uncanny reversal of the usual line of argument; namely, human rights qua protections of the person are necessary to the degree that our universality is horrifying to our personas. The bulk of us live by virtue of social identities, personas that we present to the world and protect with the aid of others who are also so endowed, not to mention broad social and governmental forces. Whether it is our nationality, our sexuality, our class, or our certificated name, our presentations of ourselves are successful only to the degree that they are recognized by others as legitimate. Hence they are fundamentally imaginary projections, projections which, of course, have quite concrete effects. Once these imaginary forces are stripped away from an individual, that naked individual, made only a person, is an object of abjection, not a container of positive right. The recognition of this repugnance must also be the recognition that human rights are there to protect this universal human and not the reverse. That is to say, it is not our universality that protects us, but rather our universality that demands our protection. The right to have rights can only ever exist as an effort in the name of our persons—it has no other ground. Thus, in contradistinction to the usual search for positive universal grounds or forms that will shield our seemingly fleeting everyday lives, only the dross of the common and tedious productions of the everyday will protect us from our truer selves.

This reversal of the universal and the particular leads, furthermore, to a second conclusion; namely, that the political exists in and for the person, not the persona. The result is easily achieved. For, given that it is the very essence of the persona to be caught in an imaginary capture of stable identification, the obverse of this stability is that anything that indicates its fragility is, generally speaking, too anxiety inducing to merit cohabitation. In other words, the imaginary persona, fundamentally linked to the sense of distinction, of border, of sovereignty of self, however tied to the nationality that anchors it, cannot stand its person, even if the person is an unavoidable and ever present condition of the persona (after all, our personas arise in and out of our persons—are layered, like the statue of Glaucus, over time in order to avoid an abject state). But if something like commodious living is the goal of any political entity, which it must be, then the reduction of the political to the protection of a subset of personas in opposition to persons is antipolitical. Put otherwise, because the person is that which we are reduced to in the state of nature, the political exists as the production of commodious living for persons in the pursuit of such living. If we are to give a name to the protection of personas in and against persons, then perhaps the best designation would be politics. To play politics is to play one grouping off of another, one set of interests against another. Within the democratic realm, this politics is, of course, the politics of parties and interests. Within the aristocratic realm, it is the play of the aristocracy against the people. Within totalitarianism, to the degree that it is possible, it is the play of the Party against the people. The political is therefore not defined as the distinction between friend and enemy, as Carl Schmitt had it[3] (and which we could call, classically speaking, politics), or even as the empty center of its possible representation, as Claude Lefort argued.[4] The political is defined as the protection of the person in and against the desire of personas or other abjectified persons, which results in the fact that the universal must be saved by the particularity of artificial political institutions.

The political thus exists in the name of the universal, but as its protection from sovereignty (when sovereignty exists in the name of a persona). Insofar as our universal condition invites destruction, however, then we cannot locate rights within that universality, but rather within its need for protection. This results in the fact that rights are not guaranteed but rather given protection by concrete institutions that must be developed from the principle of the political rather than politics. That is, rights are only a function of what humans do to protect rights—any other talk of derivation, foundation, and universal necessity merely floats. The political, and rights along with it, exists by its instantiation in the name of persons as opposed to personas. Such a reversal of the universal and the particular, whereby the particular must save the day for the universal, is exhibited best in those hoary state of nature theories that only seem to crop up, practically speaking, in the minds of conservative judges and academics. Nonetheless, from the debate between two of the great proponents of a state of nature, Hobbes and Locke, we can derive the main logic of the political that I wish to establish—desire. Desire determines the bellicose nature of the apolitical state, but only insofar as desire faces its negation. I thus argue that the state of nature is to be maintained as a useful concept, indicating an internal tension necessary to all political formation due to the fact that those who constituted political formations, humans, are themselves constituted by this problematic desire.

The necessity of the state of nature within the concept of the political is described by what I term an 'internal externality'; insofar as the state of nature is deemed external to the political state, it is nonetheless maintained internally, not as the banned *homo sacer* of Agamben's sovereign zone of indistinction, but as the split of desire that defines the subjectivity with which any given political formation must concern itself. By desire, as both Hobbes and Locke pointed out, I mean the fact that human subjectivity is defined by the impossibility of ever being fully satisfied with any object, thus leading to an endless task of accumulating ever more satisfactions in order to cover over what is essentially an anxiety about one's identity. It is Hobbes, however, who understood best that desire is anxious precisely because it depends on an individual's worry over how she or he is seen by others, what he called eminence. Desire indicates a split between what one has and what one doesn't have and, in the process, between what one is and what one isn't. To the degree that our eminence, or social status in the eyes of others, is grounded, we have more or less protected personas—socially stable identities. But to the degree that we lose those personas, we become ever more abstract beings without such protections. We become, that is, universal humans, or mere persons. To become a mere person is not merely to become an abstract universal entity, however. It is unfortunately also to become repugnant to most personas, to those who are not so stripped of their social moorings. More importantly, as we shall see, it is to become expendable.

2. Money or Life?

Your money or your life? It seems a simple proposition. But while it might be taken as a question best answered by calculations of profit and loss, a true risk analysis will place its emphasis on the worth of one's persona. We can find a nice example of this in the British hostage crisis of 2007. While controversies surrounding Iran's nuclear development, involvement in Iraq, and position as antagonist *par excellence* against the U.S. and Britain clearly informed the process, the confessions of the British captives went beyond mere theater. These confessions provided Iran with a great gain by virtue of the fact that they caused many among the world audience to wonder aloud not so much whether the captives were guilty as whether they were improperly fearful, thereby providing Iran with a certain level of success, no doubt desired if we are to judge by the manner in which the whole process was staged for world viewers, right down to the ill-fitting, pedestrian attire the soldiers were made to wear.[5]

What is important about these confessions for my purposes here has to do with the captives themselves, for in the choice one makes between money and life, money is merely symbolic for something altogether more profound. What one chooses, in other words, is whether living is more important than dignity or, otherwise put, a sense of ego in its full imaginary capture. The entire discussion around the propriety of the confessions and the weakness or professionalism of the soldiers' actions is the projection of an audience deciding whether money or life was chosen, whether the soldiers decided to keep their money (dignity/identity), or their life (loss of control/submission). Were, to paraphrase Twain, the soldiers naked or clothed? And if the former, did Britain not thereby lose in stature and influence? In this sense, one becomes what one chooses; one either becomes money and all of its symbolic attire, or one becomes mere life, left naked and impotent. That this scenario revolves around the decisions of a public audience detracts nothing from the argument; as soldiers, the captives were personas, representatives of the British state. Nor does the argument slacken when considered in terms of what kidnapped citizens, journalists, and soldiers go through without the full weight of the public eye to intervene. As will become evident later on, the self is not a unity—it is always divided internally between an indecipherable core and a persona that represents that core, even to the self. Such is why how one acts, whether publicly or privately, is always reflexive, split between its person and persona, the latter being not merely the representative of the self, but the embodiment of the social dimension of the I, and the former being the self sans such imaginary formations, left to its brute physicality and thus, left undifferentiated within the public realm, universal in its emptiness. It is precisely on the issue of what is at stake in this splitting that the debate between Hobbes and Locke resides, and, as we shall see, it is Hobbes who captures the unfortunate truth of the matter.

As is well known, Hobbes argued that the Leviathan brought us out of the bellicosity that defined the state of nature, a state so terrible that it is indistinguishable from a state of war. Locke, responding to Filmer, but clearly Hobbes as well, was not persuaded. The state of war was a subset or a possibility within the state of nature rather than its very definition.[6] While Hobbes, in a proto-Marxist moment, understood property as legitimated only by the Sovereign, Locke proposed the a priori knowledge that property is inherent in our bodies and selves, and thus the principle point of government lies in preserving this property, whether it be my living body or "the Turfs my Servant has cut."[7] It mattered little to Locke whether property is being infringed upon by a governmental or a nongovernmental force; illegitimate use of violence is violence no matter the perpetrator. Only a voluntary and properly represented majority constitutes a political society.[8]

Nonetheless, that the state of nature is ultimately untenable was not a point of contention. As Locke shows in sections 13, 90, and, particularly, 123 of the *Second Treatise*, civil government is indeed necessary to avoid the 'inconveniences' of the state of nature. If the state of nature were all that peaceful or, put otherwise, if war did not override the state of peace with a merciless consistency, we would never need to combine, and Rousseau's distant dream of an unmediated self would wake in the Real. The distinction Locke is making thereby serves the purpose of understanding the nature of government beyond its 'artificial' constructions: "To understand political Power right, and derive it from its Original, we must consider what State all Men are naturally in. . . ."[9] Insofar as the natural human is the foundation of the artificial person, the state of nature is an essential part of government, not merely an external possibility or a prehistorical moment. When Hobbes and Locke ask what sort of state we are in when government doesn't exist, they are arguing that we are always more or less living in relation to the state of nature by virtue of what political cohabitation entails. Indeed, when we consider that for Hobbes and Locke all leaders remain in a state of nature, the sense in which we always remain engulfed by the natural intensifies.[10] But even for the rest of us mere subjects, the conceptual dynamics of the state of nature qua internal to government can be seen through the very different uses of the thief in Hobbes and Locke.

For Hobbes, when faced with a decision between money and life, it is best to renounce one's dignity.[11] Locke, of course, argues the reverse, making the point that one can never predict how far a thief will go:

> This makes it Lawful for a man to *kill a Thief*, who has not in the least hurt him nor declared any design upon his Life, any farther then by the use of Force, so as to get him in his Power . . . because using force, where he has no Right, to get me into his Power, let his pretense be what it will, I have no reason to suppose, that he, who would *take away my Liberty*, would not when he had me in his Power, take away every thing else.[12]

Both positions are compelling. Mostly, thieves are only interested in money, but given that it is impossible to know for sure, Hobbes and Locke turn to the question of human nature in general. Hobbes' infamous verdict is that subjects are constituted by an unquenchable desire: "For there is no such thing as perpetual tranquility of mind, while we live here; because *life itself is but motion*, and can never be without desire, nor without fear, no more than without sense."[13] Desire knows no fulfillment because it is defined by lack, and only moments of brief felicity are to be had. There is thus no *summum bonum* for Hobbes, and although the rapacious motion that defines some does not define all, there is enough of this desire floating around that the prime goal of existence is to get out of any state that is questionable in order to reach for some sort of assurance.

Such is why Hobbesian contracts extend to thieves. The internal machinations of the state of nature are such that they suggest to reason certain laws or principles which override the terrible looping of desire. These laws are, in their first and second instances, to seek peace and to do so through contract and covenant.[14] By covenant, Hobbes means an agreement in which rights are transferred and a subject relinquishes total right in exchange for protection and stability.[15] It is only at this point of contract that the notions of right and wrong, justice and its negation come into play, for covenants are the only bridge out of a purely random realm in which right and wrong are subsumed under the will to survive: "Covenants entered into by fear, in the condition of mere nature, are obligatory. . . . For it is a contract wherein one receiveth the benefit of life . . . and consequently, where no other law (as in the condition of mere nature) forbiddeth the performance, the covenant is valid."[16] Thus Hobbes, in seeing the manner in which desire is augmented and distorted by fantasies of eminence, figures that only through an artificial and yet binding covenant can subjects release themselves from the endless power struggle that defines the state of nature, even if it occurs briefly in some anonymous alleyway.[17] In war, self-preservation is the prime goal. Covenants are the only sociable and, more importantly, *reasonable* way of achieving such an end.

While the extent of Locke's fairly blunt and consistent position on our God-given, positive rights and duties is generally well known (for instance, in the case where it is permissible for a subject to be killed for disobedience, one's property is still hands off[18]), in the *Essay Concerning Human Understanding*, Locke enumerates a human subjectivity for which property is not so obviously owned. Indeed, subjectivity in the *Essay* begins to bring Locke closer to Hobbes, but only in order to render Locke's position all the more problematic. Though the *Essay* was published in the same year as the *Treatises*, from the second edition onward, a new element was brought in, specifically in his ruminations on power. In 1694, that is, Locke begins to note what he calls an "uneasiness" in the powers of volition:

> What moves the mind, in every particular instance, to determine its general power of directing, to this or that particular Motion or Rest? And to this I answer, The motive, for continuing in the same State or Action, is only the present satisfaction in it; The motive to change, is always some *uneasiness*: nothing setting us upon the change of State, or upon any new Action, but some *uneasiness*.[19]

Here we can see that a certain anxiety now begins to infiltrate the will, an uneasiness that Locke explicitly equates with desire, thus noting that "[a]s much as we desire any absent good, so much are we in pain for it."[20] Though Locke is clear that will and desire are not reducible, he is explicit in arguing that it is desire that determines the will and is the prime motivator, if not mover, in a given decision.

While it might appear that we thus see a replication of Hobbesian desire, Locke is not quite in step, for the question remains as to what generally determines this desire. In a moment of confession, however, Locke in fact also allows that there is not necessarily a *summum bonum* that determines a given person's desire, and so "till he feels an *uneasiness* in the want of it, his *will* will not be determin'd to any action in pursuit of this confessed greater good. . . ."[21] The question thus arises as to what distinguishes Locke from Hobbes when he draws out the implications of this uneasy desire. The answer to desire is, again, reason, but that of the lonely individual. While Hobbes had no faith in a native intelligence for self-rule, Locke thought true liberty is locatable in the control of desire: ". . . and I desire it may be well consider'd, whether the great inlet, and exercise of all the *liberty* Men have, are capable of, or can be useful to them, and that whereon depends the turn of their actions, does not lie in this, that they can *suspend* their desire, and stop them from determining their *wills* to any action, till they have duly and fairly *examin'd* the good and evil of it. . . ."[22] Similarly, Locke argues in the *Treatises* that it is not until a subject has achieved the age of reason that she or he is truly ready to exercise freedom.[23]

The Lockeian subject is thus closer to Hobbes' than is often thought, though it diverges when reason prevents desire from going astray. While Locke enumerates in the *Essay* a list of the ways in which reason can go awry, it is clear that he thinks that this list is not long enough to prevent a majoritarian political structure from remaining the prime goal. Locke did admit to serious problems with human nature in the *Treatises*: "And were it not for the corruption, and vitiousness of degenerate Men, there would be no need of any other; no necessity that Men should separate from this great and natural community, and by positive agreements combine into smaller and divided associations."[24] But these problems are not enough to detract from the structure as whole. As with the great economic scandals of the closing of the twentieth century and torture at Abu Ghraib, to take a couple of examples, a few bad apples can ruin it for the greater community. The problem with this argument, however, is that it does not explain why the state of nature, a peaceful state in the abstract, in reality always ends in the state of war. That is, why are there always a few bad apples, and why do they always prevail? For Locke, government was inevitable because the state of war was invariable, which is in essence a recapitulation of Hobbes' argument. Indeed, given that it is nearly impossible to have any guarantee about one's property, no matter how God-given, without governmental power, Hobbes' argument concerning the nature of property as derivative ultimately of government guarantees begins to look plausible. No doubt, Locke's ruminations on desire bring us closer to thinking through why the state of nature is, for all intents and purposes, untenable. It leads us, as well, to ask an important question: why is this notion of uneasiness, of unfulfillable desire, not included in the *Treatises*? The answer, it seems, is that it would begin to gnaw at this individual reason, to force the question of why, if one person cannot be trusted to rule, many can. If, to borrow from Hobbes, there is fractiousness internal to our very selves that constantly endangers the political, why should we trust a *multiplication* of rulers not to return us to civil dystopia?

The point here is not to promote monarchy so much as to seek the structure of the political in regard to that subjectivity which shall constitute it. Hobbes and Locke both clearly agree that desire is a problematic and central aspect of the human condition. From there, however, they diverge. Lockeian reason is a powerful enough counterforce, particularly once education has taken its proper route, that we need not ultimately fear desire.[25] For Hobbes, however, desire is paramount, and the monarch must always be wary of its growth within the commonwealth.[26] That desire in a broader sense is definitive of the human condition is clear. Humans do not exist as fully self-contained and realized beings. They are in need of basic elements, such as food, water, and shelter. But while the latter might well be defined as mere need, need becomes complicated when it seeks the company and recognition of others. For Hobbes, it is not so much our physical capabilities as our social standing, or, as he calls it, eminence, that decides our place in the world.[27] Should we lose eminence, our ability to achieve our desires will be defeated as others overpower us. Between our mere person and our social personas, there is a division that puts into question our continued existence. It is this division, this space or gap that is never able to be ultimately filled, thereby establishing the human condition as one defined by a constant need for further recognition. This recognition is bestowed in the forms of names, sexual designation, nationality, ethnicity, class, and so on. To the degree that these forms are given approbation, our continued felicity is given greater assurance and our persona has a higher valuation. To the degree that they are devalued, our personas give less cover to our persons, and we begin to collapse into a unity of self that is unbearable precisely because it has lost its social imaginary supports. The loss of these supports has important effects in terms of the human condition that we will turn to momentarily. In any case, the central point that Hobbes adds to the debate about political subjectivity is that our self is divided between our person and our social persona.[28] It is between our self and our eminence, or our internal being and our social standing, that desire creeps asymptotically toward felicity or rushes, all too often, toward an imaginary destruction of society.

When so stripped of our social mores, our governmental modes of control, and our ability to judge one another within civil society, Hobbes' account of the state of nature contains the truth of our political condition. Being on the brink of total social decay unleashes the worst in human motives and actions.[29] In a state of social breakdown, the internal lack of the human subject becomes unbearable physically and psychologically—physically because one has no obvious means of subsistence, and psychologically because one has no sense of place, thus leading to a frenetic overactivity on the part of desire, either as a form of self-defense or as an offensive attempt at gaining more power. It is this in-between state that makes the state of nature bellicose, and it is also this lack of assuredness that leads to the virtual equality and de facto right to everything of which Hobbes speaks: since one does not know what is going to happen next, and since there are no governing bodies or higher authorities to appeal to, the state of nature is a state of war where all are reduced to the same condition of lawless survival.

Had Locke placed his ruminations on desire within his political texts, he would have, perhaps, been brought closer to the issue of how subjects consider themselves in the eyes of others, or in terms of what Hobbes called eminence. Locke veers in this direction when he speaks of the necessary tutelage of children, lunatics, idiots, and madmen,[30] and, as Uday Mehta has pointed out, notes an inherent madness in even the most normal of beings.[31]

But he does not bring the full implications of the imaginary to bear, for the concept of the imaginary Other does not make a decisive appearance either in the state of nature or the political realm. Of course, Hobbes goes awry here as much as does Locke. Though it is the case that there is no external law that indicates that property and freedom are inherent in the state of nature, there is also no positive right to everything.[32]

Nonetheless, Hobbes' account of the pull of desire, of a base fear instilled by a conception predicated on a loss, is important to the extent that it defines the political. Because human desire cannot be destroyed without destroying the human, the state of nature may recede, but it never vanishes. It is that which government strives to mollify without destroying, whatever form it takes, even totalitarianism.[33] The state of nature therefore remains ever present within governments as desire, an internal lack to each that creates a tension between all. Desire thus indicates the level to which existence is split between the I and the Other, thus placing the verification of the value of the self on the basis of social projections of its value. As such, the implication to be retained is that this division between I and Other is, like the state of nature itself, an internal externality. The split, that is, designates a distance between an individual and other such individuals, but it also indicates that this split is maintained internally within any given individual, hence producing the possibility of fantasmatic projections of what others may or may not be up to. When the Other, or the social, collapses, when it loses its rules and structures of verification and designation, then desire overcompensates and, in its failure to find a stable footing, ultimately devolves into anxiety and subjectivity scrambles in an abjection that will proliferate its enemies and insecurities and, in the process, make these fantasies concrete, as these persons interact with them in tow. Such is the precarious problem of human cohabitation; in an uncontrolled state of human cohabitation, desire will trump property every time, including life.

Indeed, as Rousseau pointed out, even in a properly republican government, when the people come together, a sort of horrifying suspension takes place:

> The instant the people is legitimately assembled as a sovereign body, all jurisdiction of the government ceases, the executive power is suspended, and the person of the humblest citizen is as sacred and inviolable as that of the first magistrate; because where the represented person is, there is no longer any representative. . . . These intervals of suspension, during which the prince recognizes or ought to recognize an actual superior, have always terrified it; and these

assemblies of the people, which are the aegis of the body politic and
the restraint on government, have been viewed with horror by the
leaders of all times.[34]

The horror that the prince feels in the face of this assembly of the people is
not simply a fear that power or control will be lost; it is a legitimate fear that
the body itself will be ripped asunder, that the desire of the people no
longer contained by law but hanging in the interim, suspended, will not
reformulate itself into a peaceful whole.[35] At such a point, the electoral
process would be the opening point toward a state of nature, a chaotic
battle for organization.[36] Hence, while Rousseau's argument is that this
horror inducing opening is a legitimate and necessary check on the concentration of represented power, there is nonetheless no guarantee during an
election that it will take place properly, that the results will come out
smoothly, that the people will even have decided, thereby causing a split
in the governing body and an uncertainty as to whether the body exists
anymore. Thus the space of suspension is aligned with the fear and excite-
ment of non-presence, the very motor of desire, which is why Hobbes was
adamant that elections ought to be replaced with the will of the Sovereign.
While it is to Locke's credit that he pointed out the desire of the sovereign,
the question of the desire of the demos would have been more fruitfully
examined.

Let me then make explicit the argument so far. The state of nature is
being posited as a metaphysical reality contained in all political formations.
It is metaphysical in the sense that it is not merely a possible or actual state,
but a condition of the political as such. This is the result, as Hobbes has
shown us, of the problem of human desire in relation to eminence in any
social formation. Given that humans are constitutionally incomplete
entities, and given that they are the very elements from which and for
which governments are formed, this very lack itself defines all governments. Insofar as political bodies fall apart due to human desire, the state of
nature can be said to exist outright in the form of civil war or total dissolution of a state. Insofar as political bodies retain their cohesion, the state of
nature exists internally as that which threatens dismemberment. In either
case, what is at stake is eminence, or the imaginary projections of individuals that motor their desire. As an example, we can see the state of nature as
defining in totalitarian and dictatorial bodies to the extent that elections
are either removed or controlled, rendering them shams, while in real or
partial democracies, it shows itself more directly as the very possible suspension of the government itself (often enough to be replaced by tyranny).

In the former, the imaginary is strictly controlled and more or less embodied by the Sovereign/Party; in the later, it is more or less left unchecked, multiplying into a greater or lesser variety of Others/Sovereigns.

While conditional, however, the state of nature is not foundational; there is neither a pure state of nature, nor a pure political social state. The two must be said to contain one another as defining co-negations. When there is political cohesion, there is the more or less intense worry over the possibility of its breakdown, represented by the idea of nature. When there is a complete breakdown, there is the drive toward cohesion, represented by the idea of the state, the republic, the monarchy, the dictatorship, the people, and so on. While the contract could be called the bridge or route out of the state of nature, desire (qua anxiety, hope, fear, loss, imagination, and lack) could be said to be the elemental or motor decline from the political state. Thus, when the state of nature arrives and announces itself as irrevocably horrible, desire rebounds upon itself and realizes that the various forms of 'having it all' and 'protecting its property (self)' are essentially failed. It therefore has to give itself up to Others or an Other, which is what every contract signifies; the willful letting go of desire's active attempt to singularly control its environment. Seeking order and control (laws of nature, reason's ruse) and desire's attempt to control order (the trumping of laws, the bellicosity of the human) codetermine one another. For these reasons, the 'state of nature' requires its inversion; namely, the 'nature of state'.

But though desire is axiomatic of the human condition, is it really true that desire stripped bare, desire sans its social mores and political and cultural guides is really a sort of hell unleashed? Even if numerous historical examples, such as Afghanistan and Iraq, seem to suggest this, is it a necessary fact, or are these merely human possibilities? Indeed, does not the Ukrainian example show us that there is the possibility of a peaceful revolt, that humans are after all not that necessarily horrible when the institutions prove to be corrupt, when it appears that the government has even attempted to poison the opposition leader? What is it about this desire that is so bad—is it not only sometimes given to excess, and is Locke not after all more or less correct, even if he does posit property and our freedom to control it somewhat capriciously, and even he has no concept of political desire? Indeed, do we not need to at least assume some concept of property in order to maintain some concept of the boundaries of power, of limiting the reach of others and institutions upon ourselves?

Unfortunately, we are not to be led to such conclusions. The universal tendency toward human surplus murder is exhibited in the stateless of

World War II, where, as Hannah Arendt argues, we see that the human being stripped of all of its social standing becomes an object of revulsion, a point of what Kristeva calls abjection.[37] Insofar as the stateless indicate desire's death, the in-between of desire without reference to a possible foothold in the realm of eminence and property, they also indicate the logic according to which desire unleashed is submitted. Without recourse to a stable fantasy of completeness, the self revolts upon itself and responds with abuse and murder. The stateless indicate that the political is very much defined by the internal antagonism of the state of nature qua human desire, for insofar as any human is reducible to this in-between, the political has to keep vigilant over such a breakdown, either by giving organization to desire in a free manner, or by making sure that those who are reduced to no-one are turned into what Lacan would call an anxiety inducing *objet a*, an excessive object to negate in order to preserve a fantasy of wholeness simply because it points all too clearly to our ontological splitting. While it is true that the Holocaust has become a knee-jerk example for anyone who wishes to make claims about the existence of evil or to negate an opponent's argument automatically, the depth of its impact is in no way to be considered shallow, as for instance in Darfur, where a debate continued for months between the U.S. and the rest of the world as to whether genocide had taken place. That such an issue has now been subsumed under the quibbling realpolitik negotiations of the larger world powers indicates its almost ordinary and, unfortunately, failed status in our present reality.[38] And it is just such ordinariness that makes the question of its causes all the more serious.

3. Stateless Nature

In *On Revolution*, in a brief discussion of the state of nature, Hannah Arendt mused that there is something to the idea that all political beginnings are fundamentally violent:

> Insofar as violence plays a predominant role in wars and revolution, both occur outside the political realm, strictly speaking, in spite of their enormous role in recorded history. This fact led the seventeenth century, which had its share of experience in wars and revolutions, to the assumption of a prepolitical state, called 'state of nature' which, of course, never was meant to be taken as a historical fact. Its relevance even today lies in the recognition that a political realm does not automatically come into being wherever men live together, and that there exist events which, though they may occur in a strictly historical

context, are not really political and perhaps not even connected with politics. The notion of a state of nature alludes at least to a reality that cannot be comprehended by the nineteenth-century idea of development, no matter how we may conceive of it—whether in the form of cause and effect, or of potentiality and actuality, or of a dialectical movement, or even of simple coherence and sequence in occurrences. For the hypotheses of a state of nature implies the existence of a beginning that is separated from everything following it as though by an unbridgeable chasm.[39]

The idea set provided here is suggestive if unclear. On the one hand, violence is something that is entirely external to the political realm. Though its prevalence in history is almost total with regard to the creation and continuation of political entities, its division is decisive. Indeed, this necessity only intensifies as Arendt continues her thought on the next page: "The conviction, in the beginning was a crime—for which the phrase 'state of nature' is only a theoretically purified paraphrase—has carried through the centuries no less self-evident plausibility for the state of human affairs than the first sentence of St John, 'In the beginning was the Word', has possessed for the affairs of salvation." Indeed, it appears that the violent and criminal beginning of all things in the world is a function of Arendtian common sense, an assumption internal to the stories people have told themselves about the way of the world.

And yet the state of nature is strictly apolitical, connected with the political though excluded from its formal enactment. What is more, in a tantalizing moment of theoretical connection, violence is brought in direct relation to the idea of beginning, a pivotal idea given its inherent relation to natality, the preeminent Arendtian concept of both the political and the human itself. However, as we know from *On Violence*, Arendt views violence as a utilitarian notion inimical to political freedom and action, to working together toward ends that are unknowable: "*Violence*, finally, as I have said, is distinguished by its instrumental character. Phenomenologically, it is close to strength, since the implements of violence, like all other tools, are designed and used for the purpose of multiplying natural strength until, in the last stage of their development, they cannot substitute for it."[40] Violence is a mere concatenation of individual strength, the goal of which is to overwhelm individual strength and, ultimately, to prevent power and freedom, or the purposeful banding together of individuals, from prevailing. We can note the similarity here to Hobbes' concept of the Sovereign, in which individuals relinquish their psychological power into a *One* who shall represent all of *Them*, except that here we see the condensation occur on a purely phenomenological plane. Either way, the Sovereign is hereby excluded from the Arendtian version of the political given its foundations in the accumulation of force in and against subjects. But this phenomenological description of violence tells us nothing about its reason for existence, nor does it say anything about why violence would have a primordial relationship to beginning.

In fact, in *On Revolution*, Arendt bypasses altogether the deeper questions of war, a preeminent form of violent historical beginning, and in *On Violence* she regards its prevalence as a byproduct of sovereignty:

> The chief reason warfare is still with us is neither a secret death wish of the human species, nor an irrepressible instinct of aggression, nor, finally and more plausibly, the serious economic and social danger inherent in disarmament, but the simple fact that no substitute for this final arbiter in international affairs has yet appeared on the political scene.[41]

Clearly, the psychoanalytic idea of the death drive is *faux*, even though a rather psychological treatment of sovereignty seems to pervade the need to revert to war. Here we find a clear begging of the question—why do nations identify with Sovereignty and independence and, more importantly, why do such ideas lead conflicting nations into war? Or, otherwise put, what is unleashed in international friction but some sort of aggression, some internal tendency toward death? More to the point, what is the ground of sovereignty? Whence comes its motivating factor such that cohabitation with the Other is negated, save for strict differentiations established on the basis of particular identities? However, despite this initial dismissal, Arendt's concept of violence does not stop at the phenomenological level, and, as we shall see, approaches an argument concerning the nature of the human that brings us close to something along the lines of a death drive and, with it, the desire of subjectivity we have been outlining.

Indeed, beyond the descriptive instrumental sort of violence that Arendt explicitly denotes, there are two other concepts or, rather, modalities of violence that she deploys in her attempt to come to terms with how humanity fails itself. As I will argue, these three notions of violence are linked to one another in such a manner that one can deduce the phenomenological mode of violence from a psychological sort, the later being ultimately grounded on a primordial biological drive to violence. We will find this deduction exhibited in Arendt's arguments concerning the stateless in World War II.

What will become clear is that Arendt's placement of the state of nature outside of the realm of the political is both necessary and impossible. Necessary because the political, as Arendt understands it, predicates its own soundness on avoiding the state of nature and the violence it does the body and freedom. And impossible because this state of nature remains a defining threat, a threat that even the freest, most stable political body carries with itself by virtue of being a collectivity of natural beings that are defined by natural life as much as, if not more than, political life. In essence, two modes of natality go to define the human condition, a natality of freedom and expression that is unpredictable and deepens our understanding of the world, and a natality of repetitive reproduction that is headless, violent, and necessary. This creates a fundamental tension in Arendt's work, a tension between the need for an open space of freedom so that a political natality may flourish and a need for limiting laws and principles of civic duty to prevent the psychotic release of a natural and potentially hellish natality. This tension is not resolved within Arendt's *oeuvre*, and as I will argue later on, this is due to the fact that Arendt fails to examine what Hobbes understood so clearly; namely, the problem of desire. All the same, it is her examination of violence in relation to the stateless that most forcefully exhibits Hobbes' arguments. This examination, unfortunately, will also show why democracy, even as Arendt articulates it, will not resolve the 'predicament of our common responsibility'.

4. Universal Oblivion

Arendt's breakdown of what happened to stateless peoples produces a frustrating and paradoxical logic whereby the universal, something that seems inherent to the notion of rights, turns into a murderous sham. This sham came into being in the post–World War I period as a result of inflation, unemployment, civil wars, and general confusion which had set off "migrations of groups who, unlike their happier predecessors in the religious wars, were welcomed nowhere and could be assimilated nowhere."[42] Through the reshuffling of nations and the creation of new and maladjusted nation-states, numbers of people were set loose without any homeland, any national protection, and thus any definite rights. Through various treaties, states were set up that grouped these stateless people together, giving some governmental power while problematically assuming the others would be treated equally. As well, certain subsets were created and called "minorities."[43] These minorities, "protected" by the Minority Treaties (which only applied to newly created states), were in effect left stranded within the world given that the League of Nations, which was to enforce these treaties, was predisposed toward the official leaders of these new states so 'hampered' by the unruly minorities. For Arendt, the net effect of these Minority Treaties was to explicate how the nation-state had devolved in such a manner that it had murdered, legally speaking, its better half: "They thereby admitted—and were quickly given the opportunity to prove it practically with the rise of stateless people—that the transformation of the state from an instrument of the law into an instrument of the nation had been completed; the nation had conquered the state. . . ."[44]

Thus the nation, an entity imagined to be bonded by blood, soil, and sovereignty, trampled over the universal rights inherent in the formal concept of the state. When the nation finally took supremacy over the state,[45] many of those made stateless became externalized irritants; aliens endlessly bandied about, placed in concentration camps and, ultimately, liquidated. Arendt argues, however, that the road from statelessness to destruction was not direct. It was the eventual stripping away of everything that gives one a place in the world, from the right to a home to the right of government protection,[46] that created the conditions proper for mass murder: "Only in the last stage of a lengthy process is their right to life threatened; only if they remain perfectly 'superfluous', if nobody can be found to 'claim' them, may their lives be in danger."[47] For Arendt, the loss of so-called basic human rights and an established place in the world created a true universalization of the human by turning the stateless into aliens, bringing forth the 'terror in the ideal of our humanity':

> The "alien" is a frightening symbol of the fact of difference as such, of individuality as such, and indicates those realms in which man cannot change and cannot act and in which, therefore, he has a distinct tendency to destroy. . . . The paradox involved in the loss of human rights is that such loss coincides with the instant when a person becomes a human being in general—without a profession, without a citizenship, without an opinion, without a deed by which to identify and specify himself—and different in general, representing nothing but his own absolutely unique individuality which, deprived of expression within and action upon a common world, loses all significance.[48]

The formulation here is striking: we become generally human by being stripped of all specific locality, nationality, culture, legal identification, and voice, left only with our 'individuality as such.' Universality hereby hinges on a loss of content, a voiding of the persona with a merely physical remainder.

With no place in the world to house our personas, we are left exhibiting only the congenital differences of our persons. Arendt argues later on that in totalitarian forms of government, this is the third and most difficult human aspect to be overcome in the production of "living corpses." After the juridical and moral persons are destroyed, the last thing to be broken is one's own natural identity, something that can be preserved through a retreat into stoicism.[49]

But why is it the case that this last deathly logical moment of the human, this absolute uniqueness that exhibits a simultaneous universality, also a cause of revulsion? Why ought it indicate a realm in which destruction prevails? What about the alien unleashes violence, and what, specifically, is this 'dark background of difference', so ominously and regressively linked to the state of nature and 'savages' by Arendt? The beginning of the passage above links this unleashing to a feeling of impotence, to the negation of the ability to act. It thus follows that the alien threatens those who have a place in the world with its loss. This threat must be inherently imaginary given that it is in fact those without such a place, the homeless, the stateless, etc., who are most impotent. They threaten not with their power, nor their capacity for violence, but with the anxiety they unleash in their onlookers. They therefore cause a clearly psychological reaction, a violent fear that exhibits itself in acts whose aim is to negate the object of fear or, otherwise put, the source of an idea. This violent source is thus directly linked to a projected sense of impotence, and we can see the logic played out in Arendt's analysis of totalitarianism as well as the Terror of the French Revolution.

It is thus strange that Arendt dismisses out of hand all psychoanalytic explanations. Noting the need to act like a science, Arendt argues that psychology and psychoanalysis provide us only with a mere checklist of moods and emotions that is as ugly as it is shallow: "Psychology, depth psychology or psychoanalysis, discovers no more than the ever changing moods, the ups and downs of our psychic life, and its results and discoveries are neither particularly appealing nor very meaningful in themselves."[50] As with Agamben, psychology is seen to have all of the gravitas of a bad crime novel. Arendt makes this claim on the basis of a distinction between the mind, which psychology, depth-psychology, and psychoanalysis do not consider, and the soul, which is their domain and is, as well, one of the most pernicious of all political factors: "The soul, where our passions, our feelings and emotions arise, is a more or less chaotic welter of happenings which we do not enact but suffer. . . ."[51] The soul is problematic for Arendt for a number of reasons but, as we can see here, the main issue is that it reduces its owner to a sufferer, one who undergoes desire as opposed to the thinker who acts and is in control of the movement of thought. The soul is thereby the realm of subjection rather than freedom and, by extension, is apolitical in lack of agency.

No less, while the soul forces its subject to suffer, its publicity produces a superego-like quality. As Arendt argues in her earlier work, *On Revolution*, the soul is the dark twin of the human mind, a space of the torn human condition containing a double passivity, one mired in the fact that we must undergo our emotions, and another in the fact that we often find ourselves acting out of a desire, need, and desperation which we do not fully understand: "And since the two-in-one of the soul is a conflict and not a dialogue, it engenders passion in its twofold sense of intense suffering of intense passionateness."[52] This passive tearing of the passionate self is located, according to Arendt, in the heart, a weltering container of emotions that can exist properly only when kept private. For Arendt, the heart is the opposite of words and deeds. While the latter can only "shine" forth and gain meaning in a public setting, the heart beats properly only in a private sphere, and is subject to a series of doubts and suspicion once made public. In essence, the heart can never fully display itself, and hence its public existence is defined by paranoia, and thus,

> The same sad logic of the human heart, which has almost automatically caused modern 'motivational research' to develop into an eerie sort of filing cabinet for human vices, into a veritable science of misanthropy, make Robespierre and his followers, once they had equated virtue with the qualities of the heart, see intrigue and calumny, treachery and hypocrisy everywhere.[53]

No less, Arendt muses that the heart begins to "beat properly only when it has been broken or is being torn in conflict."[54]

It is thus in the heart, the seat of the soul, that we find an internal division of the human self that must keep its own broken nature on a constant mend within a permanent midnight. Once the soul is publicized, its 'sad logic' of darkness and duality, of a suspicion that one can only guess emanates from its initial break from itself, comes to the fore and determines the ensuing drama that, once public, has no escape, no law or rule of order by which to orient itself. Arendt consistently argues that our sense of reality, our sixth and common sense, depends on others for its confirmation, continuation, and authenticity. Once the soul becomes the measure of this authenticity, the process of discovery and judgment will by necessity be turned into a fun house of frustration, one not dissimilar from the sorts of madness that Hobbes found to be more normal than they perhaps ought to be.

This suspicion and its impossible resolution give us a deeper understanding of the violent psychological release rooted in impotence. Arendt's thesis about the Terror of the French Revolution is that it was ignited by an adamant focus on the misery of the people and its attendant requirement of a pure access to compassion. The attempt to make goodness and purity of intention a function of the public realm by necessity results in criminality since the emotions, motivations, and movements of the heart, all elements of the soul, are not public entities and are thus not made for such inspection. We can judge the words and deeds of agents, but the search for the deeper motivation can only end in suspicion due to the heart's infinite regression. For Arendt, the public realm can only work with public objects. These are, in the case of people, not our "pure" selves, which can never escape the paranoia of Cartesian doubt, but our personas, the self that is endowed publicly with rights and a space to appear. Thus Arendt argues in *On Revolution* that when we lose our public self we are left in a state of political oblivion: "Without this persona, there would be an individual without rights and duties, perhaps a 'natural man'—that is, a human being or homo in the original meaning of the word, indicating someone outside the range of the law and the body politics of the citizens, as for instance a slave—but certainly a politically irrelevant being."[55]

Arendt clearly could have returned to the stateless here, those left with nothing but their own idiosyncratically natural selves. However, there is a dichotomy of impotent rage in the two instances. The stateless were in a sense exemplary of loss, of impotence. It was their very presence from which others recoiled or, conversely, against which they attacked. But for Robespierre and the search for the pure self, the self that is good or even the self that is completely corrupt, the very seeking of the self causes a desperately violent sort of reflexive impotence. The stateless, therefore, were an exhibition of loss, an external unbearable example of failure, while the search for the general will, the good essence, was defined by an internal failure to find any example whatsoever. Whether in the positive search for the presence of the self, or in facing a self that has completely lost its social and legal persona, Arendt reaches the same Kantian conclusion: there is no pure self, there is no self that is wholly what it is to itself, no accessible *ding an sich* of the I. It is therefore tragically necessary, once this emotive lost object is sought, that everyone fails: "Hence, the search for motives, the demand that everybody display in public his innermost motivation, since it actually demands the impossible, transforms all actors into hypocrites.... In politics, more than anywhere else, we have no possibility of distinguishing between being and appearing."[56] For all of Arendt's dismissals of the "pseudoscience" of psychoanalysis, she all the same succeeds in producing a category of violent reaction to impotence that is based on confronting suppressed fears and projected ideas of mastery. But the analysis of this psychological violence goes a level deeper, into something Arendt considers to be primordial. For behind these split hearts of darkness and horror-filled experiences of impotence churns a rhythmic, repetitive, creative, and, finally, destructive realm of biological necessity that underlies all of Arendt's fears of the social, of the political office that would become the 'living room'.

5. Biological Violence

Throughout her readings of totalitarianism and the social, Arendt consistently makes reference to a primordial, repetitive, and ultimately destructive biological ground to all things. Sometimes this biological ground is found in an ideological formation, in which case it is interchangeable with other concepts of perpetual movement, such as History. Other times this biological ground is spoken of as an almost supernatural force that takes control of us, rendering humanity into a reduced state of universality, of the merely homo. Broadly speaking, Arendt jumps between these two positions because she sees them as essentially interwoven. When an ideology of nature, history, or human misery is in control of political meaning, the *misere du monde* will by necessity bear a violent monstrosity. This primordial ground could be considered another distinction in her thought, though it only really achieves this status in her much maligned concept of the 'social', an aspect of Arendt's thought that is perhaps the most thoroughly rejected concept in her thinking. Nonetheless, the manner in which Arendt draws the social into a corresponding violence is in fact illuminating.

The social is connected primarily with the classical notion of the household. As opposed to the public realm, the private realm of the household is focused on the problems of basic living, of daily necessities such as finding and keeping shelter, eating, sleeping, and gaining the means to continue these functions. On a broader scale, the social contains such categories as economy, housing, food production, entertainment, education, and even, controversially enough, racial integration (so-called social problems). Arendt's primary concern within the social is the mindlessly functioning human being, a being cut off from thinking and acting due to the ineluctable and repetitious demands of nature: "The distinctive trait of the household sphere was that in it men lived together because they were driven by their wants and needs. The driving force was life itself. . . . Natural community in the household therefore was born of necessity, and necessity ruled over all activities performed in it."[57] Though commenting here on classical notions of the private realm, Arendt nonetheless, and to the chagrin of many, maintains that this distinction is still valid, and that it has insufferably lost its validity as household activities have bled over into society and government at large. Such blurring of the lines is exhibited in the bureaucratic state, a process-oriented form of government that in its anonymity may "even turn out to be one of [rulership's] cruelest and most tyrannical versions."[58]

What is primarily at stake in the social is the degree to which it destroys political freedom. Arendt does not dismiss the need for moments of mental evacuation: "The truth is we all stand in need of entertainment and amusement in some form or other, because we are all subject to life's great cycle."[59] The social becomes problematic, rather, when natural functions begin to become total in their reach, unleashing an underlying and inchoate violence: ". . . biological life is always, whether laboring or at rest, whether engaged in consumption or in the passive reception of amusement, a metabolism feeding on things by devouring them."[60] While the public realm requires a space of appearance so that action is in the eyes of others and is free to take exhibit itself, the biological life process is, for Arendt, a simultaneously productive and destructive underlying force, a sort of living death that underlies all of our activities and that can, given the right conditions, devour the public world, not to mention those who are deemed unfit to live in what is left over. By turning all action into necessary processes that must be taken care of, the ability to begin something new is foreclosed.

Such was the failure of the French Revolution in Arendt's eyes. In focusing on human misery and the sanctity of the heart, the French Revolution mistook economic emancipation for public freedom and in the process tapped into an underlying and hellish human factor:

What has always made it so terribly tempting to follow the French Revolution on its foredoomed path is not only the fact that liberation from necessity, because of its urgency, will always take precedence over the building of freedom, but the even more important and more dangerous fact that the uprising of the poor against the rich carries with it an altogether different and much greater momentum of force than the rebellion of the oppressed against their oppressors. This raging force may well nigh appear irresistible because it lives from and is nourished by the necessity of biological life itself.[61]

Once the biology of need was placed into the public realm, a realm for which it is not meant (as is the case for the passions), something is triggered, something prepolitical and headless in its consumption. As an absolute immanence of need subject to a constant repetition, the processes of the household overtake the human being at the cost of thought and action. For Arendt, the same removal of freedom took place in totalitarianism, whereby the endless repetitions and demands of Nature and History took the place of a truly free and open political space.

We thereby arrive at our third realm of violence. Unlike phenomenological violence, which requires the use of tools and is a deliberate action, and unlike psychological violence, which is something of a reactionary formation to conditions of impotence, biological violence is universal and necessary, always present within the demands of the organism. But what is this biological necessity, and how does its seemingly necessary violence relate to the other two forms of violence we spoke of earlier? More importantly, if it is primordial in its necessity, in what sense can we say that it is also prepolitical, as Arendt vehemently does? Indeed, what constitutes its necessity in the first place?

Within Arendt's corpus there is no direct answer. The concepts of nature and the biological have a *de facto* status brought forth in order to explain certain elements of the human condition, such as labor and the human need to reproduce and maintain oneself. While this primordial foundation crops up in a number of places throughout Arendt's oeuvre, it is never submitted to a thorough investigation or critique, standing as a sort of placeholder for all that is mindless and repetitive in our daily lives. Nonetheless, we can begin to formulate a general argument on her part by piecing together the modalities of violence that we have spoken of in relation to the state of nature. In a long passage, Arendt links the three by indicating that when political intentions seek as their goal natural, nonpolitical means, hell is the necessary result:

> Hence, when the men of the French Revolution said that all power resides in the people, they understood by power a 'natural' force whose source and origin lay outside the political realm, a force which in its very violence had been released by the revolution and like a hurricane had swept away all institutions of the ancien regime. This force was experienced as superhuman in its strength, and it was seen as the result of the accumulated violence of a multitude outside all bonds and all political organization. The experiences of the French Revolution with a people thrown into a 'state of nature' left no doubt that the

multiplied strength of a multitude could burst forth . . . with a violence which no institutionalized and controlled power could withstand. . . . The men of the French Revolution . . . opened the political realm to this prepolitical, natural force of the multitude and they were swept away by it. . . .[62]

The men of the French Revolution thus unlocked an inner possibility within the human condition that, once it is misplaced in the political realm, proceeds to destroy those who reside within it. We can thus draw the inference from the previous: there is a biological, repetitive ground to the human condition that, while necessary to the maintenance of life, is destructive of life when it is politicized. It, the biological drive, must consume, and in order to continue doing so, it must destroy. Hence, placing it within the political realm will achieve nothing other than an antipolitical consumption. No less, when propped up by the desires of the human heart and needs of the private self, the impossibility of public purity is intensified by the biological drive, resulting in a violent need to destroy. Finally, this passionate need finds as its means, ultimately, various ways to physically carry itself out in the direct or phenomenological form of violence.

No doubt, the storyline is less than satisfying. It contains a number of gaps that, like the drive it describes, beg to be filled in. Whence comes this primordial drive and how is it made political? Furthermore, if it is so separated from the proper realm of freedom, why does it nonetheless find its way there so often? Furthermore, what is its relation to the soul, an aspect of the human condition that sounds so like the natural in its infinite desire that one is left to wonder whether they share some mode of causality? But these questions are not answered in the texts, and it might very well have to do with thinking by way of faculties that prevented Arendt from seeing them as dialectically interconnected.

Still, the parallels to Hobbes here ought to be striking. On the one hand, Arendt argues that this state of nature is inherently apolitical—it is violent, destructive of social (commodious) relations, and therefore a time apart. On the other hand, it is the result of a psychological failure and natural drive. As Hobbes argues that the thoughts that motivate desire to move forth are inherently fractious and repellant to society, Arendt argues that, on the one hand, the human heart, when placed in the center of power relations, creates a destructive process due to a fear or a felt sense of failure, while, on the other, politicizing the rapacious hunger of the natural self unleashes an uncontrollable natural force. In other words, both saw in the passionate, natural self a fundamental driving anxiety that leads to violent ends. But even more profoundly, both saw that a certain sort of motion grounded everything and caused this anxiety, though Hobbes makes the more explicit case. Arendt seems to imply that the fundamental needs of the biological life processes, when combined either with an ideology of totality (as in Totalitarianism), or a search for the pure self (or the general will, as in the French Revolution), spur the passions into an uncontrollable movement of obliteration. Hobbes proposed that the fundamental motion of all things expresses itself directly and logically in the form of human desire—in our need to continue ever onward to further objects, a need that only ceases in death and is curbed only by an ideologically driven concentration of power. Arendt, in essence, sees this Hobbesian desire as the result of a combination of the heart and the natural, or the social, within the political realm. In each, what is feared is the primordial natural self, the self either stripped of a political realm (Hobbes) or the politicization of the self qua natural (Arendt).

The question then turns on what to do with these personas that both Hobbes and Arendt see as fundamental to the proper political formation. Clearly, the person, the primordial and prepolitical self, must be eradicated from the political realm if it is to avoid a violent condition. It is on this question that we can locate how what is shared between Hobbes and Arendt leads to a divergence. For as Hobbes argued that a sovereign is needed to gather up our personas into a One that will desire *for* the subjects, Arendt argued that the only way to keep the forces that lead to such deadly consequences at bay is to maintain a public realm in which our personas may be externally gathered for display, a realm of freedom.[63] We can thus note two requirements and their attendant differences:

1. There must be an essential publicity in the public realm.
   - In the case of Hobbes, this means a fully formed series of ideological state apparatuses: the public must know its place.
   - In Arendt, this means a space of appearance: the public must see itself and judge.
2. The persona is the location of agency.
   - For Hobbes, this agency is one of transfer to a unitary Sovereign who will be its placeholder and point of recognition.
   - For Arendt, this agency must be transferred to the totality of other agents who are recognized within a given public realm and who will augment its ability to act and will function, as well, as a point of recognition.

In each case, the persona is essential to the political construction in and against the person. Agency, therefore, is defined entirely by an Other, whether plural or singular, and hence in opposition to the state of nature. When stripped of our personas we are stripped of our ability to act because we have no protected space of appearance, understanding, or recognition (hence the core aspect of publicity for both). In the case of the stateless, we are turned into aliens, into 'holes of oblivion' that cause violent reactions in others. We are thereby causal agents without agency. When we are those agents of a process propped up by an ideology of purity or process, we are reduced to a constant and repetitive appetite of accumulation and destruction. We are thereby violently reactive agents without agency. When we are left in the state of nature, we succumb to an impossible desire that has no place from which to safely act out its play of accumulation within eminence. We are, as such, an agency in search of an agent. In each case, the impossibility of the self comes to the fore and obliterates commodious living. The public realm and the Sovereign both thereby function as a way of externalizing private desire from itself by publicly transferring it from the self to the agency of a persona.

Arendt's divergence from Hobbes is to be found in the fact that she believed in a persona that is free by virtue of submitting to other free personas without renouncing agency. This persona has to be able to appear, to enact its natality in the public realm, to judge and be judged by others who equally have access. Hobbesian desire is so fearful that such a public realm is merely an invitation to the proliferation of desire and thus violence. For Hobbes, then, the persona must make a second move from the public realm into the singularity of the Sovereign. The two thus share similar fears of a social breakdown into a state of nature and for strikingly similar reasons, but their conclusions are radical in their distinction. For both, the persona must be protected against the effects of the person, but the modality of this protection veers between the singularity of sovereignty and its plurality. We could continue down this line of thought, noting for instance that Arendt's disdain for the natural reaches to the point of eradicating it completely from the realm of the political, while Hobbes' fear of it meant a tight control of its reach. The two, to some degree, come to the same given that both seek a monitoring of the natural within the borders of the political realm, producing a constant surveillance of its power that results in a paranoid recognition of its conditional status.

6. Persona Non Grata

A persona is a presentation by definition, a public exhibition of the self that is neither reducible to nor separable from the natural self. As Hobbes says,

". . . a *person* is the same that an actor is, both on the stage and in common conversation; and to *personate* is to *act*, to *represent*, himself or another. . . ."[64] A persona, therefore, is something that is consciously and unconsciously held together and presented, something that is not reducible to a natural self or a unitary ego. Indeed, just as Hobbes sees that only by reference to duplicity in the self can we understand desire, he also sees that only in that way can we understand the political—a fabrication, even a political one, requires an unnatural self, an actor. Otherwise, as Arendt warns, the self, the *homo*, will be subsumed to the oblivion of the irrelevant: "Without his *persona*, there would be an individual without rights and duties, perhaps a 'natural man'—that is, a human being or *homo* in the original meaning of the word, indicating someone outside the range of the law and the body politic of the citizens, as for instance a slave—but certainly a politically irrelevant being."[65] This maintenance of the self, this presentation, gathers its necessity from what it seeks to avoid; a devolution into the unadorned self, a fall into a state of necessity and war. The persona and the political realm it implies, for Arendt and Hobbes, can only be said to exist, at least in part, by virtue of that which they continuously seek to avoid. The state of nature is therefore an internal externality, a negative yet necessary aspect of the political realm that does not wither away with the arrival of a successful organization of the people but remains as the *homo* of *homo sapiens*, as a natural and headless underground to whatever brilliant castles are constructed. It is what lies between the natural and artificial self, the person and the persona, and, finally, it indicates the space in which desire crawls without end. Its appearance underlines the reason that Twain's remark is funny rather than true—the influence of the naked is too terrible for polite conversation.

Let us then tarry with this *homo* that defines the state of nature, the political, and the call for what Arendt deemed 'the right to have rights' by virtue of its negation of the persona. It is, perhaps, felicitous to the present argument that the U.S. is chronically unhappy in deciding whether homosexuals are due the same rights as heterosexuals, and it is here that the current meaning adds to Arendt's call to the original meaning of the word—to the extent that the homo is not deemed worthy of the same rights as the hetero (and there is much room for thought here about the hetero's fear of the sameness of the homo), we can see that it elicits the anxiety of desire, calling into question the established selves that will invest inordinate amounts of will into negating this abjectified object. That the battle has made its way to a choice between civil unions and marriage indicates that the war of designation has made significant movement within the war of position. On the other hand, to return to Abu Ghraib, we can note that there has not been such a movement for the Iraqi people. As one unnamed general said to General Taguba during his 2004 investigation of the torture of Iraqis, they're "only Iraqis."[66] The adjectival modification indicates the mental result of the depletion of humanity that was necessary for setting the stage for Abu Ghraib, a depletion that began most significantly when it was decided that enemy combatants need neither a clear definition nor any rights.[67] As the logic of the stateless indicate, when a person is stripped of its persona, those who retain their personas will find the permission and necessity to do the 'unspeakable' (a word that indicates, once again, that the abjection leading to surplus murder is itself something that depends on making selves removed from common social discourse). To 'only' be an Iraqi thus gives the answer to Shakespeare's rhetorical question concerning what's in a name. To the degree that there is nothing in it, abuse, torture, degradation, and death are in a name.

As such we are returned to our main point. Desire, seeking no real *summum bonum*, requires that there be a separation of the self from its persona, and this separation, whether through an Other qua sovereign or an Other qua demos (or both), is accomplished within the public realm. The reduction of the self to a mere natural entity that contains no rights nor any valued social place becomes the Arendtian 'hole of oblivion', but is not thereby rendered invisible. Such a self becomes newly apparent for the effects upon the desire of the others, a sort of social anamorphosis disturbing, as in Holbein's *The Ambassadors*, the normal framing of events and revealing, upon closer inspection, death. Such effects are broadly reducible to overcompensation on the part of desire in order to suture its identity in the face of that which negates it, revealing as well a general ability of the human to destroy humanity. It is humanity that is destroyed because, as Arendt has pointed out, those humans who come closest to a universal state cause the most disgusted and violent reactions in others.

As such, human rights cannot be located within humanity. There is little there but abjection and the concomitant reactionary forces on the part of its onlookers. As Foucault has pointed out, in noting such facts, theory will do little to create a metaphysical block to them. Rather, it can only point to those who wish to listen where the battles can be fought, what he calls, wryly twisting the Kantian edifice, a conditional imperative.[68] Nonetheless, there is a metaphysical result to these dark ruminations on desire. To begin with, it is clear that insofar as desire is politicized, or is subject to politics, we can only be speaking of a political wherein the rule of sovereignty in the name of specified personas is at play. As such, we can locate the position of the person as forced into its place of externality—the person is that against which a "we" organizes itself, this "we" functioning on the basis of what it considers to be a proper Other (a represented subject, a charismatic leader, a complex of cultural signifiers, etc.). The loss of position within this Other designates a disintegration into the person, to the natural condition in which desire cannot coordinate according to its comfortable modes of satisfaction. But, and here we locate the significance of desire for the political, these comfortable satisfactions predicated on fabricated identities, however long evolved and however firmly established, harbor within themselves a conditioning revulsion toward any who are marked as persons—who are reduced to the point of externality defined in the state of nature.

Insofar as the political is defined as the production of commodious living in opposition to the hell of the state of nature, however, it is the case that the political, or, perhaps better put, the work of the political, paradoxically enough, is to be located in the state of nature as well. In other words, the political, properly speaking, exists in and for all persons of the world—which means the totality of the human population insofar as they are defined as a split between persons and personas. To the degree that surplus murder and the ability to disregard large swaths of humanity is predicated on the overcompensations of desire through its personas' satisfactions, commodious living and, in many cases, living itself are denied to many. Such denials are therefore apolitical because they are contradictory. If we are not to endorse the state of nature as the true goal of the political, but rather the extension of dignity to everyone in the form of protection from abjection and the presentation of the self, then we can do nothing other than to note that the political exists in the name of and for the protection of the person. A denial of this proposition is a denial of the principle of commodious living as opposed to the state of nature and is, as well, an agreement with Schmitt and Thrasymachus with him. For insofar as the friend/enemy distinction is endorsed, so is justice assumed to exist in the name of the accumulation of power for a subset of personas. But this is merely to affirm the state of nature qua war on a broad scale.

By extension, because the universal human is that which brings out those human actions that beg for human rights in the first place, human rights are to be grounded only in the name of the abject universal self. The conditional imperative posed here is thus to avoid universality as something positive, to look for what is absent in subjectivity rather than otherwise, while its positive component is to always keep a gaze on desire, to ask where the vacuums are that would ignite its drive. There is absolutely no such thing as a guaranteed human right, much less a metaphysical ground. Or, to the extent that the state of nature grounds the political in the form of the split of desire, what is being called here an internal externality, human rights are only important to the degree that their negation is located within the depersonified subjectivity endemic to the state of nature in contradistinction to the validation of personas. Such depersonified persons, so to speak, neither contain any specific rights nor do they call on the Other to hand over such rights with any binding voice. Rather, human rights must be constructed in the full awareness that their enforcement will always be subject to the desire of those powers which will claim legal status over and above them, to claim, along with Schmitt, a state of exception. To the degree that such a state is claimed, one can know with an almost automatic understanding that human rights will once again need defending. The constructions of the political, as every seventeenth-century political theorist knew, had to ensure commodious living by an artificial force. Such artificiality must once again be underlined with the full recognition that humanity, sans its personification in a more or less orderly milieu, calls upon the desire of the Other to destroy itself. The resulting paradox is that the political expresses itself truly within the state of nature as a function of the person rather than the persona. As such, and as will become clearer later on, the true expression of the political is a universal localization of persons who speak to one another, which amounts to an anti-sovereignty. Even democracy replicates the logic of the persona, and hence exists within the continuum of sovereignty that expresses itself in what Vice President Dick Cheney called the 'dark side', or what we have been calling persons.

Had Arendt taken the problem of desire more closely to heart, she may have been able to resolve the heavy tension between the social and the political in such a way that did not lead to an impossible denial of all social factors within the political. She would, that is, realize that desire cannot be destroyed but only confronted, that the social is conditional to the political. As such, the play of representations that factor into a political realm of personas that must strive to avoid the person only continues the invitation to a bolstering of identities in and against all persons. Arendtian freedom, that is, is a game of politics despite its initial intuition about the origin of the political. Thus, the political is not properly a space of freedom for representations—it is a space of appearance for the abject, for persons. Similarly, a Sovereign can only be said to intensify the logic of desire that it seeks to mollify; such is why a Hobbesian pen must be guarded by many swords. In both cases, the externality of the state of nature is repressed, avoiding in different ways the same internal condition and necessitating its return.

Be that as it may, certain factors in the argument thus far still require clarification. While it has been established through historical precedent that Hobbes' account of the ramifications of desire contains the sort of political truth that we must think through, it is not clear as of yet why desire functions in such a manner. While Arendt has pointed out three factors in our violent tendencies, each has a status that, though more complicated than Hobbes', is more or less given. What, we are left to wonder, causes this violent and consumptive drive within the human condition, one which has such terrible consequences within states of nature and, as well, political states? Why, that is, is humanity so terrifying to our personas and what establishes this split in the first place? What, to use Arendt's metaphor, tears our heart such that we are thereby made human? It is within Jacques Lacan's work that we can begin to make out a structural argument for the concepts that have thus far been presented, an argument that will provide a theoretical edifice to explain the experiential propositions that have been laid out. Indeed, as we shall see, it is a traversed body politic that will most properly represent the political, as I have described it. This notion of traversal is, indeed, derived from Lacan's concept of a subject who has moved from its persona to its person, for what is traversed is precisely the fantasy of eminence and the desirous anxiety along with it that each subject carries out of its early formation.

Notes

1 *Possessive*, 23.

2 Giorgio Agamben, *Homo Sacer: Sovereign Power and Bare Life*, trans. Daniel Heller-Roazen (California: Stanford University Press, 1998): 6. Italics in original.

3 See Carl Schmitt, *The Concept of the Political* (Chicago: The University of Chicago Press, 1996).

4 See Claude Lefort, *Democracy and Political Theory* (Minneapolis: University of Minnesota Press, 1988), chapter 1, hereafter referred to as *Democracy*.

5 "Freed Britons Are Back Home but Face Questions about Their Capture and Behavior," *New York Times*, 6, April 2007.

6 *Second Treatise*, 17.

7 Ibid., 27.

8 Ibid., 326.

9 Ibid., 4.

10 Ibid., 14.

11 Hobbes makes the following observation: "And even in commonwealths, if I be forced to redeem myself from a thief by promising him money, I am bound to pay it, till civil law discharge me. For whatsoever I may lawfully do without obligation, the same I may

lawfully covenant to do through fear; and what I lawfully covenant, I cannot lawfully break." *Leviathan*, xiv, 27. The point of this passage is somewhat ambiguous, since it is not entirely clear whether Hobbes is more worried about the preservation of the covenant or the preservation of life. However, this is cleared up once it is taken into account that the very point of the covenant for Hobbes is the preservation of life in the face of a state of nature that is in itself a state of war. In other words, there is no distinction between covenanting through fear and covenanting for the sake of legality—the legality of the covenant is predicated on the fear of death for Hobbes.

12 *Second Treatise*, 18.

13 *Leviathan*, VI, 58 (emphasis mine).

14 Ibid., xiv, 4–5.

15 Ibid., xiv, 11.

16 Ibid., xiv, 27.

17 Virtue, as Hobbes argues, "is somewhat that is valued for eminence, and consisteth in comparison. For if all things were equally in all men, nothing would be prized." *Leviathan*, viii, 1. This differential process of prizing is fundamental to Hobbes' deliberations on power—for eminence is not just the manifestation of a variety of abilities and differences in obtaining desired objects, but as well an indication of our ability to obtain those objects in relation to others who may desire the same: "The power of a man (to take it universally) is his poreent means to obtain some future apparent good, and is either original or instrumental." Ibid., x, 1.

18 *Second Treatise*, 139.

19 John Locke, *An Essay Concerning Human Understanding*, ed. Peter H. Nidditch (Hong Kong: Oxford University Press, 1991): chapter xxi, paragraph 29 (emphasis in original), hereafter referred to as *Essay* followed by chapter and paragraph number.

20 *Essay*, xxi, 31.

21 Ibid., xxi, 35.

22 Ibid., 52 (emphasis in original).

23 Ibid., 63.

24 Ibid., 128.

25 For an elaboration of the ways in which education is used to ameliorate anxiety in Locke, see Uday Mehta, *The Anxiety of Freedom* (Ithaca: Cornell University Press, 1992), hereafter referred to as *Anxiety*.

26 See, for instance, chapter 30 of the *Leviathan*, in which Hobbes outlines what essentially breaks down into an Althusserian process of extended interpellation for the subjects of the commonwealth.

27 According to Hobbes, eminence is located within one's virtue, which "is somewhat that is valued for eminence, and consisteth in comparison. For if all things were equally in all men, nothing would be prized." *Leviathan*, vii, 1.

28 Indeed, Hobbes takes this point to an odd extreme in chapter xvi, where he argues that we are not only our natural selves, but also have an artificial extension—a persona, whereby we can be represented: "From hence it followeth that when the actor maketh covenant by authority, he bindeth thereby the author, no less than if he had made it himself, and

no less subjecteth him to all the consequences of the same." *Leviathan,* xvi, 5. It is by the mechanism of the persona that Hobbes is able to make a full-fledged transference of power to the Sovereign—the Sovereign unifies the body politic by receiving from it all of its individual rights to everything.

29 Keeping in mind, again, that Hobbes did not argue that everyone acts terribly in the state of nature; just enough people to make it untenable for all.

30 *Two Treatises,* 60.

31 See *Anxiety,* 111–18.

32 Hobbes can also be read from a mechanical point of view, one that he professes from the start. The mechanical position argues that the right to everything is not a positive ontological fact, but a relational or causal one. In a situation where the social institutions that establish and profess right are broken down, the source of right is vague while the threats to one's life and limb are clear. Preservation thus requires a de facto right to everything (this idea is not fundamentally different from the legality of killing in self-defense).

33 Indeed, it is in totalitarianism that we see most clearly how leaders attempt to play with desire, mainly through negative objects of identification, such as the Jew, counterbalanced by positive objects, such as the Nation, or the People. Only by creating an enemy that is seen as an obstacle to absolute fulfillment can totalitarian regimes maintain control over the desire of their subjects.

34 Jean-Jacques Rousseau, *On the Social Contract,* trans. Judith R. Masters, ed. Roger D. Masters (New York: St. Martin's Press, 1978): 101.

35 Indeed, did not the external forces and eyes of the world help ensure that Yuschenko would enter into office? True, the orange-banded protestors produced a peaceful force in the streets and thus an internal pressure point to the government of Kuchma and Putin, but this pressure point was not only backed and observed by the EU, but funded and in many ways interpellated by U.S. government involvement. In other words, without the external organization of the U.S. and the watchful observation of Western powers, there is little doubt that the Ukrainian government would have physically stifled the pro-Yuschenko protestors, leading to a brutal recapturing of power or, possibly, a prolonged civil war as we now see in Iraq, for which no consistent, long-term plan was created.

36 And was this loss of control not felt during the 2000 and 2004 elections in the U.S? Indeed, one of the reasons given by the Supreme Court for ending the recount was the fear that the republic should disintegrate if it waited too long to make a decision. The argument was intuitively dubious given the predisposition of the court as a whole, and also given the political nonparticipation that marks the U.S. (not to mention that recounts and new elections take place as a matter of course in other countries). All the same, what is key in this example is the level to which power becomes both evident and brittle in such elections; the power relations of the system make their most obvious appearance with votes and voters being manipulated, court actions preventing democratic actions, votes being thrown out, while the electorate begins to see the whole process as one not of representation, but rather as a war of position.

37 "Abjection, with a meaning broadened to take in subjective diachrony, is a precondition of narcissism. It is coexistent with it and causes it to be permanently brittle. The more

or less beautiful image in which I behold or recognize myself rests upon an abjection that sunders it as soon as repression, the constant watchman, is relaxed," Julia Kristeva, *Powers of Horror*, trans. Leon S. Roudiez (New York: Columbia University Press, 1982): 13. Essentially, abjection is a state in which the fundamental lack in human subjectivity comes forth, breaking through the guard of our imaginary narcissistic projections. These narcissistic projections are based, as Kristeva and Lacan argue, on a primary repression of a traumatic loss that, in effect, constitutes the subject. When this loss, which is kept unconscious in our daily lives, manifests itself, a feeling of revulsion, of vertigo, of a second death, as Lacan designates it, erupts and sends the subject scrambling for a foothold. In the case of the stateless, this scrambling will include genocide.

38 See Samantha Powers, *A Problem from Hell* (New York: Basic Books, 2002), for an extended analysis of how the concept of genocide, though ingrained in international law, has failed numerous times to actually prevent genocide.

39 Hannah Arendt, *On Revolution* (New York: Penguin Books, 1990): 19–20, hereafter referred to as OR.

40 Hannah Arendt, *On Violence* (New York: Harcourt Brace & Company, 1970): 46, hereafter referred to as OV.

41 Ibid., 5.

42 *Origins*, 267.

43 Ibid., 270.

44 Ibid., 275.

45 Arendt spends many dense pages outlining the historical roots that allowed for this, including the rise of the bourgeoisie and finance capitalism, with the result of the creation of the masses, the development of racism, and colonialism.

46 Ibid., see pp. 293–4.

47 Ibid., 296.

48 Ibid., 302–3.

49 See *Origins*, pp. 451–3.

50 Hannah Arendt, *The Life of the Mind* (New York: Harcourt Brace & Company, 1978): 34–5.

51 Ibid., 72.

52 OR, 80.

53 Ibid., 95–6.

54 Ibid., 97.

55 *Origins*, 107.

56 Ibid., 98.

57 Hannah Arendt, *The Human Condition* (Chicago: The University of Chicago Press, 1998): 30, hereafter referred to as HC.

58 HC, 40.

59 Hannah Arendt, *Between Past and Future* (New York: Penguin Books, 1993): 206, hereafter referred to as BPF.

60 BPF, 205.

61 OR, 112.

62　Ibid., 181.

63　See, in particular, *The Human Condition*, chapter V, and "What is Freedom" in *Between Past and Future*.

64　*Leviathan*, xvi, 3.

65　*Origins*, 107.

66　Seymor M. Hersh, "The General's Report," *New Yorker*, June 25, 2007, 58.

67　As the attorney general, Alberto Gonzalez, expressed things in a 2002 memo, the Geneva conventions are "quaint" and, essentially, stand in the way of the prosecution of what is a new paradigm to be found in the so-called war on terror. Of course, the term 'quant' referred to certain privileges of treatment, but the broad implication of the memo, particularly in conjunction with those memos calling for increased use of torture, are no less striking given the fact that the Geneva protections being referred to were expanded and intensified in the wake of the Holocaust. Essentially, the memos ground a view that places the executive branch in control of what Carl Schmitt famously phrased as a 'state of exception'.

68　As Foucault puts it, ". . . the imperative discourse that consists in saying 'strike against this and do so in this way,' seems to me to be very flimsy when delivered from a teaching institution or even just on a piece of paper. . . . So, since there has to be an imperative, I would like the one underpinning the theoretical analysis we are attempting to be quite simply a conditional imperative of the kind: if you want to struggle, here are some constrictions and blockages," Michel Foucault, *Security, Territory, Population: Lectures at the Collège de France 1977–1978*, trans. Graham Burchell, ed. Michel Senellart (New York: Palgrave Macmillan, 2007): p. 3. Foucault, of course, dismisses any transhistorical notion of subjectivity in favor of outlining the ways in which power crisscrosses its formation. Nonetheless, he also calls, at least in the mid-seventies, for a sort of transcendental horizon of war, one in which war prevails as the background against which all political activity, even that which is peaceful, takes place. I argue that the horizon of this war is desire.

3

The Return of the Political

At this point it is quite clear that the question of the political cannot be rent from the problem of subjectivity. The issue we face concerns not so much the best form of cohabitation (monarchial, aristocratic, democratic), but what cohabitates in the first place. This question ominously arises not from within the terms of these systems, but from outside of them, from the problem of what Hobbes or Locke might have called the dissolution of government. They and many of their ilk are often seen to be arguing that this dissolution comes from and leads to somewhere. That somewhere, a sort of nowhere, they called the state of nature. The argument thus far, however, has portrayed the state of nature as something always present and thus definitive of government itself, no matter its form. The state of nature in this light becomes an internal externality, an anxiety-inducing gap within each political existence, constantly threatening and thus defining every form of political functionality. Looked at in this light, Lefort was too limited in saying that it is democracy (or, for that matter, any form that makes a claim on the primacy of political freedom) that revolves around an empty center. All political formations do.[1] But, of course, this state of nature is really another way of talking about the problem of subjectivity, about how and why we come to be the way we do and what it is about humanity, insofar as we are defining it within the modality of the person, that sends its onlookers into destructive states.

As we saw, Locke maintained a reason-oriented subjectivity within the political realm, and aimed his finger at those who would ruin it for the rest. Hobbes, on the other hand, tried to explicate why the very motion of reality can mean the failure of government. Hobbes' argument thus produced a human ontology that expressed itself as desire, a force compelled by imaginary and linguistic confusions separating us from animals and, as well, one another. It is true, Locke also identified an inherently anxious human desire, but he failed to politicize it explicitly, thereby keeping, in a sense, subjectivity out of the political realm. This foreclosure of political anxiety allowed him to avoid the question of the desire of the demos, a question that Hobbes correctly thrust into the center of his considerations. But Hobbes' account of desire and its infinite lack, though it obtained an internal coherence, could not explicate why the subject desires in the first place or why its desires accorded such fantasmatic projections that lead to existential anxiety. Put otherwise, why all this competition, linguistic confusion, narcissistic projection, and imbalance in our base nature?

By claiming that the essential substratum to all of these complexities is the continual motion of life which produces desire, and more essentially, the passions, or the straights through which desire is articulated, halted, sent into anxiety, and ultimately preserved, we are not brought closer to an answer. These passions continue motion by giving it particular forms and therefore causing different subjects, with their attendant desires, to come into conflict, but the causality of this motion remains obscure. Why do men suffer their endeavors on an imaginary plane such that their private wants conflict with their public happiness, unlike animals?[2] Why are we, as Hume would later put it, slaves to our passions, so much so that we must enslave ourselves, or our persona and its attendant eminence, to a sovereign who relieves of us our burdens?

Arendt provokes the same question, though the terms alter. The biological was seen by Arendt as a necessary though voracious consumptive tendency within the human, something to be left within the bounds of the private realm, though once let loose in the public it becomes destructive of the life it supports. This biological underpinning seems to be unleashed most when the heart of darkness is politicized, when questions of intention and desire become suspects in the political line-up. Or, on the other hand, when the political itself is destroyed, the alien comes to the fore as the indicator of an already established impotence, and once again the voracious subject rushes forth blind and dumb where the politically free persona ought to be articulating itself for judgment.

But just as Hobbes presupposed motion, language, and eminence, Arendt presupposes this biological core as categorically as she does the soul's distinction from the mind. No doubt, the distinction is not new, and thus its historical lineage allows for a certain conceptual continuity. Nonetheless, there is no argument for the necessity of its prominence in Arendt's edifice, leaving us to ponder why this heart drives our consumptive tendencies, suffering not only its own wants, but the magnetism of consumerism and ideology. Again, whence the split self and its violent, repetitive, bodily compulsions?

Despite these questions, however, we have been able to derive certain factors concerning subjectivity and its cohabitation, beginning with the base point that desire is the conditioning question of the political if we orient our view of it from the vantage of subjectivity. More importantly, to the degree that subjects are disrobed of their personas, they are either objects of revulsion, as in the stateless or the U.S. extra-legal prisoners, or agents in search of an agency, as in the current condition of Iraq and thereby all civil wars (and thus any who are straddling the abject line of subjectivity). Nor can we deny Arendt's third moment, the agents without agency who are fully propped up by ideological structures—but this is, more or less, the norm of politics as opposed to the political, a subject to which we will turn to in the next chapter. As these historical examples explicate, the desire of subjectivity indicates its division, and to be lodged between the self explicitly is to set desire alight, burning against that which is revolting or in the name of that which will put out the flame. Hence all political stability is almost invariably instantiated in the name of the persona, the form of subjectivity which is infused with the fantasy of place, but which is, as Hobbes, Arendt, and, to a lesser extent, Locke knew, itself a caricature that is there to prevent the violent self-protection to which the persona, broadly speaking, feels compelled upon encountering the person.

Thus, the result of this division of the persona from its person indicates that, insofar as a process is there to protect and embolden a given position, it submits to politics, or the act of structured cohabitation in the name of a given set of personas. But insofar as such activities occur in the name of commodious living for the maximum set of subjects, or its totality, they are functioning under the political. Politics, to put it in Lacanian terms, could be said to function according to the phallus in its imaginary form, or the $-\varphi$, whereby what is missing is filled in by the imaginary support of the fantasies of the set of personas, and its concrete expression is given form in the remainders, or whatever persons are not allowable within the set. This result is derived from the fact that to the degree that a persona is at the center of a political activity, it endangers certain persons that it meets or as happens often enough, will even create, using whatever fragments of reality are ready to hand, destructible persons in order to bolster its own identity (the Jew, the black, the homo, the terrorist, etc.). Hence democracy, insofar as it is representational and predicated on nationality and sovereignty, is a function of politics rather than the political. Its virtue is that, within its subset of accepted personas, an increased amount of freedom and protection is to be found. It is thus, as the old saw goes, the best of the worst. I will return to the issue of democracy as the issue of personas in the next chapter. At this point, however, we must excavate the grounds of the split subject that constitutes the nature of political realm, whether it submits to politics or the political.

It is the thesis of this chapter that the theoretical deficiencies and presuppositions of Arendt and Hobbes are best compensated for by the Lacanian subject. Indeed, we can already see much of Lacan's theoretical edifice given shape in the distinctions thus far argued for. On the one hand, the state of nature, or the subject outside of a guaranteed space of appearance or safety is, in its various expositions (and particularly well summed by the word eminence), either the subject submitted to a space of aggressive imaginary relations, or what Lacan called the headless subject, the thoughtless *jouissance* ridden subject of the drives. On the other hand, the persona is a fairly precise equivalent for the notion of the ego, particularly insofar as the ego is subject to symbolic dictates (what Lacan called the ego-ideal, as opposed to the ideal ego of mere narcissistic identifications first located within the mirror stage). Even more importantly, Lacan's theory of the drive, taken from Freud but fundamentally reconfigured, helps us better understand Hobbes and Arendt insofar as it answers the two related questions we left off with in the last chapter: why is the subject split, and whence this devouring biological repetition compulsion lurking in its heart? As will become clear in the following account, the movement of all subjects from wordless indistinct masses to belimed sufferers of the signifier will answer both questions, and it will do so, perhaps unsurprisingly, by way of a mugging, one that no doubt takes place within the Arendtian living room. This mugging, otherwise called the creation of subjectivity, is a decisive emergence that can be made only through the straits of sexuality, straits in which the subject is caught, in essence, between Scylla and Charybdis, or a necessary yet impossible choice that will require some death.

This choice will result, particularly in the logic of separation and the paternal metaphor, in three political implications for subjectivity. To the degree that subjectivity is forced to give up a primary desire and accept a socially acceptable version of it, it is already implicated in the processes of interpellation that Althusser outlined and of which we spoke in Chapter 1. Initiation into subjectivity, into a persona, follows the logic of ideological indoctrination, whereby the law of the Other qua Paternal metaphor is accepted so that the subject may be given a place in the world. However, to the degree that the earlier state of desire for the Other qua mother is thereby negated, the natural state of the person remains as the unacceptable drive that cannot be consciously admitted, particularly insofar as it negates the fantasy that helps prop up conscious subjectivity. Last, but not least, all political ideologies will play on this ideological condition of the subject insofar as they continue to bolster the fantasy of completion and place while using and/or creating persons to explain what are necessary failures in their code. The Jew, for instance, must be fabricated to show why all is not perfect within the Nazi system, the terrorist why democracy is an unfinished project, and so on.

Within the broader argument of the text, the Lacanian subject thus presents a structural account for why the state of nature is an internal externality, and why, given this necessary split that establishes the very distinction between the person and persona, the persona tends toward malice and destruction in the face of its abject person. It explains, as well, why personas will go looking for persons to explain and pay for the inevitable failures that define their personifications. Only by understanding this split and, with it, the imaginary structures that constitute our conscious life by virtue of a repression of our unconscious desires, can we understand why no political formation can escape the state of nature and why the 'state of nature' requires its inversion into the 'nature of state'. The political ramifications of subjectivity, insofar as it is described by the Lacanian edifice, are thus entirely necessary to understanding the current impasse of the so-called democratic consensus, particularly to the degree that it suffers a vacillation between imperialism, fundamentalism, and vapid consumer-based liberalism, all with a distinctive lack of participation by the demos. What all of these political formulations lack is a true traversal of the political subject, which, put otherwise, is a political formation that does not predicate its existence on the logic of fantasy. The remainder of this chapter will be spent in examining why subjectivity calls for such a traversal, a necessary step before we move on in the next chapter to examine whether democracy, even in its most radical form, can be said to achieve such a traversal. This also leads to a question latent in our findings from the previous chapter but yet to be broached: to what degree does the Lacanian subject shed light on our insights about the nature of the political as existing in and for the person as opposed to the persona, and, by extension, to what degree do democracy and its currently necessary attendant, capitalism, exemplify politics rather than the political?

1. Being All That You Can't Be: The Mirror Stage

As we saw in Hobbes and Arendt, the persona was conceived of as split off from the natural, a public self that can in essence be traded in words and deeds that represent the living being lurking behind it. Whether by telling one's story or transferring one's right to everything, the persona functioned not only as a way for people to display themselves, but also to save themselves from their own impossible desire. While in Hobbes this literally meant an endless and ultimately violent desire, for Arendt it meant avoiding the vile and impotent self, either the self reduced to an alien nothing, or the self that can not get control of its own dark passions. For Lacan, this persona is nothing other than the ego, and though to a certain extent the Lacanian ego functions as a savior for the subject, a way for the subject to escape its own inadmissable desires, it is also what prevents the subject from self-knowledge. The ego thus situates us along the lines of a fractured and ignorant mirage that is first formulated in what Lacan called the mirror stage.

Famously, Lacan indicated in his early work "The Mirror Stage" that the primary moment of the sense of the I, the creation of the imago, is an inversion: "But the important point is that this form situates the agency known as the ego, prior to its social determination, in a fictional direction that will forever remain irreducible for any single individual or, rather, that will only asymptotically approach the subject's becoming, no matter how successful the dialectical synthesis by which he must resolve, as I, his discordance with his own reality."[3] The image is powerful: the child, looking into a mirror, begins to recognize itself as a totality, as a complete entity. But it does so only by misrecognizing the truth; namely, that its motor skills are not fully functional and that its image is not quite what it represents. Most important in this unresolved dialectic is that the child's newly conceived sense of self is constructed via another self. Here we face a core issue: our sense of identity is grounded in alienation, in a duality of the self that blurs the line between the internal and the external while helping to demarcate it.

What makes the human world a world covered with objects derives from the fact that the object of human interest is the object of the other's desire. How is this possible? It's possible because the human ego is the other and because in the beginning the subject is closer to the form of the other than to the emergence of his own tendency. He is originally an inchoate collection of desires—there you have the true sense of the expression *fragmented body*—and the initial synthesis of the *ego* is essentially an *alter ego*, it is alienated.[4]

Key to the early mirrored self, often represented by Lacan as a relation between small others (a....a'),[5] is the manner in which it creates an internal rivalry. Because the self is recognized in an image which is separated and more perfect, fully realized, and cogent than the actual self, a basic aggression colors the mirrored image, producing the usual emotional suspects; jealousy, anger, hatred, resentment, and so on. These aggressive responses are the result of the distinction the self faces between its reality and its now identified ideality. Indications that one is not quite up to the imaginary structure now in place thus pose an anxious question to the self. The odd logic is that insofar as one is not exactly as one views oneself, one is jealous of the self that one is and, simultaneously, is not, causing the child to react negatively to the version of the self that is deficient. The punctual formula that Lacan presents (a.....a') indicates that there is also an interchangeability within this separation—my primary jealousy of myself is easily attached to other imaginary beings who might point to my own failures of perfection (meaning, for the most part, other children). In this way, one's alter ego already established in the mirror stage indicates how the formations of the 'I' are interchangeable, reflexive, and charged by vacillating emotions. To the degree that a young child is angry at others, they merely stand in for an already present anger at the self for the impossible relation of perfection set up in these early identifications.

Such is why young children are so easily caught up in rivalries over who did what to whom, whether gifts are distributed in an absolutely fair manner, sudden outbursts, displacement of blame, and so on. These conflicts are the experience of anxiety already internalized by the imaginary image—to experience another obtaining preferential treatment, or even the mere appearance of it, is to experience the already present internal failure and desire to dislodge it. It need hardly be pointed out that such aggressive, rivalrous relations are not absent from the adult formation. Suffice it to say that these issues are more or less sublimated into accepted social forms, such as sports, office politics, market competition, relational conflicts, entertainment, war, and so on. Reality TV shows and other media modalities, particularly those found on the Internet (extending, at present, our fifteen minutes of fame to a daily bread) present us with a phenomenon which we will come back to later; namely, the level to which the narcissistic imaginary relation has become an increasingly mundane facet of our lives.[6]

In the creation of the mirror image, then, what Lacan called the fantasy of the cut-up body is retroactively created. Previous to the mirror stage, a child does not differentiate between itself and others, and its self and desires are an indistinct mélange. As Paul Verhaeghe points out, these desires are nothing other than the human drives, which become increasingly partial, or polymorphously perverse, during the movement toward subjective unity: "Through the reflection process, the mirror causes the partial drives to appear to be clothed by the containing surface of the body, to be literally in-corporated . . . in the body as an experience of totality. . . ."[7] And while the mirror stage is the first emergence of what Lacan calls the precipitate subject, it is already a subject that suffers from a fundamentally misrecognized duality. Our initiation into being human thus stems on a fissure in the self that will continue to expand until either the subject performs a massive suture on itself or fails to become properly human.

Within this suturing, however, is found an already begun process of identification; the child starts to become an I through an identification with an image of itself, an image propped up and contoured by its ultimate God, its Mother, whomever fulfills the function thereof. It is important to note here that the self is both a creation in time and a retroactive effect. In other words, Lacan argues that the cut-up body is a fantasy precisely because previous to the mirror stage there was no I. There was nothing, no proper distinction, and so a sort of prehistorical time is created by the subject in order to cope with the fact that, historically, the subject did not exist. In essence, the fantasy of the cut-up body functions in the same way as does the thoroughly abstracted version of the state of nature; there was a time when all was randomness, a time before the coherence of our political/subjective state. We will, of course, return to this issue, but suffice it to say that both positions are correct (there was/was not such a previous time), and it is precisely the impossibility of resolving these two positions that fully defines both the state of nature and the precipitate subject.

As noted, the internal dialectic of self to self found in the mirror stage is already mitigated by another, the Other. The parent, often enough the mother, has been there from the start, holding the child up to the mirror and, according to Verhaeghe, helping to achieve the process of mirroring simply by responding in certain ways as opposed to others, ways which give the child a concept of itself as more complete than it really is.[8] As Lacan puts it:

. . . where the subject sees himself, namely, where that real, inverted image of his own body that is given in the schema of the ego is forged, it is not from there that he looks at himself. But, certainly, it is in the space of the Other that he sees himself and the point from which he looks at himself is also in that space.[9]

In essence, then, the subject begins its identification through an inverted form that is constitutive and false. Aggression occurs within this separated self that derives from the fact that the image is off-kilter. The Other is already contained within the image, though obscured by the self-centered ego that is being formulated in this early moment of identification. As Joel Dor puts it: The child recognizes himself in his own image only insofar as he senses that the Other has already identified him with this image.[10]

Whether it is by express declaration, such as "That's You!," or other more implicit expressions, the image the child identifies with is guaranteed by the Other in contradistinction to the fact that the child has as yet little control over its capacities, much less a sense of itself as a self. And, indeed, the failure involved in the success of the ideal ego will unfortunately only intensify in the next logical moment of subject formation: alienation.

We can pause to note here that we can begin to locate those dark motivations that Arendt and Hobbes spoke within subjectivity by recourse to a very mundane experience—that of a child being propped up by its mother and hailed, as Althusser would say, into an existence that is already shot through with contradiction and failure. Insofar as subjectivity gets its first bearings in an imaginary plane, it is already conditioned by a basic failure to live up to itself, and this sets the stage for certain modalities of jealously and aggression that are well expressed by Hobbesian eminence and the Arendtian torn heart that cannot, for the sake of itself, find its pure expression.[11] Each modality, of course, is predicated at base on impotence, for such is what defines the uneven division between the self and its imago.

2. Money or Life: Alienation and Existence

Perhaps one of the most basic assumptions about child rearing is that of the mother-child bond. Despite increasing reports of infanticides in the press and the growing numbers of women suffering postpartum depression,[12] the idea that a mother loves her child unconditionally remains powerful (mother's day's express *raison d'être,* whatever anxiety one goes through in getting a card sent in time). According to Lacan, this bond, and with it motherhood, is a myth that the child suffers in a determinate way (though the mother is herself the very result of that same myth). The reason for the mythical status of this undivided love becomes apparent in the anxiety the child suffers during the process of alienation from the Other, which is itself the condition of our speech.

Bruce Fink offers a concise way of understanding the underlying cause of the child's sense of alienation:

> Perhaps the simplest way of putting this [cause of alienation] is as follows: Why would a child ever bother to learn to speak if all of its needs were anticipated, if its caretakers fed it, changed it, adjusted the temperature, and so on before it even had a chance to feel hunger, wetness, cold, or any other discomfort? Or if the breast or bottle were always immediately placed in its mouth as soon as it began to cry? If nourishment is never missing, if the desired warmth is never lacking, why would the child take the trouble to speak?[13]

In the early mother-child relation, a necessary miscommunication defines the dyad, causing a sort of dual-channel anxiety as to what the other is saying. One can already note how the early fusion of mother and child within the womb, often carried over into the early stages of infancy, can only occur as a mode of remembering filtered through the sense of distance or alienation that causes each to speak to one another. Because there is no shared language between the two, one must be improvised, and this improvisation is necessitated by unfulfilled needs. A child thus begins to speak on the basis of missing things that at first appear practical; lack of nutrition, warmth, cleanliness, the bottle or the breast. But within these objects of need lurks an insubstantial yet all encompassing object, an object which has no clear outline or use value. This object is the desire of the Other, and its logic is that of the missing piece, the unfinished puzzle. Essentially, the child interprets these lacks on the part of the mother as her unsatisfied desire, and therefore dutifully puts it upon him or herself to find a way to fill in that missing piece, leading thereby to a second form of alienation, one more fully situated in the Other.

While the mirror stage introduces the emerging subject to the logic of *méconnaissance*, of a sutured mastery and its attendant rivalry, alienation proper inducts the subject into the realm of the signifier and thus to a decision that will ultimately split it in two:

> In a field of objects no relationship is conceivable that engenders alienation apart from that of the signifier. Let us take for granted that no subject has any reason to appear in the real except for the fact that speaking beings exist therein. A physics is conceivable that accounts

for everything in the world, including its animate part. A subject intervenes only inasmuch as there are, in this world, signifiers which mean nothing and must be deciphered.[14]

What Lacan means by a signifier is not at all clear. On a very basic level, what is at issue is the fact that, as Fink points out, if a child is going to get its needs met, it must attempt to communicate. But insofar as the child does not yet have language, a tragicomedy of errors ensues. Here is where the signifier becomes important for Lacan. The primary or, as he called it during the mid-sixties,[15] unary signifier stands for nothing other than the desire of the Other, or the desire of the mother. Thus while the child clearly has needs that must be met, the child also suffers a question that must be answered: what does the Other want, what are they saying to me, why are they doing what they are doing? This is what Lacan means by saying that there are signifiers that mean nothing—a signifier is the empty word or expression of the Other that a child is forced to decipher in terms of what may or may not be the Other's desire.

Such is why Lacan calls the primary signifier the unary signifier. It comes to stand for the object of the mother's desire that will bring back a supposed unity between the two. Whether through lapses in attention, personal needs, or a direct desire for other things, a child notices eventually that its parents are not completely absorbed in her or his needs, a fact that is difficult to take given that these needs and wants hinge entirely on the caregiver. As such, this dichotomy causes the child to suffer from alienation and have to give up on its desire for full attachment; in other words, since there is no true unity, no familial Rosetta Stone, a child begins to internalize the lack of unity. Lacan argues that this acceptance is, all in all, forced, and the force of the situation derives from the obscure nature of the signifier. At base, what any child must choose between is being and meaning.

On the one hand, being stands for a complete immersion in the Other, an undifferentiated symbioses. Conversely, meaning stands for the internalization of language as the mediating factor in the relationship. The situation is forced, for the most part, because language is already being given to the child in the stead of the mother's absence. Lacan's commentary on Freud's account of Little Hans gives a good explication of the situation a subject-in-waiting suffers. In Freud's famous account, a young child who is apparently well loved makes use of his toys by consistently tossing them away and bringing them back, expressing as he does so 'fort' (gone) and 'da' (there). Freud reads this process as the replication of the mother's withdrawal, one whereby Hans partakes in a process that all children do as they attempt to "make themselves the master of the situation."[16] Lacan, however, inverts this mastery into the exhibition of the level to which the child cannot master that which he desires to most:

> If the young subject can practice this game of *fort-da*, it is precisely because he does not practice it at all, for no subject can grasp this radical articulation. He practices it with the help of a small bobbin, that is to say, with the *objet a*. The function of the exercise with this object refers to an alienation, and not to some supposed mastery, which is difficult to imagine being increased in an endless repetition, whereas the endless repetition that is in question reveals the radical vacillation of the subject.[17]

The *objet a*, the missing part of the relationship, is the desire of the Other, and thus Hans does not master this game because he literally does not know, in the sense of Cartesian self-conscious awareness, what he is doing.[18] Hans is not playing a game so much as becoming who he is, as Pindar put it, by expressing what is happening to him. Fundamental to that expression is the fact that *da* is defined by *fort*, that his new presence only occurs in the wake of his mother's absence. Hans is thus becoming a subject by metaphorically internalizing his loss. That he does so with an object, and that this object takes on its meaning through words indicates what is at stake in the signifier: the signifier is the stand in for the loss of the mother, the *objet a*, that little piece of the Other that the subject can neither produce nor find, neither be nor have, save for various incomplete proxies.

No doubt, such proxies can and will eventually be politicized. Indeed, we can already note that the dilemma of the subject, the dilemma of a choice between being and meaning, indicates that the precipitation of the subject describes, in advance, the logic of the state of nature. For insofar as being a subject means submitting to the signifier of an absence and therefore language, to enter a political society indicates submission to an Other—it thus also indicates that the person, the being that has been stuck in the state of abject choice, must be repressed by the political entry. To put it in Hobbesian terms, my right to everything, or my right to the entirety of the m(O)ther, is denied by choosing a coherent, structured meaning. In its stead, I will give my representation, the articulated persona that is fungible and thereby structured like a language. If I don't, I signal my resistance to the structure that is being offered as a way out and remain within a realm that is beyond the acceptable protocol.

Indeed, just as Hobbes and Locke exhibit the meaning of the political through the metaphor of the thief, Lacan likens Little Hans' situation to being mugged. In section16 of Seminar XI, he argues that the subject suffers a vel of alienation, an either/or situation encapsulated in the phrase "your money or your life!"[19] Lacan's answer to Hobbes and Locke, however, is to point out that the situation is lose-lose. If I choose money, I will likely lose my life and with it my ability to enjoy the money. But if I choose life, I lose a bit of what I have chosen since it is through my money that I enjoy life. What is worse, as with the British prisoners, I am haunted by the fact of submission—of having given into the forced choice, even if no one would blame me. Similarly, a subject, if it is to choose life, what Lacan calls ex-isting,[20] will lose full being, a fusion with the Other: "If we choose being, the subject disappears, it eludes us, it falls into non-meaning. If we choose meaning, the meaning survives only deprived of that part of non-meaning that is, strictly speaking, that which constitutes in the realization of the subject, the unconscious."[21] By ex-sisting, I forsake access to the supposed pleasure, that pound of flesh, to be found in the Other, what Lacan calls *jouissance*. As such, I will be haunted by the sense that something is missing, though it cannot be named. Experiences of being mugged will only bring the sense of an existential loss to the forefront, though an explicit connection to the original loss is, structurally speaking, inexpressible.

But one can resist. Psychosis is thus the state in which a subject refuses the signifier, refuses to accept meaning, and clings to a realm in which the signifier does not create a distance from that ultimate signified, the desire of the Other.[22] Most subjects make the neurotic choice of accepting that their desire and the desire of the Other will be mediated by language, that their ultimate wish will be banished to a forbidden realm that circulates only in the unconscious. Arguably, this gives us a clue as to the existential basis of the phrase that you cannot have your cake and eat it too—you can have the object (i.e., a relationship with the Other) only insofar as you do not enjoy it (i.e., you do not continue enjoying the Other).

It is thus only by a baptism through language, so to speak, that subjectivity begins to fully structure itself:

> But, certainly, it is in the space of the Other that he sees himself and the point from which he looks at himself is also in that space. Now, this is also the point from which he speaks, since insofar as he speaks, it is in the locus of the Other that he begins to constitute that truthful lie by which is initiated that which participates in desire at the level of the unconscious.[23]

Here we can see the level to which the imaginary function of the ideal ego is expanded into the realm of the Other. As the desire of the mother, what the Other wants, becomes entangled in the logic of the signifier, the subject is further fractured, losing yet another aspect of itself as complete or whole. As Hobbes phrased it, he is "as a bird in lime twigs, the more he struggles the more belimed." While the child desires to be the fulfillment of the mother's desire (hence Lacan's famous dictum that man's desire is the desire of the Other[24]), that attempt at fulfillment runs into the impossibilities of language. We can also venture the following Hobbesian result: if the 'normal' subject is neurotic, as opposed to psychotic, then the normal subject is also Hobbesian. Even before we are fully aware of what is at stake, we choose life in the face of the brigand, we choose to contract in the hopes that at some later date, perhaps, we will not only continue to live, but to do so felicitously by means of the Other (Sovereign) who will provide us with the rules and laws of our continued existence on the basis of the fantasy that the Other knows what is going on. We don't, on the other hand, tend to choose being, a complete possession of all that is meaningful and dear to the self, at whatever cost, as a Lockeian position might propose initially, though not ultimately. Rather, our personas are transferred under the terms and conditions of that incalculable sovereign, the Other.

Insofar, then, as we are mainly Hobbesian in our subjective being, from our split desire to our tendency to contract with the thief, who is, no less, our m(O)ther, subjectivity and its political ramifications are bound together by the problematic logic of the state of nature. The opening unto subjectivity, that is, indicates the sort of abject vacillation that the state of nature imposes or, more accurately put, reveals in those who are subject to it. To thus be submitted to a state of nature is to be returned to that anxious deciding point that is wholly dependent on external circumstances, circumstances which for the most part provide mixed signals at best. Subjectivity enters unto the scene by way of a forced choice that requires a fundamental loss, producing a kind of inherent if hazy nostalgia that permeates our existence. To be stuck into the state of nature is thus to revisit this vacillation, except, as will become clear, with the proviso that what one vacillates between is not being qua fusion and meaning qua language, but the possibility of a political persona and a violent, abject nothingness. In other words, there is no physical m(O)ther in the state of nature, which is why those who come bearing politicized versions of her promises are all the more desirable.

3. Signifying Nothing

But though it is the case that there is difficulty in interpretation that haunts the initial relationship between the subject and its other, it is not at all clear that this initial problem must remain problematic thence forward. At this point we reach the core structuralist component of Lacan's theory of the signifier, one which explicates an inherent impossibility within language itself that has nothing to do with our general ability to speak, write, and communicate.[25] Rather, Lacan argued that the Saussurian model of the signifier and the signified leads to the conclusion that the signified, the meaning or object that a word indicates, is fundamentally elusive given that it is not anchored to its signifier.[26] Contra logical positivism, there is always a new combinatory that can come along and create new meaning, new signifieds, due to the chained structures of language: "We can take things no further along this path than to demonstrate that no signification can be sustained except by reference to another signification."[27] Just as words in dictionaries lead to more words, dictionaries become outmoded, and words are dropped and replaced. Indeed, language could be said to be somewhat democratic to the extent that meaning is inherently representational, never landing on its terminal definition.[28]

But the meaning of a word is slippery also by virtue of its temporal construction within a given sentence. While the different phonemes and graphemes are being heard or read, their actual meaning depends on the last one received. Meaning is thus retroactively constructed, insisting its way along but never consisting of any particular articulation: "Whence we can say that it is in the chain of the signifier that meaning *insists*, but that none of the chain's elements *consists* in the signification it can provide at that very moment."[29] Should the sentence end differently, its contents will be altered. As we can see, however, any given sentence is not open to infinite meanings; the last word seals the deal, as it were. This final term that ends the diachronic sliding of differential meaning construction is called by Lacan the 'button tie', the term that sews together the previous.[30] All the same, there is obviously no final say on any given utterance as new expressions will affect the timbre of a previous meaning.

The creation of new meaning, however, is not arbitrary. The system is, as Lacan points out, subject to certain laws of combination. Lacan marks metonymy and metaphor as the mechanisms by which the infinite or "incessant sliding of the signified under the signifier" is accomplished.[31] We can already see how metonymy, whereby a part comes to represent a whole ("wheels" for a car, for instance), functions in the production of meaning. In attempting to express the meaning of something, every formulation only obtains a partial meaning. Thus metonymy, according to Lacan, can be seen as the gap that any meaning effect creates: insofar as every signification fails to be a full signification, and insofar as this failure is a function of other possible combinations, metonymy is that very empty part or partial-ization of all attempts at meaning. Metonymy thus signifies how language is necessarily incomplete: "The repeating interval, the most radical struc-ture of the signifying chain, is the locus haunted by metonymy. . . ."[32] All utterances become a vocalization of their intended meaning and simultane-ous failure to express full meaning, a sort of stand-in for totality that marks its absence nonetheless. Metonymy, like a specter, haunts language.[33]

The metonymic specter leads us to the problem of the drive, which is one of the most difficult concepts in psychoanalysis.[34] For Freud, the idea of the drive provides a way of talking about our fundamental life force, or the way in which we are internally propelled toward activities that satisfy our needs for survival, reproduction, and, above all else, pleasure. Freud viewed the drive as a bridge between the body and the mind, but unlike animalistic instincts, which are not submitted to language and interpreta-tion, the drive is a "borderland concept between the mental and the physical. . . ."[35] Thus the drive is something that is *represented* in consciousness, and it is this representation, when it turns out to be too disturbing to handle, that is ultimately repressed. Accordingly, one does not repress one's drive *per se*, but how it is conceived.[36] Freud's insight about the unconscious thus turns upon the manner in which the physical becomes mental, the way the heart blooms already torn, as Arendt suggested, from a disturbingly corpo-ral root. The elaboration of the drive can therefore be seen as an elaboration of the biological roots of Arendt's social, as well as Hobbes' motion, once connected to desire, thereby helping to explain how the devouring body could become a political *thing*.

Lacan takes the Freudian drive and reconceives the concept of represen-tation by incorporating it within structural linguistics. As it turns out, such corporal representatives suffer the logic of signifiers we have just noted. The fact that these signifiers function under certain linguistic logical constraints, such as metonymy, leads to Lacan's famous dictum that the "unconscious is structured like a language."[37] Lacan thus examines what happens to this primary constant force when it encounters the Other and does so through her words. In that drama, the *mise en scène* of the subject, one can witness a cornucopia of failed desires that eventually leads the emerging subject to full subjectivity, though one that still waits. As such, we can thus explain how the specter of metonymy haunts the subject at two levels. On the one hand, alienation at its core forces the subject into a linguistic universe, a universe in which desire, the subject's and the Other's, is transposed and cut up into words. Because these words themselves are equivocal, the subject is forced into a process of constant deciphering, a deciphering that means that as soon as the subject has 'got it', she will soon 'lose it'.[38] "It," the desire of the Other, will forever be obscured by the various significations that are transmitted between child and parent, and its loss is the loss of the subject from itself. This loss of the self is precisely the subject's fading, a disappearance between the lines, or between signifiers. The gap in meaning is the linguistic expression of the gap in being, and hence all words will metonymically represent by means of the missing piece the totality of the desire of the Other.

As such, the subject's drive, the expression of an internal want and a need to return to homeostasis, or for pleasure and release, gets an equivocal response from the Other. There is, therefore, a dialectical relationship between the drive of the subject and the answer of the Other which goes thus: insofar as the Other responds to the subject's drives less than whole-heartedly or even with disapproval, the subject attempts to modulate her or his expressions. As Verhaeghe points out, this creates primal repression, by which is meant nothing other than that the unconscious is built on what is inexpressible or that which cannot be put into words and, most importantly, cannot be assimilated into the desire of the Other.[39] Given that the unconscious, which is where the drive is relegated to in repression, circulates around a lost or missing object, we can see why Lacan argues that, contra Freud, there is no *ganze Sexualtrebung*, no fully formed drive.[40] The drives are inherently partial because they are constructed around a missing element, seeking satisfactions sculpted around failures of satisfaction and unable to be consciously accepted.

From precipitate or inchoate subject to actual subject, a truly Hobbesian logic determines our being such that there is no ultimate good, no *sunnum bonum* that could satisfy us completely. However, as Hobbes also understood, the pathetic ironic motor within this lack of an ultimate good is the subject's belief in its nonetheless. That is, the subject encounters an Other that bears with it the promise of fulfillment, a promise that remains unconscious but newly translated through language into other possibilities of fulfillment. But, as we have seen, insofar as language can never provide the great good of which it constantly speaks (a great good that does not, in itself, exist in any case), there is always a new greater good to take its place or, should one encounter the last straw of failure, the possible unhinging of imaginary constructs, thus releasing the force of the drive unmitigated. For the most part, however, we remain within the systematic tension created by the relation of a conscious, linguistic existence that creates sublimated versions of satisfaction over and against a partialized, ever circulating, and repressed drive that does not, for all of our structural improvements in the name of the Other, go away. Politically speaking, the result is that whatever modalities of a perfected state one creates, there will by necessity be a return of the repressed insofar as perfection does not define subjectivity. Or, to the extent that politics promotes a cohabitation predicated on the perfected and conscious yet imaginary persona, the person will, in various ways, always emerge in the contradictions of the beautiful structure, thereby expressing the symptom of politics, or the return of the political. All systems, like all subjects, have their symptoms, their indicators of the gaps within the fantasy that structures and motivates their continued existence. Beneath that fantasy, however, lies our drives that unacceptably seek the Other nonetheless, emerging every so often in ways that must be repressed once again or, what is also the case, staged in the form of external bad objects which can, through such staging, be invested with these distasteful energies. Subjectivity, and thereby political subjectivity, is thus defined by the tension between our neurotic need for an Other who will provide the imaginary promises that only language can construct and the unacceptable though continuous *pulsion* of its drives.

However, Lacan makes a somewhat controversial argument with regard to the drive. One can read him as arguing that what the drive represents is an immortality that we lose at birth. As he says in Seminar XI, this immortality is nothing other than the libido:

> It is the libido, *qua* pure life instinct, that is to say, immortal life, or irrepressible life, life that has need of no organ, simplified, indestructible life. It is precisely what is subtracted from the living being by virtue of the fact that it is subject to the cycle of sexed reproduction. And it is of this that all the forms of the *objet a* that can be enumerated are the representatives, the equivalents. The *objets a* are merely its representatives, its figures.[41]

Verhaeghe takes this argument literally, arguing that it is reasonable considering that in parthogenesis the possibility of immortality is retained since the self continues onward indefinitely, while in sexual reproduction, the continuation of the species requires the death of the individual.[42] However, Lacan does not directly say this, using rather a myth to make the point (the myth of the lamella, which is rather presciently descriptive of the alien babies in Ridley Scott's *Alien*). What Lacan argues, then, is that the living being loses its immortality in its birth as a subject, not in its birth as a human. This is the subject of the signifier, the subject that must exist in the Other at the cost of losing its being, and what is indicated by sexual reproduction is not the act of physical reproduction, but the process of sexuation, of dealing with the desire of the Other: "The relation to the Other is precisely that which, for us, brings out what is represented by the lamella—not sexed polarity, the relation between masculine and feminine, but the relation between the living subject and that which he loses by having to pass, for his reproduction, through the sexual cycle."[43] Lacan thus argues that this tells us why the drive is inherently a death drive. It is so because by becoming a subject, a persona realized in and through a deciphering of the desire of the Other, the subject suffers a loss, a death of its self qua an irrecoverable being.

The *objet a*, as we saw above, represents this loss as the desire of the Other of an unvarnished fullness and fusion: "The *objet petit a* is not the origin of the oral drive. It is not introduced as the original food, it is introduced from the fact that no food will ever satisfy the oral drive, except by circumventing the eternally lacking object."[44] The drive circulates around this loss, in the form of a particular object, whether the breast or something else fulfilling the same function, but the object is inherently nonexistent—it is void, a missing thing, one desired all the same. Indeed, the force of the drive is found in the relationship between the pleasure of the body and the demand of the Other. Though the drive desires a rest from pleasure, or homeostasis, it is inherently mitigated, frustrated, confused, and pleased by the ways in which the Other bears upon it.

True enough, were the drives to reach full realization unproblematically, psychoanalysis and, more importantly, the question of the self would disappear. We would obtain our satisfactions and move on. But there is something utterly inappropriate about pleasure for most, something that is felt as forbidden, dirty, unrespectable, and so on. Pleasure is often gotten on the sly, behind closed doors, and for reasons that generally are felt to be upsetting by subjects (hence phrases like 'it's too much', 'crossing the line', 'one just doesn't do that', and so on, all indicators of how pleasure beyond certain bounds is insidious). Ultimately, the drive and its inappropriate compulsion is rendered unconscious due, as Lacan argues, to the instantiation of the paternal metaphor, or the acceptance of the Law by the subject. Here the subject-in-waiting becomes a socially acceptable subject as such, giving up its desire for total immersion in the Other and setting upon the task of finding its own way with regard to the external world (the Symbolic realm). Here, as well, we see that the forced choice was made; the subject, more often than not, chooses life, and, as we shall see, unwittingly seeks its lost money everywhere it goes. However, we can already see a way in which the drive is its own inhibition: since it seeks an impossible pleasure through the Other, the drive is clearly structured in terms of a gap, a void, a missing piece, otherwise called *objet a*. The drive is thus impossible: "The subject will realize that his desire is merely a vain detour with the aim of catching the *jouissance* of the other—insofar as the other intervenes, he will realize that there is a *jouissance* beyond the pleasure principle."[45] In other words, the subject-in-waiting, the emerging subject of the drive, seeks something more than just a satisfaction, more than a return to calm: the subject seeks the *jouissance* of the Other. Again, the desire of the subject is the desire of the Other, a desire embodied in a lost object that is compulsively sought as a fusion with one who is forbidden through the paternal metaphor. This compulsion, this constant force, is that which, once subjectivity has been born, is too much, is beyond the pleasure principle and thus taboo.

Politically speaking, this force is what drives political identification with other personas and the revulsion at subjects who are reduced to mere persons. To the extent that a subject is ensconced in its identity, it obtains a modicum of pleasure and comfort in a stabilized identity that contains, nonetheless, that inherent anxiety circulating around a forbidden drive. Hence, the anxiety of which Hobbes and Locke spoke, and which meant a biological tendency toward destruction for Arendt, is to be found in the pleasure of the body as it is crossed over and partialized by the desire of the Other. The structure of its dismissal into the unconscious will be outlined next, but it should be noted that its dismissal is required if one is to become a subject proper—to enter society requires a repression of a direct desire for the Other. To be stripped of one's social personifications is to be desublimated and hence to return to the abject state of choosing between money and life, if such an offering is made. In the eyes of others, it is to instill the fear of the loss of the persona, the fear of being returned to such an abject state. Such is why the stateless, who had the least power of any, could instill a sense of impotence in their onlookers. Their universality, which really indicated their lack of a social persona, did threaten, but only with that loss which everyone has already. Hence, they threatened with awareness.

It must be pointed out, as well, that to the degree that a persona is at stake but not well established, the feelings of aggression, jealousy, and hatred of which we spoke earlier will be rendered more explicit and raw. Such is why a civil war is one of all against all—the intensity of the loss of the persona releases the unkempt, childlike aggressions toward the self as failed but projected onto others, aggressions that need the soothing answers of an Other who knows. But because pure fusion remains unacceptable within social bearings, it requires a public law to limit it, just as Hobbesian reason suggests. Does this mean, then, that public personas, once established, will not then commit atrocities? Obviously not, and insofar as the drive remains, an Other that calls upon it to commit these atrocities, particularly against persons, will be gladly answered, though generally under the condition that such acts remain unofficial.[46]

4. The Paternal Metaphor and its Phallusy

We can thus far see why Lacan insists that within alienation, and therefore the subject itself, there exists an essential lack of meaning, a fundamental indecipherability and loss that is, insofar as the child accepts the signifiers presented to it, accepted and internalized. Since the subject-in-waiting cannot fully decipher what the Other wants, and then must repress its desire to seek that answer, the *Kern unseres Wesen*, the core of our being, as Freud put it, functions as an unnerving and basic absence. This meaning that must be given up is experienced by the subject as a fading, an aphanisis. This lack of meaning is what Lacan called the *objet a*, and later (a), the cause of desire. Desire, in other words, erupts as the seeking of that which was lost, thus underlining and explaining Hobbesian desire: there is no *summum bonum* because it exists only in its loss, only as a retroactive imaginary construction. As such, only particular objects can stand as metonymic placeholders for what was never quite there in the first place. On the flip side, however, this desire qua missing piece also indicates the drive insofar as it is repressed, rendered unconscious. The problem is that the drive does not disappear; it insists infinitely. Furthermore, the subject's identification with the desire of the Other through the positive signifiers given to it also functions as a defense against this very drive, the subject's increasingly unconscious pleasure seeking.

The subject must decide between the driven demand of the body and a nonsensical yet meaning-ridden demand of the Other, though there is really only one acceptable choice. This bodily drive that is relegated to the consciously unacceptable realm, a prohibited *jouissance*, is what Lacan calls the Real, the encounter with which occurs, so the subject thinks, "as if by chance."[47] What the subject encounters in the Aristotelian *tuché* is the primarily repressed trauma of the lost yet desired connection with the other, the pleasure that the distance of identity shores up. Whether it is the accident of a slip of the tongue, the randomness of a strange dream, or a desire that is not compatible with one's professed values, the drive continues to reemerge within our socially acceptable personas and expresses itself as the stumbling blocks over which they trip.[48]

Alienation is thus a way of talking about our entry through desire into the public world, into the realm of language and meaning, discourse and discussion, and the search for answers as it expresses itself in codified, historicized, and more or less established forms, an entry whose opening is predicated on an absence, as we have seen. Alienation is, after the relatively private process of the mirror stage, a more publicized process of identification within relations of meaningful dissemination and creation that Lacan refers to as the Symbolic realm, best exemplified currently by television, news, movies, the Internet, education, and the like. However, the Symbolic gift, as it were, comes fully filtered through the Other in alienation. By beginning to accept language as the ultimate mediator of one's approach to the desire of the Other, the subject starts to receive and create an understanding of the various external meanings that will come to define him or her: "It is in the very act of speaking that I make this formalization, this ideal metalanguage, ex-sist. It is in this respect that the symbolic cannot be confused with being, far from it. Rather, it subsists qua ex-sistence with respect to the act of speaking. That is what I stressed . . . by saying that the symbolic bears only ex-sistence."[49] This ex-sistence, this forcing of the subject outside of itself not only in terms of meaning but in terms of the Other with whom there was a supposed fusion, is primary if the subject is to succeed as a "normal," "functioning" human being.

One can think of this ex-sisting as the movement between two forms of the Other. The first Other, generally speaking the mother, functions primarily along imaginary lines.[50] Early on, the caretaker is the entirety of the child's world, and the anxiety of alienation stems for the sense that the world as such is being lost. This being pulled out of oneself through the Other qua mother, or caretaker, is accomplished by means of the new Other, the Father, or instantiation of the law. Lacan represents this as the movement from the unary signifier, or S1, to the binary signifier, S2.[51] In primary repression, we see a number of things occur with regard to these signifiers. On the one hand, the second linguistic process takes place, that of metaphor. Insofar as the desire of the mother is forbidden, it becomes evident that this desire is controlled by the Father, or the paternal function/metaphor. It is this paternal metaphor, or S2, that comes to take the place of the unary signifier. By seeing the father as the placeholder and regulator of the mother's desire (and thus anyone's access to it), the child makes a substitution and, at the same time, a repression. The binary signifier, in other words, stands metaphorically for the desire of the mother as it becomes the core of the child's unconscious, a word or group of words that indicate what is forbidden.

Lacan's main example of this, as we saw earlier, is the *fort* / *da* game of little Hans. In expressing his alienation, Hans is also expressing his acceptance of the loss, the *fort*, of his mother. The bobbin, or the *petit a*, is the remainder of the process of primary repression. Lacan uses Freud's concept of the *Vorstellungsrepräsentanz* to explicate this idea.[52] As Lacan translates it, *Vorstellungsrepräsentanz* means representative of the representation, which, otherwise put, means nothing other than the representative of the mother's desire:

> Hence the division of the subject—when the subject appears somewhere as meaning, he is manifested elsewhere as 'fading', as disappearance. There is, then one might say, a matter of life and death between the unary signifier and the subject, *qua* binary signifier, cause of his disappearance, the *Vorstellungsrepräsentanz* is the binary signifier.[53]

The unary signifier represents the desire of the Mother, the binary the Law of the Father. By becoming the unary signifier's representative, the binary signifier takes its place and, for the subject, becomes an anchoring point allowing an acceptable linguistic place in the world.[54] The paternal metaphor, according to Lacan, is the zero point, the button tie which stabilizes and gives a structuring meaning to all further expressions. As noted earlier, the button tie is a diachronic element that anchors meaning and gives the elements within a sentence a retroactive coherence. As we can see now, the paternal metaphor accomplishes the same effect with regard to the subject's identification with the Name/No of the Father, a name which is an identification and a prohibition; the subject now achieves stability in regard to the wavering alienation it previously suffered from. Without this button tie, the subject is essentially psychotic.[55]

Primary repression, then, is the institution of a speaking subject and the creation of a persona who is ready for the symbolic realm (as opposed to the possibly psychotic and generally abject person that is stuck in a forced choice). This gives us a view of the level to which the rules of structural linguistics do and do not determine the subject. It is clearly not the case that there is no subject. We are not reduced to being mere effects of a system. Indeed, as we have seen, there is freedom insofar as the subject makes a choice, however limited. Furthermore, the linguistic effects of language are not entire to the extent that the unconscious is only structured like a language. More importantly, there is a basic nonsense about the whole process given that the unary signifier is a sort meaninglessness that literally drives the subject out of itself. The primary signifier has little to do with its general meaning—rather, its power resides in its relation to the desire of the Other, which indicates that each subject is always particular in the way that they come into existence; that is, each will butt up against and ultimately accept a certain representation, a certain signifier, and in a certain way, thus making each individual's drama distinct, even if the fact that all must go through the drama is not in and of itself special.[56] In any case, we are now in a position to understand Lacan's phrase that a signifier is what represents a subject to another signifier. What occurs whenever a subject speaks is his or her place with regard to the binary signifier: "My definition of the signifier (and there is no other) is as follow: a signifier is what represents the subject to another signifier. This latter signifier is therefore the signifier to which all the other signifiers represent the sub-ject—which means that if this signifier is missing, all the other signifiers represent nothing."[57] Though we are not aware of this, for we cannot be, whenever we speak our words are anchored in and colored by their relation to the primarily repressed signifier, the Name/No of the Father which, furthermore, is colored by that which it wards off, the unary signifier, the desire of the Mother.

It is important to note, however, that this father is not necessarily tied to a real father, or even the presence of a father.[58] Rather, it is insofar as the mother expresses a desire for another presence, expresses a law that she herself is submitted to, that the subject comes to understand that the desire of the Other is for something else; namely, the father. Here we enter into a rather touchy issue in Lacan, one so subject to debate that it merits more space than will be given here. For, according to Lacan, a phallus is at stake both with regard to the desire of the Mother and the Law of the Father. However, before we do so, it is important to note a couple of points regard-ing issues that we left off with in Chapter 2. One of the most problematic elements in Arendt's presentation of the primordial biological underpin-ning of humanity was the profound effect it had on the split subject—in other words, why does the subject qua homo, qua reduced, tend to produce violent reactions in those who maintained their personas, and why do the latter, once deprived of freedom, tend to become massively destructive consumers? Here we can begin a much more articulate answer: because, to the extent that we see others reduced to drive, reduced to their original condition of unmitigated desire for presence of the Other, we are reminded of our own repressed inner conflict—the abjection of the other touches off our own abjection, an abjection that is central to the very alienation that was fundamental in our creation (abjection, being, after all, a two-and-fro, an uncertain and noxious back and forth between obliteration and presence). The self that is comfortably in and for itself cannot stand to see the representation, so primal, of its primary loss.

On the other hand, to the extent that subjects are relegated more and more to private realms of desire, they are also brought closer to the repetitions of desire unchecked by any overriding paternal authority, creating a pleasurable level of repetitive accumulation, but one that is attended by a gnawing sense of anxiety and emptiness. Though, as we shall see later on, desire is not drive, the two are closely linked, desire being but a fantasmatic way to deal with what is inappropriate in the drive. As Lacan says: "The subject sustains himself as desiring in relation to an ever more complex signifying ensemble."[59] What mass society and capitalism are able to achieve is a desire-based mode of existence, one that uses signifying ensemble of images, ideas, and sounds by which to further provoke desire, though in the form of some object or another that can only promise but never finalize desire. But such is also an existence that more and more precariously verges on falling into the psychosis of drive the less there is any preventative factor. As we have seen, it is the prohibition of the paternal function that keeps desire separated from drive, even though the object of desire and the object of drive are the same (the difference being that the drive functions in the Real of the body, while desire functions in the Imaginary, in fantasy).

In our current historical configuration, however, the paternal function has been weakened—there is no clear authority, though we can witness a quite strong desire for one in the images projected by presidents such as George W. Bush[60] and movements such as the Promise Keepers and Al Quaida. What the Arendtian 'living room' reveals to the subject more and more is not some blob of a biological underpinning, but the anxiety-ridden, excessively pleasurable, and ultimately empty nature of its drive. The constant repetition of desire, after a time, ends in a voided feeling, an overabundance spilling into abjection (which is why addiction is, in essence, applicable to any repeatable activity). Turning, then, to Hobbes, we can clearly indicate why desire is both impossible and fundamentally repetitive. Its impossibility stems from the fact that it is based on an object that does not exist as represented. While Hobbes argued that desire never ends because there is no ultimate object of satisfaction, Lacan argues that desire *begins* because there is no ultimate object of satisfaction (the *objet a* is the cause, not the object of desire). We desire what doesn't exist, and then later on we are forbidden to have it. This repression, this forbidding of an impossible object, is what creates the compulsive repetition at the heart of the subject; we are driven to constantly turn around a missing piece, a void at our core.[61] Such an essential void raises the generally unwanted issue that Agamben dismisses from the start: is democracy, which itself revolves around an empty center and promotes the freedom of constant choice and accumulation, particularly when packaged with capitalism, a good config-uration for such subjectivity? Do the two not, in essence, succumb to logic of accumulation that the masculine role suffers in its need to have the phal-lus? This, of course, assumes that there is such a phallus in the first place.

Just as the 'social' is Arendt's conceptual pariah, the 'phallus' is Lacan's *persona non grata*. While Lacan is often seen as theoretically useful or inter-esting, particularly with regard to his mirror stage, many have decried the phallus as nothing less or more than a full frontal endorsement of patriar-chy. Perhaps one of the most notable negations of the importance of the phallus comes from Judith Butler, who accuses Lacanians of trying to have it both ways:

> Are we using the categories to understand the phenomena, or mar-shaling the phenomena to shore up the categories 'in the name of the Father', if you will? Similarly, we can try to accept the watered-down notion of the symbolic as separable from normative kinship, but why is there all that talk about the place of the Father and the Phallus? . . . Lacanians are hard-pressed to justify the recirculation of patriarchal kin positions as the capitalized 'Law' at the same time as they attempt to define such socially saturated terms in ways that immunize them from all sociality or, worse, render them as the pre-social (quasi-) transcendental condition of sociality as such.[62]

In essence, Butler is dismissing Lacanians for proposing the phallus as both historical and indicative of a sexually neutral transcendentalism. Since the very concept of a phallus is inherently tied in with the penis, and since the phallus is itself fundamental to the Law and the creation of subjectivity as such, the Lacanian concept of the phallus is proposed as a de facto endorse-ment of male-centered heterosexual social arrangements. For Lacanians to attempt to argue that the phallus is merely an abstract notion that need not be considered necessary or metaphysical is a shell game that fails in its very execution.

We can trace the thrust of this dismissal back to Butler's earlier text, "The Lesbian Phallus," in which she articulates this argument in the following way: "To claim for the phallus the status of a privileged signifier performa-tively produces and effects this privilege."[63] Or, in other words, Butler is making the Austinian argument that naming the phallus as privileged is itself the very creation of the phallus's privilege. The question then arises; why the phallus, something so tied to the penis and thus male 'superiority' itself? Why not alter the notion of the phallus and claim the priority of a lesbian phallus: "When the phallus is lesbian, then it is and is not a masculinist figure of power; the signifier is significantly split, for it both recalls and displaces the masculinism by which it is impelled."[64]

The point of Butler's critique is thus that to place the phallus in the position of the secondary signifier, as that which enacts subjectivity itself, is to effectively say that the phallus is good, that we should continue on with it. As Austin had it, words can be deeds; their use can constitute an action. If the word in use, phallus, for instance, is itself performing a damaging action to half the population in the world, it might very well be a good idea to not use that word. But though the performative argument has much to recommend it, its application to the phallus is not convincing. Lacan does not argue that the phallus is a transhistorical truth, but rather that it has played a primary role in Western culture. Indeed, we can see its latest display in the recent battles over gay marriage. The Christian and conservative right finds the hetero-phallus so in jeopardy that many of them are willing to make the heterosexual matrix a federal institution.[65] It is difficult to imagine that if Lacanians were to begin using a term such as the Lesbian phallus, institutionalized heterosexuality would begin to disappear. As Fink puts it:

> Psychoanalytic practice suggests, as do other practices, that in Western culture in general, that signifier [of what is desirable] is the phallus. Though many claim that that is no more than a preconceived notion, psychoanalysis claims that it is a clinical observation, and as such is contingent. It is verified time and again in clinical practice, and thus constitutes a generalization, not a necessary, universal rule.[66]

Indeed, it is unclear where the idea that Lacan intended either a transhistorical or approving view of the phallus came from. As he puts it in Seminar XX: "The body's being is of course sexed, but it is secondary, as they say. And as experience shows, the body's *jouissance*, insofar as the body symbolizes the Other, does not depend on those traces."[67] The traces to which Lacan refers are the physical sexual characteristics that result from the germ, the sexual reproductive cell. In essence, Lacan is arguing that the physical body is, insofar as it is sexual, a secondary sexual trait, the primary issue being the question of the desire of the Other.[68] Altering the conception of the phallus might be a theoretically good way of solving the issues at play, but it does nothing for analyzing the actual current cultural configurations that go into making subjects insofar as they are subsumed under the vexing logic of desire.

Indeed, it is arguable that this is much ado about nothing, since what analysis attempts to alleviate the subject of is the way she or he comes to be oriented with regard to the phallus, a representative of something that does not exist in the first place. The phallus is a sign of a fundamental failure. Its expression as a glorified object of reverence in many cultural manifestations indicates one of the primary problems of subjectivity that psychoanalysis wishes to cure. As such, the phallus symbolizes an existential failure, and those structured as women tend to navigate it much better than those structured as men. If one prefers another name for the phallus, one more neutral in its content, though no less problematic, perhaps a best bet would be *lack*, the primary 'Thing' that the dynamic of the phallus plays out. Hence, the Lacanian response to the idea of a Lacanian endorsement, conscious or otherwise, of the superiority of the masculine phallus is that the very concept is itself destructive of such superiority. The Lacanian phallus is essentially impotent. Such is what the castration complex exemplifies.

5. *Che Voi?* From Separation to Desire

The object is a failure. The essence of the object is failure.[69]

Lacan is rather consistent in pointing out that the phallus is neither the physical penis nor its image, but rather what is missing within desire: "It is thus that the erectile organ—not as itself, or even as an image, but as a part that is missing in the desired image—comes to symbolize the place of *jouissance*. . . ."[70] It is thus clear that Lacan posits the phallus as a negative factor (he calls it -φ in its imaginary form), something that is not present but rather the symbol of lack. The phallus, furthermore, is the bar between the signifier and the signified, or the symbol of the missing signified (which is, after all is said and done, the desire of the mother). We can thus see that the phallus stands for everything that the subject wants but, structurally speaking, cannot have. It stands, that is, for the desire of the m(O)ther, and insofar as the subject accepts that this desire is unobtainable, the subject succumbs to a castration complex.

Indeed, the phallus qua loss is that which motivates the symbolically acceptable personas that the bulk of us inhabit as a means of dealing with the underlying anxiety of our unacceptable original desires. Because the Other cannot be had, thus denying our being, we begin the process of meaning creation, one that is essential in its division and fabrication to understanding the complex relations of personas and their general abhorrence of persons, who, as reminders and explicit remainders, are too unbearable in what they indicate about subjectivity. The castration complex is thus the acceptance on an unconscious level of loss, one filled with anxiety. Anxiety is thereby caused, according to Lacan, by the inability of the subject to solve the deadlock of the Other's desire:

> Desire begins to take shape in the margin in which demand rips away from need, this margin being the one that demand—whose appeal can be unconditional only with respect to the Other—opens up in the guise of the possible gap need may give rise to here, because it has no universal satisfaction (this is called "anxiety"). A margin which, as linear as it may be, allows its vertiginous character to appear, provided it is not trampled by the elephantine feet of the Other's whimsy. Nevertheless, it is this whimsy that introduces the phantom of Omnipotence—not of the subject, but of the Other in which the subject's demand is instated . . . and with this phantom, the necessity that the Other be bridled by the Law.[71]

Desire occurs because every given satisfaction on the part of the subject never seems to accomplish a full fusion with the Other who remains inscrutable and preoccupied, thus creating the difference between a given satisfaction and the lack of a full satisfaction. This constant remainder produces the infinite nature of desire that Hobbes pointed out. Receiving bits and pieces of the Other, the subject is essentially frustrated. Between a given satisfaction and satisfaction as such, we find the phallus as the missing object—the failure at the heart of the image of complete harmony a subject will create over and over again to suture desire's anxious failure.

With such a logic in play, the subject as sutured is ready-made not for any given ideology, *per se*, but ideology as such. Here, then, the Lacanian subject provides the *modus operandi* for Hobbes' ideological blank slates. Our receptivity to ideology is predicated not on our complete absence, but the fact that our identities are created out of the original anxiety that absence produces in us. Thus ideologies, which always predicate themselves on some version of an Other as container of truth and acceptance, are socially acceptable modes of fusion. The nature of their imaginary and linguistic formations, however, preclude them from resolving desire's deadlock. They can ameliorate it, provide it a new answer, but they cannot fulfill it. Hence, ideology founders not on its own imperfections, but the fact that it serves an imperfect customer. Hence, as well, the proliferations of reasons, otherwise known as enemies, for the various failures that any given ideology will exhibit.

Still, the comfort is there, and the Father qua law provides an answer to this vacillation, giving the subject a separated identity and thus a distance from the primary Other. By being cut off from the Other, the subject is relieved (since, as the quote above indicates, the desire of the Other can be overbearing and because alienation is unbearable) and accepts a basic loss or, to put it more correctly, basis itself on an accepted loss. This acceptance of loss institutes the subject's castration, though unconsciously so. Castration, then, is nothing but the paternal metaphor qua representation of the acceptance of the loss of the desire of the Other (i.e., money or being). The Father is seen to have that which the mother desires, the phallus, and the subject, in its masculine form, thus identifies with this symbolic formation. In this sense, then, the paternal metaphor is the first experience of ideology proper. Due to the "father's" supposed possession of the phallus, the father and its laws becomes an object of new identification. Hence, the Law of the Father accomplishes not only the personification of subjectivity as a socially acceptable and recognizable entity, but as well outlines subjectivity's predisposition for authority-based answers to the problems of existence, or ideology.

This gives us a fairly clear sense as to why the Lacanian phallus is the symbol of a lack. Whether in its imaginary function (within every beautiful image there lies the subject as missing, or -φ), or in its positive Symbolic function (Φ, the Name/No of the Father), the phallus indicates an absence, something simultaneously lost and barred. Thus castration anxiety is the expression of a sense of failure on the part of a subject, either a failure to have or to be the phallus for the Other, or, later in the logic of subjectivization, a failure to fully conform to the ideal of the symbolic Other.[72] The question arises, then, as to how the subject actually accomplishes this identification, how the subject incorporates the phallus, the answer to which lies in separation and the fundamental fantasy.

In order for the subject to bear the burden of alienation, two factors must contribute. On the one hand, the paternal metaphor comes to the rescue by giving the subject a way out of the vacillations of separation anxiety. The subject begins to attack the lack in the Other, hacks away at the meanings between the lines: "By separation the subject finds, one might say, the weak point of the primal dyad of the signifying articulation, in so far as it is alienating in essence."[73] By separating from the Other, by seeing the Other as less than complete, as also lacking, the subject is able to constitute his or her own desire. Such is the motivation behind the why of the child, the endless and seemingly random questioning that children put forth to those supposed to know: ". . . all the child's *whys* reveal not so much an avidity for the reason of things, as a testing of the adult, a *Why are you telling me this?*"[74] In asking so many questions, the child is separating by constructing a theory, in a sense, for what the Other wants: *Che Voi?* However, as Lacan further argues, this constitution does not avoid deception, for the subject accomplishes this feat of engendering by means of a fantasy. By constructing a fundamental fantasy, a subject formulates an unconscious way of copping with its loss.[75] With the primary repression goes, in essence, a reason for what must be relented in the choice that was made, one which is really an inversion since the subject creates an unconscious imaginary scenario whereby the loss is found.

The fundamental fantasy is thus what is always at play in the way that a given subject desires, in what turns on a given, as we might now put it, person/*a* (which may very well turn off another). The *objet a* is, as we have seen, the cause of desire qua missing object, while the fantasy gives desire a particular coherence: "The fantasy is the support of desire; it is not the object that is the support of desire. The subject sustains himself as desiring in relation to an ever more complex signifying ensemble."[76] Within the fantasy, which gains in complexity as time marches forward through ever more signifiers, the subject exists explicitly as more or less satisfied, but implicitly as missing, as fading. The very need for a fantasy only occurs due to this loss, and that missing piece is the *agalma*, the essence of the subject as completing and being completed by the Other, of which there are countless ways to fantasize. We can fruitfully return to Hobbes here. Lacan controversially argued that Freud thought the choice of object does not matter, is, in fact, "a matter of total indifference."[77] While Freud did not use these exact words exactly, the fact remains that Freud thought the object choice secondary to its function—objects are external, may come and go, may remain, may be displaced, and so on, but they ultimately are at the service of the aim, or satisfaction.[78] Here, Lacan is more Hobbesian than Freud. Since there is no final organization of the drives for Lacan, we are stuck with the impossible desire of Hobbes, whereby objects differ among different subjects, but none shall find an ultimate satisfaction. Hence the movement from a person, or an abject being in the throes of decision, to a person/*a* lies in that little object, the *objet a*, insofar as it indicates that the loss will be replaced by the fantasy of its being found. A persona, which allows and lubricates our sociality, is predicated on its unconscious fabrication, one which, as we have noted, sets us up for whatever Ideological State

Apparatuses may come our way. As such, subjectivity is already instantiated into existence through what is essentially an ideological movement—an
identification with a socially codified identity allows the subject a place
that is not subject to the deleterious state of alienation (nature). This instantiation uses, no less, a law, a name, and a series of signifiers that are
continuously supported by acceptable social institutions.

Does this not mean, then, that Lacan would further concur with Hobbes
that we need a strong unifying force, a Sovereign who will personify the
subject and thus relieve it of all of its impossible internal satisfactions?
Indeed, is the paternal metaphor not merely an updated form of the sovereign, a familial version of the sovereign whereby, as in the Oedipal myth,
the subject gives up its right to everything, renounces the primal horde,
and accepts the integration of its imago into the symbolic formation of an
identity? The answer to this question is negative, due mainly to the fact
that though subjectifization occurs by means of symbolic identifications,
this identification itself is not only false, it is a hindrance to the subject in
terms of living a fully authentic life. The identification of a subject with an
authority as intense and condensed as a Hobbesian Sovereign would serve
only to increase the deadlock of subjectivity, to further alienate the subject
from its drives. But this answer is not as easy as it sounds. For as we have
seen, identification provides subjectivity a way out of the deadlock of
alienation. By identifying with symbolic images and by renouncing one's
right to the Other, the subject is released from the vacillations of alienation
and the whimsy of the Other. The paternal metaphor rescues the subject.
Are we thus left with yet another impossible situation for the subject?
Perhaps.

The subject is rescued only by giving up *jouissance*, by repressing that
which it wants most in the world, a desire that is placed under the subter-
fuge of acceptable fantasies. The very reason there is such a thing as a
compulsion to repeat is due to the fact that what was given up is not gone—
within the drive, within the unconscious, forbidden desire continues
nonetheless. Such is the meaning behind Lacan's phrase, "doesn't stop not
being written." In terms of our symbolic, speaking existence, we can signify
what we mean, clarify our sense of reality, and articulate ourselves in a
rational manner. But in terms of our unconscious selves, within that which
is repressed, which is rendered unspeakable so that we may speak properly,
we encounter a basic nonsense at the heart of our being, a nonsense which
will not go away. It (*Es*) doesn't stop not being written insofar as it can
never be articulated in the symbolic realm, and it doesn't stop insofar as it
remains the *Kern Unseres Wesen*, the unseen motivating force behind all of

our actions and, more importantly, everything that we think we are in control of: "People repress the said *jouissance* because it is not fitting for it to be spoken, and that is true precisely because the speaking thereof can be no other than the following: qua *jouissance*, it is inappropriate."[79] Since the underlying desire of the subject is inappropriate, the subject suffers an internal splitting such that it is at odds with itself. By subjecting itself to the second Other, the symbolic Other, the subject escapes the primary Other only by covering over its desire for the later. The rescue of the Other, it seems, is incomplete. In order for the subject to 'not give up on its desire', it must retrace its steps, a process that Lacan called traversing the fantasy. Only insofar as a subject can break the deadlock of its identification and realize the false nature of its fundamental fantasy can it truly enjoy itself, however missing that self might ultimately be.

Indeed, a sort of Hobbesian presumption of total mastery exists in the Lacanian subject, or at least in its mainly male formulation. Insofar as the subject is castrated and identified, it clearly accepts the loss of the Other. But insofar as the subject maintains a fundamental fantasy of completion, of having it all, the subject refuses to accept this loss. Between loss and its renunciation lies the subject, and this vacillation explains the more or less unconscious assumption of one's right to everything, even if this assumption is, in explicit symbolic or social terms, unacceptable. What is worse, the drive seeks it without stop. The duality of the subject, the excessive desire for and obtaining of *jouissance* found in the drive and, in sublimated fashion, the fantasy, provide for us an anxiously split being. The therapeutic goal, therefore, is to return that persona, through its symbolic formation, and through its fantasy, back to its original drive formation, to reencounter its person. It should be clear, however, that to the degree that the person is not accepted by the persona, there are three broad results:

1. The persona is oriented toward ideological answers given its ideological roots.
2. The persona will find the person reprehensible to its fantasy insofar as the person brings to the fore the false nature of said fantasy.
3. Ideologies, like all structural fantasies, will require explanations for their failures. Given the level to which they elicit revulsion and promote anger and hatred, persons will generally perform this role.

These conclusions thus beg the question of what political exit is available to subjectivity given the largely negative conclusions just enumerated.

6. Traversing the Fantasy

There are men who are just as good as women. It happens.[80]

Traversing the fantasy is perhaps the least covered aspect of Lacanian psychoanalysis, but there is good reason for this. Because the purpose of analysis is a process of de-identification, to provide a map of what the end point ought to look like, it seems, would only reintroduce identification. A similar logic is at play with Lacan's vexing use of algorithms—because they are more or less devoid of meaning they preclude an imaginary identification, forcing the reader into the voided yet excessive realm of the Real.[81] Traversing the fantasy, then, functions as a second level of separation insofar as the subject finds a way to separate from the second Other, the paternal metaphor, that allowed for the first separation. This second separation is the realization that 'there is no Other of the Other', that the Other, who is seen as all powerful, who is supposed to know, is also impotent and ignorant.[82] It is, as well, a return to the drive, to *objet a*.

According to Lacan, such a traversal, also called a traversal of identification, takes place in the analytic context by means of the desire of the analyst. While some theories of psychology propose that the ego ought to be bolstered, for Lacan, the ego is the problem. It is precisely because the fantasy at the base of the ego is too strong that one cannot overcome it, and the analyst's role is to play the *objet a*, to become the object of desire insofar as it is absent for the subject. By doing so, the subject is confronted with its own desire, but in its unconscious formulation; the subject, that is, confronts its drive as it circulates around *objet a*. In the mode of subjectivity that is supported by fantasy, this object manifests itself in all sorts of beautiful constructs of happiness. In the analytic setting, it is reduced to its bad form, its failure, a piece of shit: "*I give myself to you, the patient says again, but this gift of my person—as they say—Oh, mystery! is changed inexplicably into a gift of shit*—a term that is also essential to our experience."[83] The self is transmogrified into shit for the reasons we have enumerated: at one's core lies a failure to comport properly and completely with the desire of the Other, an inability to answer one's own and the Other's demand. The fantasy, in unconscious form, keeps alive the belief that somewhere, somehow, the desire of the Other can be completed. The assumption or belief behind the disappointment of "that's not it" is that somewhere else "it" will appear and one's problems will be solved. The fact that such is not the case can be seen in the ultimate middle- to lower-class fantasy: winning the lottery. While the economically destitute imagine that winning will alleviate all of life's problems, those who do win often find themselves in a realm of further burdens and losses, whether of friends, lovers, or the money itself. While winning the lottery appears as a way of reversing the effects of one's initial mugging, the fact is that money, like the signifier itself, is yet another representative of a lost *jouissance* (hence its repetitive, fungible nature). Indeed, the surplus *jouissance* that a sudden allotment of extra funds provides can be traumatic given that the whole structure of subjectivity is an attempt to control and condition a *jouissance* that was deemed unacceptable in the first place. The winner, in other words, is ironically faced with an intense initial loss, of having to eat its cake.

In the analytic setting, transference, therefore, is often the attempt to block one's own excretion, to become loveable in the eyes of the new Other, the new persona who is supposed to know.[84] The analyst's objective is to situate him or herself such that this is rendered impossible, to make desire inscrutable, thereby making *objet a* emerge within the drives (gaze, voice, anal): "It is at this point of lack that the subject has to recognize himself."[85] By identifying with something that is impossible to identify with, a subject is essentially released from that which, ironically, freed him or her in the first place; identification with the Other and its attendant fantasy. This means, as Lacan argues, that the subject must face its drive, must come to accept that what seemed like an accident, a misfortune, is in fact the subject's very own being qua loss of being. The subject must, that is, subjectivize this loss, take responsibility for what seemed external and accidental, whether in the form of unacceptable desires, impossible memories, subversive tendencies, or any other form that the symptom takes. Hence Lacan's quite specific reading of "*Wo es War, soll Ich werden*"; where it was, there I must come into being. I must realize myself in *Es*, It, drive, not *Ich*, not I.[86] I become free as loss, as desire for an Other who herself suffered the same tragedy.

Arguably, then, Lacan returns us to a new form of authenticity, a newly chosen self that seems to appear very much like a reintroduction of the ego. Insofar as I am able to move through my symbolic assumption and undergo a destitution of my assumed fantasy, I come out on the other side by choosing not faith, not a belief in the other, but myself qua *jouissance* ridden drive. As Verhaeghe and Declercq put it, I choose myself, create my being anew: "As a creation, it is indeed a creation *ex nihilo*, that is, one not based on any previous identity, which in one way or another would be tributary to the Other. Hence the implicit, but very important, meaning of separation in Seminar XI: *se parer*: to give birth to oneself."[87] Is this, however, not the ultimate return to the American Dream, the idea of pulling oneself up by one's bootstraps, of creating oneself and one's fortune by pure individual will power? The answer is clearly no. While there is a process of self-engendering, a creation *ex nihilo*, the nothing that one comes out of is the lack in the Other. For the subject, there still remains the manner in which her or his drives came into partial being in relation to that lack. The subject comes to accept this loss, and comes to accept the enjoyment that was forbidden within it. This move is freeing for the subject not only to enjoy, not only to be released from the mystery of the symptom, not only to no longer believe that "the truth is out there," that there is someone who "knows," but also to create anew, to achieve a love that is not bound by conscious law and unconscious loss: "There only may the signification of a limitless love emerge, because it is outside the limits of the law, where alone it may live."[88] Insofar as the subject no longer labors under the burden of a supposed Other, and insofar as the subject assumes its symptom as its own, love and creation, life and its enjoyment are no longer hemmed in by what is ultimately a fantasy. Of course, one only achieves this position with regard to the self by reading through the network of the signifier, a long and arduous process full of traps and deceptions. Such is why the desire of the analyst, a desire that is ultimately to be mapped out by the subject, is reduced to *objet a*. As well, the presence of the analyst's desire shatters the pure individualism of the American fantasy, downgrading the persona to a person/*a*.

This brings us to a final subject in Lacanian thought which we can only briefly cover; the problem of subjective positions in regard to men and women. In most of the references thus far, the sexuation, as Lacan put it, of the subject has either been vaguely intimated or even assumed as male. This would seem to reproduce the oft-repeated claim of, as Butler would have it, a masculinization of the subject, a supposition of a male supremacy in subject formation. Indeed, as we saw earlier, the phallus takes a predominant position in subjectivization, even if it is in an imaginary or symbolic form, and even if the greatest thing a phallus could ever reveal is nothing. All the same, there is a sense in which most subjects succumb to a sort of masculine formation, what Lacan calls phallic *jouissance*. Such is the result of castration, the fact that a subject really only ever enjoys on the basis of a fantasy of enjoyment, each object of pleasure merely being yet another repetition of that failure to find the ultimate object.

However, it is the case that men and women, which has nothing necessarily to do with anatomy, tend to identify in different ways—men with their paternal counterparts, and women with their maternal leads:

On the side of the Other, the locus in which speech is verified as it encounters the exchange of signifiers, the ideals they prop up, the elementary structures of kinship, the paternal metaphor considered qua principle of separation, and the ever reopened division in the subject owing to his primal alienation—on this side alone and by the pathways I have just enumerated, order and norms must be instituted which tell the subject what a man or a woman must do.[89]

In other words, once alienation produces the signifier in the subject, a subject will receive in the signifier the various ways it must take on its secondary identification. Of course, this process does not always go smoothly, and all subjects do not choose as the Other would have them do so, but clearly the process of identification provides the subject a treasure trove of familial and cultural images to glom onto in order to formulate a separated identity. Important to castration for the male and the female positions alike is that it involves a loss of the Other, a loss of fulfillment. What is most interesting in Lacan, however, is the level to which women are able to better cope with this fact and accept it. Thus is why the feminine structure, for Lacan, is the preferable one—women as a whole are already more attuned to loss than men, and thus a man's ultimate goal is directed toward existing within this path.

Thus Lacan argues in *Seminar XX* that there is a feminine *jouissance* that does not succumb to phallic *jouissance*, that is not stuck within the signifier. Masculine *jouissance* is entirely bound to fantasy, to *objet a* as the ultimate object of completion which never arrives. In this sense, masculine *jouissance*, the obtaining of one object after another, is not much different from capitalism. Since the later is predicated on an accumulation without end, on a competition in which one seeks to be the winner but in which there is no ultimate resting point, capitalism and masculine sexuality are more or less parallel. Indeed, the parallel becomes stronger when it becomes clear that though the theory of capitalism argues for the benefits of competition, the implicit desire behind capitalism, as Adam Smith saw so long ago, is absolute mastery, or monopoly.[90] Thus, as the law of capital, competition, is motivated by its exception, monopoly, so the law of the castrated subject, repression, is accepted on the basis of a fantasy of its exception, or having the Other. The castrated subject secretly believes that it can overcome its castration. On the other hand, women, though subject to castration, are also forced through the process of identification with the One who does not have the phallus, and are thus forced to create themselves *ex nihilo*, on the basis of an understanding, however unconscious, of negativity. Early on, Lacan identified the feminine position with the masquerade.[91] Later, it appears, this process of self-creation indicates the very core of the cure itself; insofar as Woman does not exist, she understands that her existence is predicated on a loss and a creation within this loss, that there is no Other of the Other. Woman qua nonexistence already, more or less, occupies the beyond of analysis, the position of 'absolute difference' qua void and natality. In this way, a subject who is released from the fantasy is released from the burden of phallic *jouissance* within masculine subjectivity.[92]

One who is not released from phallic *jouissance*, then, succumbs to a Hobbesian bad infinity of desire. Its logic is that of the 'yet one more'. To the degree, that is, that each object fails to live up to the hidden fantasy of completion that anchors subjectivity, 'yet one more' object will be required to maintain desire's asymptotic approach. The persona thus functions according to this accumulating 'yet one more', staging new scenarios of completion and failure, new triumphs in the face of new adversities, and so on. Were a persona to be traversed, it would have to admit that yet one more is only an indication of an already present failure of the persona to overcome its person, which is its unconscious desire that must be admitted to, accepted, and thus released. How does this traversal bear on the political then, particularly given the ideological implications of our subjectivity?

7. The Return of the Political

Before answering, let us first outline the manner in which the issues noted in Hobbes and Arendt are given a ground in Lacan. As we have seen, the repetition of Hobbesian desire is based not on a universal substratum of motion, but in how desire of the Other transforms the constant life force, resulting in the partialized and impossible death drives. Because the persona is but the result of subject's defense against a loss and a prohibition, desire exhibits an internal repression that maintains itself through fantasy. Lacan is essentially in agreement with Hobbes insofar as desire is impossible and leads to a tendency toward the dissolution of situations when left unchecked. Since there is no great good, even though the subject believes in it nonetheless, each particular satisfaction is not enough and headed for an eventual dissolution. While a unifying persona, a Sovereign, would seem an attractive solution to the issue given that it can shore up the subject's impossibility by transferring it to a new Other, we see in it merely the intensification of the subject's deadlock. The problem was always that the Other was supposed to have the phallus, the completion of desire. By creating a massive authority, the subject surely can satisfy its need for an Other in the know, but that Other cannot satisfy the subject's true demand: a real satisfaction to end all satisfactions. Such an Other, whether it is a Sovereign, a teacher, a scientist, an analyst, a successful capitalist, or what have you, is merely an instantiation and further provocation of one's fundamental fantasy. As we have seen, this tells us why leaders who project a possible utopia invariably must turn to a unifying enemy of some sort: because there is no perfection, and because the relationship is based on the promise of one, an external object must be designated to explain why things have not resolved themselves. This *fremde Objekt*, whatever form it might take, not only provides an explanation for why things are not going so well, but also provides subjects a way to invest their enjoyment in a negative form: by hating the other through the Other, the drive is able to partake in an excessive and permitted enjoyment, however dark.

Lacanian theory also provides insight into the Arendtian subject. The reason that an other who is manifestly impotent (the stateless, immigrants, the poor, minorities, and so on) can cause those who are not to create contradictory fantasies (such as the Nazi Jew's incredible omnipotence and simultaneous femininity, or the terrorist's omnipresence, fearful audacity, and cowardice), resulting often enough in literally unspeakable violence, is indeed due to the dark division of the soul, which is now locatable. Arendt, it turns out, was right in her speculation that the heart only begins to beat on the basis of an original ripping, but that ripping is due to the Other, the one who brought the soul into being in the first place. Because the desire of the Other is internalized as lost and never found, the persona of the subject comes to represent a fantastic answer to an impossible situation: generally speaking, rather than being the way in which one articulates one's story from the point of view of true natality, the subjective tendency is to submit to a repressed fantasy of the impossible, to maintain beneath it all the absolute faith in a promised land. Impotent persons thereby represent these negative aspects of the subject qua repressed: the subject as inadequate shit, the subject as nonbeing, and thus the revulsion of the self when it meets its own lack (they are, in Lacanian terms, Real objects, objects no longer properly adorned by imaginary or symbolic gowns, or imaginary rivals, the self as possibly more perfect, perhaps enjoying my *jouissance* in a way that I cannot—often enough, in fact, they are both, depending on the needs of the moment).[93]

We can also now understand why Arendt is correct that the internal self is impossible to exhibit in a public realm and why it leads to a necessary downfall of self-recrimination and, often enough, mutilation. Since the self is already in existence due to a failure, and since the self is predicated on a basis of self-recrimination for this failure, attempting to exhibit a purified I can only end in tragedy. In each case, one confronts the excessive *jouissance* of the drive, either internally or externally, in self and other, as forbidden. As such, the drive as that which circulates around what is most desired, forbidden, and impossible, around *objet a*, causes the conscious self to be confronted with its death. For most subjects, this is too much to handle, and we have already outlined certain historical cases of this.

It should be pointed out with regard to the fundamental fantasy that it operates on two levels. For each individual, the fundamental fantasy is linked to the binary signifier in an unconscious fashion, motivating the subject in ways that are not consciously acceptable. However, the links of the persona and its accumulation of further signifiers allow for mediated and more explicit social fantasies that can be participated in without suffering a too conscious awareness of what has been forbidden. To the degree that these fantasies function simultaneously on conscious and unconscious levels, ideologies are able to tap into various modalities of subjectivity in express and implied ways. In essence, then, subjectivity is already an ideological entity insofar as its acceptance of the law as a prohibition and a name instantiates it into the realm of speech and acceptability. The persona's formation, that is, is an interpellation (as in the Policeman's "Hey, you!") of subjectivity that can establish a workable structure for future forms of ideological interpellation. No doubt, subjects are distinct in their histories, and hence every ideology has its opposition. Nonetheless, ideology is the promise of what is secretly desired by the generally neurotic populace: an answer to the question of desire, a fantasy of totality, and a number of foreign objects to invest our basic aggressions with as an explanation for why the fantasy remains an incomplete project. These foreign objects, as we have already discussed, are generally nothing but the place-holders of our own empty selves that we can bear only insofar as they are to be eradicated—persons (thus, the language of the person devolves quite often into the language of the pest and the rodent).

But if ideology requires its *fremde Objekt*, then political formations that partake in ideological structures predicated on a privileged person/*a* are, as I noted at the conclusion of Chapter 2, contrary to the political. That is, insofar as it is accepted that commodious living is the goal of the political, and insofar as this commodious living ought to be provided to the largest group of humans possible, which is all humans, the universality of the person is aligned with the universality of the political: the political exists as the promotion of commodious living for all persons and opposes the exclusive nature of the politics of personas. The political is therefore anti-ideological to the degree that it negates political instantiations that would use persons as their negative others in order to explain why the gaps have yet to be filled, thereby leading to the antipolitical result that many persons will be denied rights, imprisoned, tortured, or killed in order to maintain a given set of personas. Appropriately, these persons are invariably placed outside of the law (national, international, religious, etc.), whose existence in the name of the father is also in the name of the persona. Once they are there, the ability to unleash the prohibited *jouissance*, mingled as it is with its aggressive attachments to the imaginary other we spoke of in the mirror stage, is intensified and made necessary. Politically, these aggressive expressions are either left off the books in such places as 'black/hard sites' and detention camps, or through subversive legalistic moves, such as wars perpetrated on the base of false information in order to kill what are "only Iraqis." That Iraqis had nothing to do with 9/11 is beside the point: to the degree that they are mere persons, they are interchangeable with any other object of abjection.

Broadly speaking, the accepted answer to this situation has and remains the promotion of democracy. The repeated logic is that democracies promote freedom and do not attack one another. While the latter proposition must be submitted to a Clintonian "that depends on what your definition of democracy is," the former is much more difficult to dismiss out of hand. It is generally true that within certain representative democracies, the increases in freedom and choice are clear. As opposed to autocratic regimes, democracies provide much more space for expression and, to use the terminology thus far employed, increase the number of acceptable personas closer to the universality of the person than any other form, save for theoretical communism. But democracy suffers its own issues which in recent years have become more apparent than ever. Just as human rights have suffered from a lack of a positive universal ground, democracy itself suffers an inherent relativism, which is not pure nihilism, but rather a competition of fantasies that takes place over a void. Nihilism proper holds the position that all is meaningless, but democracy proliferates meaning, holding that all positions are meaningful. This proliferation of meaning is, however, also a proliferation of personas, each coming to represent the empty center and provide its own fantasy of its fulfillment. As such, over time the constant repetition of 'yet one more' answer within democracy subjects its subjects to an increasing anxiety about the fundamental meaning of their existence, one only punctuated by the phallic *jouissance* of capitalism. Such an intensification of the subject's alienation provides too many possible strongholds of separation and makes extra-democratic positions attractive (thereby explaining why thoroughly interpellated democratic subjects who have obtained economic status are also joining the so-called "terrorist networks"). Perhaps, then, one could say that while democracy is of itself not nihilistic, believing as it does in a basic human capacity for freedom and choice, it is always threatened, through its empty core, by a nihilistic implosion.

When, as we are now experiencing in current times, there is no sure or generally accepted mode in which to explain the meaning of existence, which, otherwise put, means that there is no Other to the Other, then we are faced with a collection of selves caught in a series of imaginary captures incessantly, if slowly, imploding. In this way, totalitarianism and fundamentalism increase in desirability since they provide a stop gap to the constant sliding of the self under its own fading. Otherwise put, democracy replicates the problem of subjectivity in its loss. Unfortunately, even the proponents of a Lacanian response to the current deadlock of modernity, post or otherwise, do not have any clear idea of how to escape this sliding. For though they propose democracy as a political form of traversal, they in fact articulate why democracy is a political form of alienation, which can be encapsulated within the logic of representation insofar as it accepts the necessity of individual and national sovereignty and, with it, the primacy of the persona. Such is what the next and final chapter will attempt to elucidate.

Notes

1 It is telling that the system most opposed to democracy in most theories (save for those which see it as democracy's necessary remainder), totalitarianism, is described by Arendt as an onion; a many-layered system of controls that peels away to a void or "a kind of empty space" at the center of which a leader directs the totality. Though there is a leader there, the implication is that he or she is a vacant object of identification, lacking any true or full content. See BPF, p. 99.

2 As Hobbes says, the passions begin from our endeavors, and endeavors begin in the imagination since we must initially conceive of what it is that we are going to do (see *Leviathan*, vi, 1). As I have been arguing, this is where Hobbes sees the problem begin to take shape—between perception, conception (or projective imagination), and the force of desire, or, otherwise put, between what we have at present and what we think we want in the future, a gap of anxiety erupts that sets us in motion toward the quelling of that anxiety. Since there is no final resting place, however, there is no rest to anxiety. We must, rather, transfer the anxiety onto a One who shall desire for us.

3 Jacques Lacan, *Écrits: A Selection*, trans. Bruce Fink (New York: W. W. Norton & Company, 2002): 4, hereafter referred to as *Écrits*.

4 Jacques Lacan, *The Psychoses: The Seminar of Jacques Lacan, Book III*, trans. Russell Grigg (New York: W. W. Norton & Company, 1993): 39. Hereafter referred to as SIII. See also Jacques Lacan, *The Four Fundamental Concepts of Psychoanalysis: The Seminar of Jacques*

Lacan, Book XI, trans. Alan Sheridan (New York: W. W. Norton & Company, 1998): 257, hereafter referred to as SXI.

5 The "a" is short for the French *autre*, or other. In Lacanian theory, the fact that the a is lower cased indicates that we are speaking about the imaginary plane of the ego rather than the symbolic realm, in which case Lacan generally uses the capitalized *Autre*, or Other.

6 For a more detailed account of the mirror stage, see Joel Dor, *Introduction to the Reading of Lacan: The Unconscious Structured Like a Language* (New York: The Other Press, 1998): 95–7, hereafter referred to as *Introduction*.

7 Paul Verhaeghe, *On Being Normal and Other Disorders: A Manual for Clinical Psychodiagnostics* (New York: The Other Press, 2004): 163, hereafter referred to as OBN.

8 See OBN, 163.

9 SXI, 144.

10 *Introduction*, 159.

11 One example, perhaps, of a life without such a base imaginary jealousy of self would be Werner Herzog's version Kasper Hauser, for whom insults and injuries function as confusions and lead to a desire not to live with others rather than indignity, incensed competition, or anger.

12 The increased awareness of postpartum depression is perhaps best exemplified in the media face-off between Tom Cruise and Brooke Shields, the former arguing that there is no such thing as a chemical imbalance (which is merely a corollary to the fact that psychology is a pseudoscience in the Scientologist framework), the latter quite sure that Cruise has and never will experience the complications of childbirth. Perhaps most interesting about the interchange is the level to which Cruise, the masculine imago *par excellence*, came off in a classic hysterical form, passionately deriding the Other (science) as lacking in truth as it perpetuates a conspiracy against the masses.

13 Bruce Fink, *The Lacanian Subject: Between Language and Jouissance* (New Jersey: Princeton University Press, 1995): 103, hereafter referred to as *Lacanian Subject*.

14 Jacques Lacan, "Position of the Unconscious (1964)," in Feldstein, Richard, Bruce Fink, and Maire Jaanus, eds., *Reading XI: Lacan's Four Fundamental Concepts of Psychoanalyses* (New York: State University of New York Press, 1995): 268, hereafter referred to as *Position*.

15 Later on he would come to see the primary signifier as the Name-of-the-Father, the master signifier. See Jacques Lacan, *On Feminine Sexuality: The Limits of Love and Knowledge: The Seminar of Jacques Lacan, Book XX*, trans. Bruce Fink (New York: W. W. Norton & Company, 1998): 143, hereafter referred to as SXX.

16 Sigmund Freud, *Beyond the Pleasure Principle*, trans. James Strachey (New York: Norton & Company, 1961): 16.

17 SXI, 239.

18 Such is why Lacan places subjectivity against the Cartesian Cogito. It is not in the thinking that the substance of the self resides, but in the loss that one repeats unconsciously.

19 See SXI, 212. Here Lacan makes it clear that he is borrowing from Hegel's master/slave dialectic, though in Lacan's reworking, there is no final resolve or recognition of equality. There is, rather, yet another misrecognition that normalizes the subject.

20 To exist thus means to accept meaning, to accept language in all of its uncertainty, a situation that, as we saw, Hobbes was well aware of with his dueling scientists. As Fink points out, Lacan takes the notion of ex-sisting from Heidegger's use of the Greek notion of *ecstases* in *Being and Time*. Essentially, the ecstatic base of Dasein indicates its temporal incompletion, its being outside of itself in regard to the past, present, and future. Perhaps, as we shall see, more importantly for Lacan is the fact that the temporality of Dasein's fundamental being is a being-towards-death. See SXX, p. 22, fn. 24. See also *Being and Time*, II.3.

21 SXI, 211.

22 This sort of dramatic moment of the 'forced choice' is one of the primary techniques used in action and sci-fi movies. For instance, in the film *The Chronicles of Riddick*, the evil Necromengians invade planets and offer them a choice between conversion to their religion and death. On a political level, the forced choice was put to good use by the Bush administration, whose common mantra is that they are more than happy to work with those who are in agreement with their policy. In other words, those who wish to work with the administration can do so as long as they already agree.

23 SXI, 144.

24 See, for instance, SXI, p. 38 and Jacques Lacan, *The Ethics of Psychoanalysis: The Seminar of Jacques Lacan, Book VII*, trans. Dennis Porter (New York: W. W. Norton & Company, 1992): 14, hereafter referred to as SVII. It should be noted that the genitive construction "desire of the Other" is intentionally ambiguous. Not only is our desire a desire for the Other, it is also a desire that models itself on the Other's desire (how one's mother, for instance, wanted things, described things positively, and so on). Indeed, one desires only insofar as one encounters the desire of another in the first place. It is also the case that our desire is based on being desired by the Other. Perhaps the most succinct expression for this form, which is more or less what Lacan calls love, is the title of Cheap Trick's song, "I Want You to Want Me."

25 Just as when he stated that there is no sexual relation he did not mean that people were not having sex.

26 As Lacan himself notes, he is indebted to both Saussure and Roman Jakobsen for these insights. See *Écrits*, 167, footnote 13, and 286.

27 *Écrits*, 141.

28 To carry the metaphor, which is not without content, dictatorships attempt to infuse and solidify language, to maintain its control as a corollary to the control of the dictator. Orwell's brilliant creation, Newspeak, is perhaps the greatest literary exemplification of such a process.

29 *Écrits*, 145.

30 See *Écrits*, 292.

31 Ibid., 145.

32 SXI, 271–2.

33 For another clear explication of this process, see Mikkel Borch-Jacobsen, *Lacan: The Absolute Master*, trans. Douglas Brick (California: Stanford University Press, 1991): 182.

34 Even Bruce Fink, a practicing analyst, is less than satisfied about the subject: "Drives, instincts, and their representatives all remain, it seems to me, to be far better elucidated." See *Lacanian Subject*, p. 188, fn. 11.

35 Sigmund Freud, *General Psychological Theory* (New York: Touchstone, 1991): 87, hereafter referred to as GPT. See also Sigmund Freud, *Three Essays on the Theory of Sexuality*, trans. James Strachey (Basic Books, 1962): 34. As Paul Verhaeghe points out, Freud was using this notion of the drive before he so named it, calling it in 194 a "quantitative energy factor." See OBN, 246, including footnote 11.

36 See GPT, 106.

37 It should be noted that Lacan meant what he said: the unconscious is structured *like* a language, it is not in itself a linguistic structure. The relationship between the unconscious and language, which will be explored latter, is thus a logical one insofar as the two share certain key mechanisms which are, to be specific, metonymy and metaphor.

38 A Lacanian reading of the term "it," as it is used in phrases such as "s/he's got it," "the It-factor," and "what it is," all phrases that indicate an inexplicable yet fully desirable 'something', is merely a socially sublimated way of talking about this object of the drive', or lost satisfaction. Or, to return to Freud, *Id* is a translation of the German word for it, *Es*.

39 See OBN, 213–17.

40 Here we also find a fundamental break that Lacan makes with Freud; there is no finality to the drive, which remains inherently partial. See chapter 14 of SXI.

41 SXI, 198.

42 OBN, 255.

43 SXI, 199.

44 Ibid., 180.

45 Ibid., 184.

46 Here an analysis of Lacan's account of Kant with Sade would be fruitful, though we do not have the space. Nonetheless, it is with this point that we can begin to think through why atrocities are a requirement of civil wars—because the pleasure of the drive, mixed by its inherent self-aggression that is displaceable on to all others and not kept in check by an internalized social law, is released, violence and violent sexuality become prevalent, and in a way that is not necessarily reducible to male aggression. Hence, in Abu Ghraib, males and females alike took part in the various modes, including sexual, of torture. However, in this situation, it is difficult to say completely what went on, given that it appears that these abuses were sanctioned. As such, they may have taken place in the known if unofficial name of the Other, hence releasing the normally repressed drives, but in order to satisfy the chain of command. In any case, the photographs bear witness to the level to which the torturers were able to enjoy themselves in the process.

47 SXI, 54.

48 As Lacan puts it: "The place of the real, which stretches from the trauma to the phantasy, in so far as the phantasy is never anything more than the screen that conceals something quite primary, something determinant in the function of repetition . . . is what, for us, explains both the ambiguity of the function of awakening and of the function of the real in this awakening." SXI, 60.

49 SXX, 119.

50 It should be clear that the use of 'mother' and 'father' have little to do with biological sex—they are rather the general terms assigned to these roles which, broadly speaking, are more often than not fulfilled by these biological sexed placeholders. But the latter does not

matter—what is important is the role that is being produced, whether the person is the object of desire and the Other who desires, or whether they are the instantiation of the law.

51 Later on, Lacan will call S1 the paternal metaphor, rendering more obscure the desire of the first Other. See, for instance, *Feminine Sexuality*, 143.

52 See GPT, 106.

53 SXI, 218.

54 See, for instance, Lacan's first graph of desire on page 291 of *Écrits*. The child, as Lacan puts it, disconnects "the thing from its cry," leaving behind the realm of imaginary signs and taking up the representations of signifiers.

55 The clearest formulation of this can be found in *Écrits*, 190. There Lacan's equation shows how the Name-of-the-Father comes to cancel out the Mother's Desire, leaving the subject to grapple with desire through the ever flowing metonymical straights of language. *Verwerfung*, or foreclosure, indicates a situation in which the metaphoric operation fails to take place, as in the case of Schreber's psychosis. See SIII for a detailed account of the latter.

56 Such is why each has her or his own signifier, which depends on the occasion of its connection as metonymic stand-in. This also indicates why, as Hobbes and Locke, among many, have pointed out, what fulfills a given individual's desire is entirely relative. Except we can locate that relativity to the emergence of the subject—later objects of desire will conform in one way or another to the initial signifier by various routes of association.

57 *Écrits*, 304.

58 See, for instance, *Lacanian Subject*, 56. As Lacan argues, there are three fathers, just as there are three registers to subjectivity: the real father, the imaginary father (whom the subject comes into conflict with during the Oedipal phase), and the symbolic father, the Other proper, otherwise known as the ego-ideal. Similarly, the lost object has its three registers: the Real object, which is generally difficult to encounter, the imaginary object (*objet a*), which is found as a missing piece within the fantasy, and the Symbolic object (the phallus), which is a socially acceptable object of acquisition or identification.

59 SXI, 185.

60 Who moved, interestingly enough, from the likeable imaginary other (a....a') to, post 9/11, the strong leader, or A, though we cannot ignore the elderly, experienced support of the vice president. His third stage, of course, is the failed father, the Other with cracks necessitating a new separation.

61 This fusion with the Other that does not exist does not mean that pleasure does not exist either. There is pleasure, a quite real pleasure of the body, but its drive, its need to repeat is based on a total immersion that cannot be had while, socially speaking, its attempt to create this immersion is inappropriate and must produce an essential separation via various forms of sublimation.

62 Butler, Judith, Ernesto Laclau, and Slavoj Žižek, *Contingency, Hegemony, Universality: Contemporary Dialogues on the Left* (London: Verso, 2000): 152–3.

63 Judith Butler, *Bodies That Matter: On the Discursive Limits of "Sex"* (New York: Routledge, 1993): 83.

64 Ibid., 89.

65 This is rather ironic given the general conservative complaint that government is too big and invades our capacity for private self-determination, not to mention the fact that 'states' rights' was a euphemism for segregation (on this score, however, the conservatives failed to make the leap in the Schiavo case). This irony is replayed in the attempt to destroy the filibuster in order to place conservative judges on the bench; the filibuster was previously used to prevent the enactment of civil rights laws. However, all irony disappears when one views political mechanisms as objects of utility within the war of position rather than sacrosanct elements of a precious democratic artifice. This problem will be returned to in the next chapter.

66 *Lacanian Subject*, 102.

67 SXX, 5.

68 Perhaps the best response to this notion of a privileging of the penis and a transhistorical prejudice for the masculine phallus occurred within one of Mustafa Safouan's seminars:

Question: The vulva can function as phallus according to Luce Irigaray.

Safouan: I never heard of a society which took that course suggested by Irigaray: She is a girl because she has a vulva, he's a boy because he hasn't a vulva. This would be a very smart way of solving the problem, and I have no objection to it. But once the phallus is taken as the signifier of the difference of sex, this is its function. It is a function that can be changed or not changed; one can dream of change and work for a change. At another level of the problem, the phallus is not a signifier of the sex but a signifier of desire. This is indeed why I subscribe to your question.

See Mustafa Safouan, "Direction of the Cure, the End of Analysis," Literature and Psychology v46 (2000): 11.

69 SXX, 58.

70 *Écrits*, 307.

71 Ibid., 299.

72 See OBN, 171.

73 SXI, 218.

74 SXI, 214.

75 ". . . fantasy is really the 'stuff' of the I that is primally repressed, because it can be indicated only in the fading of enunciation." *Écrits*, 302.

76 SXI, 185.

77 SXI, 168.

78 See GPT, 87–8.

79 SXX, 61.

80 Ibid., 76.

81 In SXX, he calls this 'mathematization'. See 131.

82 See *Écrits*, 303.

83 SXI, 268, emphasis in original.

84 See section 20 of SXI.

85 SXI, 270.

86 See *Écrits*, 120–1.

87 Paul Verhaeghe and Frederic Declercq, "Lacan's Analytic Goal: *Le sinthome* or the Feminine Way," in Luke Thurston, ed., *Re-Inventing the Symptom: Essays on the Final Lacan* (New York: The Other Press, 2002): 70.

88 SXI, 276.

89 *Position*, 276.

90 The normal reading of Adam Smith takes its leave from his rarely used metaphor of the 'invisible hand', whereby it is contended that the only thing we really need to know about the ethics of capitalism is that to the degree that private interest is unregulated, its own greed will lead to the good fortunes of the public at large. However, closer readings of Smith indicate that he was not entirely sanguine about purely unregulated markets, noting that "[p]eople of the same trade seldom meet together, even for merriment and diversion, but the conversion ends in a conspiracy against the public, or in some contrivance to raise prices. . . . But though the law cannot hinder people of the same trade from sometimes assembling together, it ought to do nothing to facilitate such assemblies; much less to render them necessary," Adam Smith, *An Inquiry into the Nature and Causes of the Wealth of Nations*, ed. Kathryn Sutherland (New York: Oxford University Press, 1998): 129. The current pro-capitalist position negates the warning that Smith provided in order to promote positive results of deregulation. Despite the various so-called scandals of current finance capitalism, the urge toward ever greater profits, an urge defined by the goal of mastery found within a monopoly, produces the following figure: the capitalist as analogous to the father of the primal horde, one whose power is so absolute that laws do not and ought not apply until his excesses become unbearable to the sons (stockholders, employees, workers, politicians). But, as we can see, the capitalist must submit to a law nonetheless, which here, in its perfected state, is no other than the law of desire, or *More (Encore)!* Hence, excessive wages for executives are explained as necessary for promotion of capitalism, whether or not the distribution, the secret discussions, or the law is ultimately on the side of the worker.

91 *Écrits*, 279.

92 Of course, as we have already argued, this does not mean that those who have female sexual organs are necessarily structured as women, nor does it mean that all those who are so structured are already traversed. It only means that the feminine structure itself is closer to such a position.

93 While there is not enough space to go into this, the two are indeed distinct, though often mixed up. While the other qua piece of shit is the *objet a* as revealed nothingness, the other qua rival is an imaginary foe that is supposed to enjoy, one who is stealing my *jouissance*. The former, to use the Lacanian triad, is the object in the register of the Real, while the latter is the object as it is exhibited in the register of the Imaginary. Hence the stateless, in their apparent nothingness, exhibit the void of the self qua desublimated Real, while the immigrant is stealing our good jobs and, perhaps, enjoying more than I in the 'strange ways' in which it does so, hence falling into the position of the imaginary rival full of mysterious potency. Of course, the two positions are easily interchangeable according to the needs of a

given situation for personas. In other words, to the degree that the imaginary other becomes too unbearable, it is often turned into the real other, paving the way, as in the stateless and Abu Ghraib, to various forms of excessive violence. An analysis of this later dynamic from the abject point of the view of both sides with regard to race and culture can be found in Frantz Fanon's *Black Skin, White Masks*.

4

The Personification of Democracy

We have travelled a long and dark path, arriving thus far at a ideological subjectivity that is ripe for imaginary associations and, in the same moment, unlikely to submit to any political formation that would provide it with their traversal. In the same breath, it has been proposed that the only authentic political formulation would side with the person in opposition to its projected persona (or person/*a*), a political formulation that is therefore unlikely in the resistance it would promote in the demos. Indeed, it seems painfully obvious that insofar as subjectivity is formulated in favor of personifications seeking an Other to the Other, there is very little hope for any solution that does not in some fashion or another promote a kind of tedious political repetition compulsion. Still, there are many who argue that we need not really look too far, that democracy itself already provides us a present and practical solution to the dilemmas of, to begin the list, totalitarianism, false imaginary projections, apathy, the right to have rights, and so on. Hence the answer is right under our noses, and the prevalent insecurities of globalization need no new revolutionary path (for it would be, no doubt, inherently totalitarian and, what is worse, unpragmatic), but, simply put, *more* democracy. The problem, therefore, is not that we don't have an alternative, but rather that we have not sufficiently realized the powers of the current consensual formation. We need, therefore, not revolution, but radicalization.

Hence, radical democratic theorists tend toward promoting the essentially antagonistic nature of the democratic form, thus formalizing and internalizing the friend/enemy distinction that Schmitt provided so many years ago (the enemy becoming, in essence, the competitor).[1] In contradistinction to this, my argument is that the political must exist in and for the person, not, as in politics, the person/*a*. To the extent, of course, that democracy negates the unary control of totalitarianism, one cannot complain about the freedoms and opportunities that it provides. However, to the extent that democracy continues by virtue of sovereignty (of the individual, the state, the nation), it is less than clear that it sufficiently breaks the bind of a subjectivity submitted to the imaginary vicissitudes of the person/*a*, nor whether it does not, in the process of producing an anxiety within its ever revolving Other, open the door to totalitarianism by virtue of its very construction nonetheless. I will thus bring this formulation of the political in the name of the person to bear on some of the primary thinkers of radical democratic theory, including Claude Lefort, Ernesto Laclau, Chantal Mouffe, Jannis Stavrakakis, and Slavoj Žižek. Two main questions are at play within this encounter: (a) to what extent does radical democratic theory avoid the bind of subjectivity explicated thus far, and (b) should radical democratic theory fail to do so, to what extent does Lacanian theory provide a supplement to complete the project. It is my view that Lacanian theory is necessary to understanding subjectivity and thus the political, but not in the manner in which its proponents to date have formulated it. Indeed, the one moment of clear difference from the general radical democratic theory, found in the Lacanian act that Žižek calls for, tells us little about what political agency is, for its inherently passive nature can only produce a sort of Heideggerian waiting. Rather, we ought to begin thinking through the political as a simultaneous universalization of the principle of the person along with its localization of actual persons meeting and discussing whatever issues are pertinent to them, but within the principle of anti-sovereignty.

No doubt, these ruminations are timely. The obviousness of democracy has undergone certain curious attacks, many in part due to its clear historical triumph. Once carried forth by near holly words such as freedom, citizenship, rights, and representation, to utter an antidemocratic sentiment, given its necessity after the end of history, amounted to political sacrilege. However, the bald imperialism of the Iraqi occupation undertaken in the very name of democracy made many somewhat confused as to what freedom is being fought for and who "hates" it. It had, as well, produced a good number of individuals who have now identified a set of Western persons who are the negations of their personas. No doubt, there are still clear reasons to be attracted to democracy. It affords, in many of its forms, choice in various arenas, a structure for political involvement, a level of distance from one's neighbor, and relief, sometimes only eventual, from overtly oppressive leaders. Each element has a value that would not be difficult to argue for, but, on the other hand, the sum of these values does not necessarily add up to the final word in what is possible or, more to the point, best in the realm of the political. Indeed, for each positive aspect, one can describe its undesirable counterpart, such as the confusing hydra of too much choice alongside a suspicion that the choices are, in the end, not essentially distinct; a dearth, within many democratic countries, of much voter turnout (not to mention actual political participation); an aching lack of community; and, last but not least, a tendency toward leaders who will act in authoritarian ways nonetheless.

The tension inherent in these two presentations of democracy are what, one may surmise, leads to Churchill's quip about democracy being the best of the worst. After all, as I have been arguing thus far, subjectivity, when one examines it closely, is not an entirely attractive entity, and any functioning political system will necessarily reflect this. Thus, after all is said and done, the greatest argument for democracy is that it embodies the listed tensions in such a way that none can dominate wholeheartedly. Hence, the myth of communism is that it can realize all of the good within the democratic project and avoid the bad, thus producing the ironic fact that the politics of social realism is really a fantasy that does not understand the reality of the human condition. We ought, then, to pragmatically accept our limits and move on with whatever comes next within the democratic framework.

While such a conclusion inspires a determined resignation to our minimum, it is also limited in the scope of its account of the effects of democracy. It must be noted, first off, that democracy is not radically separated from its opposite, totalitarianism, because it partakes, as I have argued, in the logic of politics and thereby the persona, or, in the Lacanian formulation, the person/*a*.[2] Most democracies are, as Alain Badiou puts it, parliamentarian and thereby productive of a representational gap between the persons subject to a given political formation and those who wield its relations of power.[3] Insofar as this representation is itself the Hobbesian displacement of one's persona to another persona who shall function as a stand-in, democracy is a fractured version of the totalitarian displacement of the plurality unto the singular Sovereign. The two are not inversions so much as versions of a shared logic differentiated by degree, one splitting the sovereign and the other unifying it. The opposition is thus within this fragmentation of the persona, but in neither case is the persona itself denied.

Hence the democratic consensus does not alleviate subjectivity of the deadlocks of its desire. Indeed, as the primary thesis of this chapter argues, democracy proliferates the negative aspects of desire insofar as it is a constant repetition of the logic of 'yet one more'. Democracy is thus exemplary of the phallic *jouissance* of accumulation, a constant additional presentation over an empty center or void that is too disturbing to have in itself. It is arguable that given the presentation of subjectivity that we have seen within the Lacanian edifice, democracy gives its subjects precisely what they want—a kind of voided object, a gift of presence that produces, once opened, nothing. That gift would be appropriate, however, to a polis that is traversed and capable of accepting its nothing. But democracy does not truly provide a traversal; rather, it provides the fantasy of its own fulfillment, over and over again. In this sense, democracy replicates the alienation of the subject, giving it at one point an answer to its issues and then, at another, taking it away. Democracy could thus be said to be predicated on a series of crises that are, due to its representative nature, always deferred to the Other who must be punished if they are not solved in a satisfactory manner. The subject of democracy, however, must remain in the living room of its accumulations, submitted to its private desire and left to decipher a larger meaning. As such, a double fantasy takes place within democracy. Individually, each persona functions according to her or his fundamental fantasy which will be carried out in a given way. In the plurality, on the other hand, this fantasy submits to a representative who will produce the public version of the Other, of a public answer as to how the fantasy of the self will be taken care of. Hence it is no wonder that many do not participate within representative democracies as they complain nonetheless about how the system fails to represent them. To the degree that the representational artifice functions from afar, one need not participate. On the other hand, to the degree that this artifice is itself an assumed personification of the demos, the Other/s will be blamed for everything that has not been accomplished.

The inherent anxiety of the current democratic configuration is thus not difficult to parse out once we see democratic subjects as subjects of desire. In its repetitive personification of the empty center, democracy structurally provides an answer while taking it away. While we cannot dismiss the positive aspects of democracy mentioned earlier, we cannot be surprised by those seemingly unnecessary negative aspects either. For instance, democracies, which are said not to invade one another, have a long history of imperialist expansion nonetheless. As well, they have no qualms about invading democracies that are labeled illegitimate, either explicitly or tacitly (hence the C.I.A. is an active presence in countries such as Venezuela). These decidedly undemocratic actions, not to mention the lack of participation in most representative democracies, are not accidental, but are rather the expression of the distance between the person and the persona. In essence, insofar as democracies replicate the quandary of desire, their inability to fill in the gap between the person and the persona with full satisfaction requires an answer, or negative objects that are, for the most part, persons.

Parliamentarian democracy is thus a function, like totalitarianism, of politics and not the political. Its repetition compulsion in the name of a new persona who shall represent the demos fails by virtue of its very success. Its failure, however, will be a boon to those in power who wish to use it, for they can capitalize on the vacuums of desire by augmenting the negativity of given objects, or persons, to explain what has gone wrong and to promote regimes that are structured to maintain such a logic. As such, our first thesis is that democracy only replicates the logic of desire, thus predicating itself on a phallic *jouissance* that cannot but, by definition, suffer an anxiety due to the fact that it cannot satisfy what is essentially a fantasy of satisfaction. However, Slavoj Žižek, critiquing the bad infinity of the radical democratic camp proposes a solution of traversal. As we noted in the last chapter, a subject that is not a sufferer of its fundamental fantasy must go through, or traverse, it by disidentifying with the fantasy and come to terms with its true desire. While democracy proliferates desire, Žižek argues that a militant act wherein the fundamental fantasy is denied will provide us with just such a proper Lacanian modality of the political. However, there are serious issues with the Lacanian act as it is submitted to mass political situations, the primary one being that it negates agency insofar as one is merely left to wait for such an act to occur. Thus, the second thesis is that no matter how radical democracy is, it will always reproduce the logic of 'yet one more' and, in the process, produce power vacuums that will inevitably be filled by foreign objects, or persons. On the other hand, even when a fully radical traversal is proposed, as is the case with the act, agency is rendered passive and one is left to wonder what to do until it comes. The options are thus set between a repetition compulsion predicated on a phallic addition and an apocalyptic waiting for end-times.

However, if the radical position is unavailable, this does not mean that democracy is thereby negated in full. Rather, democracy can be retained, but it must be done so as an anti-sovereignty. That is, the notion of representation, of a division between us and them, must be relegated to the desire laden realm of politics and supplanted by the nature of the political, which is the promotion of commodious living in the name of the one universal instantiation of the human, or the person. Hence the political formation proper will exist in and for the person, and its political existence will have to function as the lack of borders within the entirety of the planet in conjunction with a constant local meeting of all persons in the discussion of how their existence shall be shared. In this way, the political is universal in that it applies to the universal human and is borderless, and it is local to the extent those persons must physically and regularly meet with one another to the exclusion of none. The three thesis of this chapter can thus be rendered as such:

1. Democracy replicates the deadlock of desire insofar as it is submitted to phallic *jouissance*.
2. Radical democracy only intensifies the logic of 'yet one more' and thus continues the game of politics or, in its Žižekian formulation, negates political agency by producing a passive act that must be waited for.
3. The true formulation of the political is found in the principle of the 'everyone already' such that it is anti-sovereign (submits to no politics of the persona), universal (exists in and for totality of persons), local (requires that all persons engage with one another locally), and productive of commodious living for all rather than some.

In essence, then, the following serves as a critique of both democracy and radical democratic theory, but in order to better understand the nature of the political. The rational for this critique is that radical democratic theory has done well in uncovering the core principles, formally speaking, of the democratic project. But in so doing, it has also uncovered basic problems of the same project. While it seems rather premature to make the argument that authority figures are currently dethroned, that we are living in an essentially psychotic culture due to a full forced questioning of all leaders and a rampant, consumerist individualism, it is clear that we exist in an anxious world, one that corresponds more to the Lacanian notion of alienation than psychosis; in other words, the desire for authority, for a place, has not abated, and there are many who are willing to provide it—the Bush administration and Al Quaida being but two obvious examples. It could be said that, on the one hand, neither succeeded in defeating the other, while, on the other hand, such was their success. Hence, Osama Bin Laden and the Bush administration received what they desired when the U.S. invaded Iraq—a grand and vague war between competing ideologies: a war with no end, a war of "infinite justice." As such, the questions concerning, say, the truth of Islamic tradition or the weapons of mass destruction are subject to the whim of political necessity because they are irrelevant. What is at stake in desire is not a reality that can be footnoted, but the manner in which personas can be fortified in the name of their possible domination (and better to have a total war so that the continued existence of negative persons can be propped up at will to explain whatever failures come next). In opposition to these stagings of desire, then, we must turn to the true nature of the political, one that can only be understood, however, as the supercession of democracy in its most extreme form.

1. The Gutting of the Sovereign: Lefort's Democratic Void

The one unifying factor in radical democratic theory is a belief in disunity, in antagonism as democracy's premiere political gift, seemingly a gift of nothing. The space which allows for this disunity has its most concise expression within Lefort's account of the political void. For Lefort, once the political body historically lost its sovereign head, a democratic space was left behind that contained no determinate content but was felicitously productive nonetheless. Lefort narrates the process as follows:

> Power was embodied in the prince, and it therefore gave society a body. And because of this, a latent but effective knowledge of what *one* meant to the *other* existed through the social. This model reveals the revolutionary and unprecedented feature of democracy. The locus of power becomes *an empty place*. . . . The important point is that this apparatus prevents governments from appropriating power for their own ends, from incorporating it into themselves. The exercise of power is subject to the procedures of periodical redistributions. It represents the outcome of a controlled contest with permanent rules.[4]

If we were to redraw the image on the title page of the *Leviathan*, the gigantic plume in the Sovereign's left hand would be carved into implements for each who inhabit the body. Their first act would be to erase the contents of the sovereign's head, leaving it as a vessel in which the body politic could constantly rethink itself. The sword of force, now the right hand of the people, would be subject to the form of the body itself, subservient to its protection rather than an extension of the whim of the Sovereign. Such is Lefort's reworking of democracy. The centerpiece of this new mutation of the political is itself an empty place in which power can no longer be singularly claimed. In Lacanian terms, there is no Other or *One* who would tell us who we are, who could show us how to count as a *one* among the *many*. Identity is at play, albeit according to rules of contest that are themselves not. Democracy is thus the empty box, the form without content, or the form whose content is the form itself. Democracy is in this way not dissimilar to Lacan's Heideggerian potter who fashions something out of nothing, whose very creation of a container can only proceed on the basis of the void around which it is fashioned. Like the vase, democracy is "an object made to represent the existence of the emptiness at the center of the real that is called the Thing, [and] this emptiness as represented in the representation presents itself as a *nihil*, as nothing."[5] Democracy, like the signifier, is fashioned *ex nihilo*, from and out of nothing, and its activity can proceed only so long as there is an empty space within which it can interminably recreate itself, thereby making democracy essentially metonymic.

Lefort continues by disincorporating the body altogether, designating an inherent split within a power that is "the agency by virtue of which society apprehends itself," one that "marks a division between the *inside* and the *outside* of the social."[6] He thus demands that the Hobbesian inscription be left blank altogether, indicating that democracy is "a society without a body," one which undergoes "the *dissolution of the markers of certainty*."[7] The extremity of this position is not to be missed. Although many defend democracy on the basis of its supposed peacefulness, democracy expresses here a society that does not know itself and cannot give itself a full identity, much less rely on an external identity to buoy its voyage forth. For Lefort, however, this is not total dissolution. This lack of identity becomes a sort of unity whereby every "division . . . is constitutive of the very unity of society."[8]

Of course, the contradictory proposition that division is constitutive of unity begs elaboration. Lefort's position seems to be the following: insofar as the King's head has rolled, and along with it a definitive social body, the identity of society is subsumed under debate as the formal negotiation of what society shall be. Hence, the unity of society is guided by the formal principles of debate and division. Because all share in this debate, theoretically speaking, everyone is connected by its form. In his essay on human rights and the welfare state, Lefort spells out the necessary ramifications of our divisive unity:

> The existence of that gap [between political authority and adminis- trative power] means that the representational imperative is still efficacious. Ultimately, that imperative is incompatible with the full implementation of the norm for two reasons. First, it both necessi- tates and legitimates the expression of a multiplicity of positions on the part of both individual and collective social agents. Secondly, it proves to be indissociable from freedom of opinion, of association and of movement, and from the freedom to express conflict through- out society.[9]

The agonistic indetermination of democracy requires certain preconditions, certain formal rights which become, one could say, the quiddity of democracy. The many in their wild variety must be able to speak to one another, and in order to do so they must be able to move and to congregate, to express themselves in alliance and opposition, which means that they must have a space in which to act. Lefort's argument about unity qua division thus obtains an initially plausible reconciliation: we are united in our division insofar as we all fail to contain a fully constituted identity *and* we have equal possession of those rights which allow us to attempt to establish our identities nonetheless.

Here we reach the crux, I believe, of Lefort's argument. Only insofar as there is a clearing can there be a democracy. Rights, civil or otherwise, positive or negative, cannot exist, democratically speaking, unless the space of their contestation is maintained as open. Attempting to close the space of presentation can only be seen as the attempt to fill the void and in the process silence the people, whether they are a part of the masses or otherwise: "As a result, no artifice can prevent a majority from emerging in the here and the now or from giving an answer which can stand in for the truth." [10] So long as the space remains open, no content or, for that matter, contestation of a given content, can override what Arendt would call our space of appearance. Right thus depends on the articulation of right, depends not simply on the vertical ability to speak truth to power, but on the horizontal interplay of the voices of the demos. Perhaps, then, a better metaphor at this point for the Hobbesian sovereign would be a amoebic body of citizens with no head but an avaricious digestive tract, an empty center that is constantly in need of nutrition but never satisfied. Each representation of the body politic enters the empty center, attempts to represent a fullness of the polis, a definite form, only to eventually be shat out and replaced by another representation of fullness by virtue of the democratic constitution.

Thus, once the democratic space is opened, its *raison d'être* becomes the crisis of the legitimate, as Lefort argues, or the question concerning the nature of the space itself. Democracy contains an internal contradiction that it is, theoretically speaking, happy to maintain: it is the fundamental legitimization of the debate over what is legitimate, requiring only that the debate over legitimacy remains infinite. Such is why Lefort endorses the democratic process as the very grounding of the right to have rights, though he means it in a way that differs from Arendt's use. While Arendt posed the phrase in light of a totalitarian obliteration of rights, indicating something yet to be had, Lefort rather endorses democracy as its achievement.[11] We will return to this point later on. Suffice it to say that the right to have rights is maintained by democracy, according to Lefort, simply because the democratic space requires its existence. Appearance itself would disappear with the loss of this space, and appearance as the ability to reappear, to contest what appearance itself is or means, is the basis of democracy.

To return to our previous conclusions, insofar as power indicates in democracy the level to which there is a division in society, one that is both inside and outside of it, the state of nature parallels its logic. As we noted earlier, one of the prime arguments against democracy has been that it brings us too close to an inherent division that fractures society, too close to that within the human condition that tends to negate the possibility of commodious living. But here the division, the internal externality, is lauded—it is that which gives democracy its meaning and greatness. Because democracy allows those internal divisions within society to express themselves, allows things considered external to have a chance at occupying, for a time, the empty locus of power, it obtains unity within disunity, coherence within anarchy.

No doubt, given our ruminations to this point, it is less than obvious that democracy achieves, in and of itself, such a self-stabilizing anarchy. Indeed, what Lefort does not describe here is what within democracy's stability prevents its decline. No doubt, the logic is clear and not to be argued with, but the formulation in the paragraph above is telling: the majority constantly provides a 'stand in for the truth'. The draw of truth, therefore, remains a necessary component, and the personification of democracy, its constant representation by personas who provide a version of truth, thus indicates its play within politics rather than the political. In other words, in the same breath that democracy's division grounds basic rights it separates the representatives from the represented the personas from the persons, the stand-ins from the truth. Democracy is no less productive of fantasies than other forms of government, but these fantasies are plural. But, as such, we only see here the formal structure of the democratic game. It is with Laclau and Mouffe that we see its full articulation into a process and, no less, a political form of engagement. The questions that remain from Lefort's account are thus carried over to Laclau and Mouffe: is this democratic process really so unifying in its difference, or does this democratic void rather provide subjectivity with anything other than the alienation of proliferating fantasies of utopia? And if the latter, what remains of utopia's remainder, the person?

2. Laclau and Mouffe's Hegemonic Strategy

Laclau and Mouffe, through their analysis of Marx, Althussar, and Gramsci, can be said to have taken Lefort's insights into the democratic space and submitted them to a systematic praxis. Fundamental to their argument is the notion that the indeterminacy of the political space is commensurate with the indeterminacy of subjectivity. Hence, the *radicality* of democratic politics is located in the fact that "each term of this plurality of identities finds within itself the principle of its own validity, without this having to be sought in a transcendent or underlying positive ground. . . ."[12] Within the democratic space, no individual subject has an a priori identity, thereby functioning as a floating signifier seeking articulation, though in opposition to others within the given set of social relations. We can note the *ex nihilo* logic of democracy thus applied to subjectivity: with no core, there is a productive nothing within what we call a person, a nontotality that affords us freedom and competing interests. Furthermore, this radical pluralism is *democratic* "to the extent that the autoconstitutivity of each one of its terms is the result of displacements of the egalitarian imaginary."[13] It is with the latter that we discover the level to which Laclau and Mouffe have expanded Lefort's insights.

While in basic agreement with Lefort's notion that the social is divided over a democratic void,[14] Laclau and Mouffe formulate a strategy of antagonistic left-oriented politics. Though *Hegemony & Socialist Strategy* is a polemic against the decline of the Left, it is also an attempt to explicate democracy in light of new social movements, to understand the "logic of the social."[15] Once the latter is understood, it seems, the former will have the proper tools with which to engage politically. In that sense, the idea of 'displacements of the egalitarian imaginary' gives us a sense of what is at stake: the equality of differences at the center of democratic theory is something that at all times can only ever be imagined—it is a formal fact of democracy which does not and, more importantly, cannot be an actual fact. Equality therefore must be constructed around an imagined sameness that negates real differences in the name of some concrete goal. Equality thereby exists by virtue of a falsehood or, more correctly, is a virtual truth predicated on inequality. For example, in order to establish the equality of the 'sexes', their differences must be ignored. More importantly, the question of what shall constitute a member of a sex is also generally a limited category. Furthermore, it is only those who fall outside the parameters of a democratic consensus who may attempt to displace its assumptions.

This displacement is possible precisely because the open space of democracy is itself a site of contestation:

> . . . There are hegemonic practices because this radical unfixity makes it impossible to consider the political struggle as a game in which the identity of the opposing forces is constituted from the start. This means that any politics with hegemonic aspirations can never consider itself as repetition . . . but must always mobilize itself on a plurality of planes.[16]

Thus any attempt at hegemony can only succeed by rethinking the various networks of those who may oppose and those who may join. This is made possible because of the internal split of the social: "The irresoluble interiority/exteriority tension is the condition of any social practice: necessity only exists as a partial limitation of the field of contingency."[17] Because society is not a totality nor are its constituents fully formed identities, the notion of a complete or final representation of society is foreclosed. Even if such a representation were to arise, it could only ever be as the fantasy of a totality.

Such is the case for Laclau and Mouffe due to the discursive nature of reality. Reality's discursivity even enters into its materiality because the latter can only be reached and understood within a system of discursive differences.[18] In essence, Laclau and Mouffe are arguing that any meaning effect can only be understood by virtue of how it is articulated in relation to other meaning effects. If one wanted to analyze an institution as nondiscursive, frustration would result because the very tools of analysis and objects to be analyzed are, they argue, already discursively constructed in opposition to other discursive objects. Like Lacan, Laclau and Mouffe take Saussure's radical argument about meaning as a relation of differences and apply it to society as such: every given object is relationally constructed and thus does not have an a priori meaning. As well, they apply Wittgenstein's argument about the material performativity of the language game to discourse: language is a material enactment of meaning, something that lives within the very process of enunciation itself.[19] To say 'slab' is to enact the meaning of 'slab', and to verify that the slab is not, for instance, a pillar or a block. But while all reality is discursive for Laclau and Mouffe, we do not find a complete creation of reality—discourse does not say it all, and this inability of total expression is what allows for antagonism.

While language presents us with a system of signifiers defined by their differences, antagonism stands for that within discourse and society which escapes articulation, exhibiting beyond language what is repressed within society: "If language is a system of differences, antagonism is the failure of difference . . . for every language and every society are constituted as a repression of the consciousness of the impossibility that penetrates them."[20] Antagonism is thus a 'metaphor' for the disruptions of society, for the repressed underlying impossibility of any identity fully becoming itself. Any antagonism within society is as such the sight of living beings who are the repressed, existing externally as the metaphor of impossibility. They are, in Lacanian terms, the *objet a's*, and in Arendt's discourse, the alien, the remainders of a nothing that must be ignored, separated, debased, or eradicated in order to achieve, however futile, identity. They are also, as Lefort has shown us, the very division that constitutes society's impossible nature, the outside of power that goes to define its internality. It is only because the identity of those who maintain a hegemonic hold is itself incomplete that an articulation through new equivalences is rendered possible and these remainders, or persons, have the logical possibility of locating a space within the recognizable. Equivalence and difference thus indicate the last and final terms within hegemony.

For Laclau and Mouffe, the radical nature of society is located in its simultaneous objective and negative character. While a series of identities do in some respects exist in relation to one another, and many of them obtain equivalence and thus participation in a similar grouping, they are also distinct elements that do not obtain a full presence to themselves, indicating that neither full equivalence (we are all the same) nor full difference (we are entirely distinct) is possible. This leads to a logic such that the increase in equivalence, the attempt to reach a point of pure suture or sameness intensifies the underlying differences, thus bringing out the antagonism within the social:

> . . . certain discursive forms, through equivalence, annul all positivity of the object and give a real existence to negativity as such. This impossibility of the real—negativity—has attained a form of presence. As the social is penetrated by negativity—that is, by antagonism—it does not attain the status of transparency, of full presence, and the objectivity of its identities is permanently subverted.[21]

Laclau and Mouffe use extreme equivalence to explicate a situation in which there is a basic, divisive opposition with few or no conceptual bridges, such as in the colonialist creation of symbolic divisions (the intensification of caste systems in India, the racialization of the Tutsi vs. the Hutu), or, more recently, the Sunni/Shia divide. Antagonism is that which cannot be annulled in equivalence, functioning thereby as the return of the repressed within a stabilized social formation.

A society structured on extensive differences, such as that of the welfare state, enables a proliferation of different subject positions. Antagonism is the point to which those positions are not able to either link themselves in equivalence or accept themselves in difference. Since they have an objective existence but not discursive expression, they exist, but do so outside a communicable paradigm. They insist while never quite consisting of a meaning, functioning thus as internal externalities to the state, or, according to our earlier formulation, the nature of state. Their negativity, as we saw above, is productive—just as Lacan and Lefort argued, the level to which something is placed outside of expression but is present all the same creates a process whereby nothing seeks to become something. Seeking to find a voice in the empty space of the democratic adventure, the limits of the discursive within the system of equivalences and differences erupts, making the status quo both impossible and nervous, thereby motivating a reaction (whether it is acceptance, negotiation, or violence). Again, the attempt at a constitutional amendment in the U.S. to define marriage as heterosexual is a clear example of this process, but insofar as it submits to the accepted modalities of codification.

While Laclau and Mouffe find in Gramsci the presupposition of a unified class and singular hegemonic centers,[22] they define hegemony in modern democratic situations as the attempt to create links between a myriad of subject positions from various points of departure. Central to hegemonic formations, insofar as they are democratic, is that they are "constructed through regularity in dispersion, and this dispersion includes a proliferation of very diverse elements: systems of differences which partially define relational identities; chains of equivalences which subvert the latter but which can be tranformistically recovered insofar as the place of opposition itself becomes regular and, in that way, constitutes a new difference. . . ."[23] The main point here is that while historical blocks can be formed, the open nature of society, in which differences can never be fully sutured, prevents a final utopian telos. The withering of the state, the end of history, and all such visions are thus rendered merely fantasmatic. To quote Margaret Thatcher, "there is no such thing as society."[24]

Thus when feminist groups mobilize, for instance, they must do so under a campaign of articulated intelligibility. In order to become effective hegemonic movements, movements which obtain the consent of their opposition, not just power over them, they must find, as Gramsci put it, an organic link, a way to connect their position with those who do not share it: "All struggles, whether those of workers or other political subjects, left to themselves, have a partial character, and can be articulated to very different discourse. It is this articulation which gives them their character, not the place from which they come."[25] Like democracy itself, the position of those groups that combine to form it is inherently partial and, incomplete, subject to a void or absence which allows for a parasitic or symbiotic relation to other positions. It is insofar as the group latches on to forms of expression which resonate that they are able to leave the place of being merely external or unheard, as outsiders to the antagonism, and to enter into the endless dialectic of creating a new legitimate order. A cultural example of this rearticulation is the notion of the metrosexual, the 'straight man' who contains all the previously clear signifiers of the 'gay man'. It is precisely because these 'gay' signifiers have obtained a level of acceptance, of common currency, that they are able to be internalized by the heterosexual subject.[26] This confusion is, no doubt, a boon for corporations as skin care products slather themselves over the emerging male market. All the same, it also exemplifies a successful strategy of articulation, at least within the marketplace, whereby a previously antagonized position is slowly integrated into the previous norm.[27]

It is at this point that Laclau and Mouffe propose that this is not only a new social logic, but as well the mainspring for a new socialist strategy. Left behind are the concepts of the economically determined proletariat subservient to the logic of economy, no longer useful are the neoliberal assumptions of property and freedom. 'Man' fails to exist so much that his loss of existence is reduced to a 'polysemia', an endless discussion about what it indeed might yet be. The descriptive idea of radical democracy as emanating from the antagonistic nature of social formations also obtains a prescriptive democratic position: antagonism is not only real, it is good, and the Left ought to take the lack at the center of democracy and intensify it: "The task of the Left therefore cannot be to renounce liberal democratic ideology, but on the contrary, to deepen and expand it in the direction of a radical and plural democracy."[28] As they go on to note, this can only be achieved by the ever increased integration of subordinated groups within a positive conception of society, but one clearly divided by the division and negativity central to hegemony: there will never be a total or totalitarian resolution of differences, and the social space wherein various subjectivities vie for identity must always be subject to 'the subversive logic of democracy'.[29]

Here, however, there are two problems, the first to do with the utopia, the second *jouissance*. In the case of utopia, Laclau and Mouffe state emphatically that society (and, one would have to add, subjectivity) can never be considered an object with a scientifically discoverable essence. Such, they say, would "be the height of utopianism."[30] But Laclau and Mouffe claim that utopianism is inescapable all the same. The requirement of utopia could, arguably, function as a critique of Lefort's notion of an inherent unity within the democratic void—democracy with no meta-principle is insufficient for an actual hegomonic political project: "This is because the logic of democracy is simply the equivalential displacement of the egalitarian imaginary to ever more extensive social relations, and, as such, it is only a logic of the elimination of relations of subordination and of inequalities."[31] While democracy means eliminating inequality, the positive social moment is both a creative notion, a notion of a positive order of society, and a negative notion, the idea of destroying present social conditions in order to create the world anew: "without 'utopia', without the possibility of negating an order beyond the point that we are able to threaten it, there is no possibility at all of the constitution of a radical imaginary— whether democratic or of any other type."[32] Here Laclau and Mouffe become mercurial, charging that it is impossible to simply leave the Left with a management of the possible, with what might be called 'pragmatic politics', which is merely an updated version of *realpolitik*, and claiming that we cannot devolve into a simplified fantasy of totality. But if neither is possible, what, exactly, is the utopian position of this so-called radical imaginary?

While it seems plausible to point out a de facto tension between any positive social movement and democracy's negative constitution, when speaking of a movement's idealization of itself, it is unclear what it means to stand between the two poles and still designate it as both 'positive' and 'utopian'. While Lefort indicated a formal unity in our division insofar as we are unified by a shared space for obtaining rights, Laclau and Mouffe unintentionally point here to what we desire within it, which constitutes the imaginary factor within this unity. Utopia negates negation and, insofar as it is the sight of those who fight for it, it cannot be legitimately predicated on a 'suspension of disbelief'.[33] Either there is a belief in the truth of the process one fights for, or one is up to something else. If Lefort does not note the fact that the totalitarian moment of the imaginary is a part of the unity of the democratic void over and above the unity of difference, Laclau and Mouffe do not see the manner in which this imaginary indicates something more than a mere problematic relation in the democratic process.

The indeterminacy of the utopian thus brings us to the deeper issue of *jouissance*. As we have seen within our analysis of subjectivity, the problem of desire and, more importantly, *jouissance*, makes direct uncertainty nearly impossible to bear. Laclau and Mouffe do not shy away from using Lacanian concepts such as the Symbolic, the Real, and even the Imaginary (though in their own fashion), but the subject of *jouissance* is absent. Laclau himself acknowledges this fact, arguing that "something remains incomplete in my argument without a category such as *jouissance* (or another that plays a similar structural function)."[34] However, the project in fact fails without an account of *jouissance*. If it is the case that there is no inherent ideal or universal instantiation of society or the subject, it is also the case that subjects create for themselves such an ideal all the same. This is what the problem of *jouissance* has shown us: the subject is barred from itself not simply because there is no essence on earth, but also because the signifier, as it is delivered from the Other, bars the subject from its *jouissance* along with its idea of what that *jouissance* is. Bars it, however, in such a way that the subject accepts this limit, chooses and internalizes it, no matter how forced the choice. As such, it is the fantasy, repressed in its fundamental form, and express in its allowable, socially ideal types, that fills in this gap, and allows the subject to have an asymptotic and essentially failed relationship with *jouissance* as the drive, nonetheless, circulates a little too close. In stark terms, the social fantasies that imaginary utopias provide allow subjectivity to latch onto an external and acceptable form of the completion of desire, no matter how impossible its formal reality may be. To the degree that subjectivity is so constituted, that we are, as Hobbes and Lacan understood, ideologically constructed, we will not fail to be hailed into new utopian formations nonetheless. What is thus missing from the displaceable and incomplete subjectivity of the antagonistic democratic space is its fundamental desire for an end to displacement.

As such, insofar as the impossibility of the subject and, along with it, the social, is a function of repression and fantasy, of a traumatic *jouissance* that insists all the same, the idea of a radical democratic project which does not account for this leaves subjectivity in the lurch twice over. On the one hand, as an answer to *jouissance*, an impossible radical imaginary is merely confusing—it does not alleviate the burden of utopia inherent in a lost fusion that secretly drives us (and while it is theoretically true that democracy tells us that the fantasy of utopia is impossible, democracy in its de facto existence has yet to fail at promising various sorts of utopia nonetheless). On the other hand, the radical nature of the imaginary construction merely replicates the subjective deadlock, providing the subject with more of what it already has: an impossible and fantastic utopia predicated on the bad infinity of yet one more antagonism that may or may not (though, really, won't) suture antagonism itself.[35]

Hence, if it is the case that society is impossible, that democracy functions on the basis of a productive negativity, and that subjects are nonetheless functioning under a fantasmatic and impossible relationship to *jouissance*, then democracy acts as a mere amplification of the impossibility of desire, indicating the constant phallic achievement of small goods with no final good. It thereby exhibits the Arendtian biological voraciousness in which the production of democracy eats itself up, spitting itself out in new formations without end and without, more importantly, any principle of stabilization. Let us put the point in even starker rhetorical terms: if a subject can traverse his or her fantasy in the analytic setting, what makes us think that democracy would have a similar effect when radicalized for a whole population? Why isn't democracy, especially when radical and only "utopian," not a platform for the increase in anxiety and paranoia that leads, as we have already seen, to undesirable outcomes? Is this argument about the unity, traversal, and 'utopia' of democracy not, as Hardin would put it, a fallacy of composition yet again? Nor are these questions merely stuck in a theoretical vacuum. The use of fear to motivate democratic countries into wars with falsely constructed enemies shows us the level to which democracy alone as the guarantor of freedom and rights is not particularly strong. It thus seems questionable that radicalizing democracy will strengthen it rather than underline for subjectivity its weaknesses. To use Laclau and Mouffe's own terms, the intensification of a socialist strategy, one that increasingly empties out the Signifier of the social, also empties out the content of the fantasy, making it increasingly void of specific content and revealing the Real, the unbearable *jouissance* of a direct social antagonism. As such, a socialist strategy of intensified articulation so described, even if it is inherently democratic and egalitarian, asks society to face that object of antagonism directly and without recourse, and as such threatens it with organic crisis.

3. Lacan as Theorist of Democracy

Perhaps, then, we can find an answer to these questions in Yannis Stavrakakis' *Lacan & the Political*. The thoroughness and clarity of Stavrakakis' treatment of Lacan within the political realm is unparalleled, and given that this text is preoccupied with how Lacanian theory can be applied to the political, it appears to be our best bet for breaking through the issue of democratic traversal.[36] Indeed, while Stavrakakis is clear that

Lacanian psychoanalysis would agree with much of what Laclau, Mouffe, and Lefort have argued in terms of society, subjectivity, and democracy suffering from an unfillable gap, he is also aware of the problem of *jouissance*:

> What is at stake in the Lacanian conception of fantasy is, as we have already pointed out, enjoyment (*jouissance*). If the effects of the normative idealist or Enlightenment-style critique of racism are severely limited, if this critique is not enough. . . , this is because, to use one of Sloterdijk's formulations, it 'has remained more naive than the consciousness it wanted to expose.'[37]

The 'fantasy of utopia' lives off of what Stavrakakis himself points out as the impossible *jouissance* of the subject, a *jouissance* that is impossible because, as we have already noted, it presupposes a perfected state (I have it for the Other, the Other has it for me) which is prohibited (I cannot have it, it is inappropriate), thereby leading the subject to desire via its underlying yet infinite fantasy of utopia expressed through sublimated modalities ('x' exists, and if only 'x' were obtained, things would be perfect).[38] Insofar as *jouissance* continues to insist in opposition to a socially acceptable fantasy, a relation of friction exists between: (a) the social imaginary, or the way in which societies construct stories about their own coherence and privilege; (b) the individual imaginary, or the way in which a subject invests him or herself in that social imaginary in order to maintain a distance from and relationship to *jouissance*; (c) the individual's own repressed relationship to the disturbing Real; and (d) the antagonisms that must be repressed in order for this web of imaginary relations to maintain its sheen.

So how is it that a Lacanian political formation would undercut the libidinal investment in the fantasy? How would the underlying lack at the center of society and the individual be made, all irony intended, desirable to individuals qua individuals and qua participants in a social group? According to Stavrakakis, by emphasizing more deeply democracy itself, by bringing out its internal emptiness. So doing provides us a hope that is not predicated on utopia:

> Is it then possible to retain this element of hope without incorporating it into a utopian vision? Can we have passion in politics without holocausts. . . ? The experience of the democratic revolution permits a certain optimism. Democratization is certainly a political project of hope. But democratic discourse is not (or should not be) based on the vision of a utopian harmonious society. It is based on the recognition

of the impossibility and the catastrophic consequences of such a dream. What differentiates democracy from other political forms of society is the legitimization of conflict and the refusal to eliminate it through the establishment of an authoritarian harmonious order.[39]

We can note a slippage in this passage that is found in most radical democratic theory. On the one hand, it is argued that democracy provides us with optimism and a project of hope. On the other hand, we are told that democracy cannot and ought not, and here the slippage begins, be mired in utopian fantasies. It is this move between what cannot happen and what ought not happen that is at issue. It is quite clear that democracies can provide their own vision of a utopia, whether it is the finally free world, the totally administered state in which all needs are met, or even a freedom grounded in religion. That democracy can be shot through with utopian visions, even if it ought not, indicates that Stavrakakis is begging the question: what sort of hope does a Lacanian politics provide us sans utopia, what libidinal passionate attachment can we have to the empty center?

At this point, unfortunately, we are reverted to where we ended with Laclau and Mouffe. Stavrakakis argues that what we ought to aim for is "the creation of a democratic ethos. . . . The emergence and maintenance of democratic forms of identity is a matter of identification with this democratic ethos, an ethos associated with the mobilization of passions and sentiments, the multiplication of practices, institutions and language games providing the conditions of possibility for the radicalization of democracy. . . ."[40] Again we must focus our attentions on the antagonism of society and enter into it so that the repressed may be represented and find a place among the recognized and articulated demos. As a part of this democracy, we ought to believe in the impossibility of society and democracy along with it, we ought to identify with the symptom that structures, however negatively, our social being (or lack thereof). On the same page, Stavrakakis rhetorically asks: "Isn't it something worth fighting for?"

It is unclear. One of Stavrakakis' tasks is to respond to the main critique of Lacanian political theory; namely, that by emphasizing impossibility and lack, the citizen is left with nothing to think of or believe when thinking about political engagement or, for that matter, social existence. Indeed, Stavrakakis' formulation of one of Sean Homer's criticisms is devastating: "If psychoanalytic theory does not engage in ideological construction, in trying to fill the gap in the social, other ideologies and discourses do and will continue to do so."[41] Indeed, what about a Lacanian political alternative will prevent it from being invaded by nefarious utopian discourses?

What is desirable, in other words, about Lacanian political theory given that, as the theory itself tells us so vehemently, and as Hobbes pointed out some time ago, subjects are fundamentally driven by their desire in a way that they have little control over it.

Stavrakakis is not unaware of the fact that democracy, as Laclau and Mouffe argued, is subject to situations of organic crisis whereby society is so partialized and torn asunder that there is no sense of stability whatsoever, thus providing for totalitarian fantasies of recovery.[42] But practically speaking, the idea of a democratic ethos is problematic due to the fact that it is predicated on identifying with absence. As we have seen, in the analytic situation, one must identify with one's symptom in order to understand that it is conditional, however nonsensical it ends up being. Identifying with this symptom is a way to work through the utterly blinding power of fantasy. Similarly, Stavrakakis enjoins us to identify with our social symptoms, to predicate our democratic hopes on our social failures, on our exclusions:

> By saying 'We are all Jews!', 'We all live in Chernobyl!' or 'We are all boat people!'—all paradigms used by Žižek. . . , we elevate the symptom, the excluded truth of the social field (which has been stigmatized as an alien particularity) to the place of the universal—to the point of our common identification which was, up to now, sustained by its exclusion or elimination.[43]

One cannot help but be struck by a similarity here with the Arendtian argument for the universality of the stateless. As we saw, to the degree that the stateless were stripped of all particularity and left as merely human, they were a cause of revulsion and annihilation. Here the universality of the stateless is the democratic moment *par excellence*, the heart of an ethos in which we circle around the traumatic and thus Real gap repetitively and asymptotically because, as we know, we cannot really touch the Real in an articulate, organized way. Thus Stavrakakis argues the following: "this gap should be viewed as opening the optimistic possibility of democracy as opposed to totalitarianism or radical fragmentation; a possibility that rests on the recognition of the constitutive character of this gap. . . . Democracy depends on an originary disharmony or disorder."[44]

As with Laclau and Mouffe, what we fail to find here is any persuasive reason why such circling is desirable, why it gives us hope, on any level, and how, according to our original question, it would counter the acute and chronically powerful problem of the relation between *jouissance* and fantasy. While it is clear that democracy has an affinity with the Lacanian subject qua traversed insofar as it is a political institution that recognizes its own emptiness (there is no Other to the Other, there is no final democratic representation), it does not follow that it actually precludes people from believing that there is someone who knows the truth all the same.[45] In fact, there seems to be a critical contradiction at play within Stavrakakis' argument: if we must identify with democracy as a disharmony and disorder, we must therefore identify with the lack of a project, the impossibility of ever achieving a state of affairs that is stable and, more importantly, existent. We can push the contradiction even further. Insofar as democracy is the institution whereby people vie for admittance to the representation of the empty center, it depends on the fact that people believe they know best how to occupy that center. In other words, the only reason to occupy this center, save for mere power, is because one has a concept of what it ought to look like. Democracy thus depends on the competition of representations, and those representations depend on the belief that they are true. To identify with the idea that they are impossible, that they are merely 'disordered' means to not really believe in them and, as Homer argued, have no strong desire to pursue them.

We are thus led to a formal problem with Laclau, Mouffe, and Stavrakakis' antagonisms. Insofar as radical democratic theory depends for its existence on antagonism, it cannot be a prescriptive theory. It can describe the impossibility of society, it can outline the fact that exclusion is central to society, but it must maintain all the same the fact that exclusion is central to society. In other words, such theories hold forth the essential nature of antagonism, which allows for a continuous contestation of the center. But this descriptive aspect precludes a prescriptive move toward any particular position. To attempt to represent democracy in its radical form with a democratic ethos accomplishes either of two things: (1) it achieves redundancy, since it is merely descriptive of the social condition as such, or (2) it is self-negating insofar as any attempt to represent the essential nature of the democratic project is itself undemocratic. If a radical democratic ethos attempted to install itself as the one and true representation of democracy, then democracy itself would fail to exist as an ever contested and empty location. Should the radical democratic theorist protest that the position is fine because it takes into account its own failure, its own open nature, we are reverted to the problem of redundancy which, put otherwise, begs the following question: what, in its particulars, is your ethos anyway? How does it distinguish itself from democratic practice as such; for example, equality, liberty, suffrage, and the like? Such is why radical democratic theory retains coherence as a critical descriptive theory and does well in analyzing certain real life cases. But when it attempts to portray itself as an actual political position, it becomes empty, and *must*—its content is a lack of content, its focus is antagonism, and thus its representation is negative.

Of course, a counter response might point out that there is a positive content insofar as more are drawn into a chain of equivalences, thereby extending inclusion. But this response fails to account for the fact that a radical democratic project must represent its other half, antagonism. Such is evident in Laclau's arguments concerning the relation of the universal and the particular:

> We can say that, as a result of this constitutive gap: (1) the more extended the chain of equivalences that a particular sector comes to represent and the more its aims become a name for global emancipation, the looser will be the links between the name and its original meaning, and the more it will approach the status of an empty signifier, (2) as this total coincidence of the universal with the particular, however, is ultimately impossible—given the constitutive inadequacy of the means of representation—a remainder of particularity cannot be eliminated.[46]

The broader the inclusive nature of a universal representation, argues Laclau, the more empty that representation becomes. As such, the more inclusive they are, the more universal claims deny difference. Furthermore, since the approach to true universality is asymptotic, there is always some necessarily excluded representation, some *objet a* that implies the contradictory or antagonistic nature of the so-called universal representation of the demos. As such, a radical democratic position must laud inclusion and exclusion at the same time, must require that the excluded be brought in and that there continue to be exclusion nonetheless, else democracy as such, like a desireless Hobbesian subject, dies. The hope that a particular struggle raises is mitigated by the fact that the broader its success the less it truly represents difference and, more fundamentally, the more powerful its triumph the more clear some antagonistic force has been ignored or denied. Radical democratic theory, practically speaking, cancels itself out.[47]

Thus, while it may seem theoretically and even ethically expedient to seek a political realm such that any utopian imaginary is constantly fought off or, in other words, such that fantasy is fully traversed, none of these theories explain how this is to be accomplished on a large scale. While the therapeutic situation provides us with a model of what an individual traversal would look like, the political realm is an entirely different beast, driven as it is by a plurality of subjects who are to be gathered under one banner, whether radical or not. The presupposition thus far, it is true, has been that we cannot understand the political without understanding the individual, or that the political is in many ways an expression of the psychological structure of those who constitute it. Thus we can see why fantasies of totality tend to be desirable to individuals since it answers the question of just what the Other wants for and from them. Political representations therefore work because they speak to our fantasies. But just because subjectivity gives us many insights into the nature of the political and its failures, it does not then follow that a political body that resembles the end point of traversal will, in and of itself, be sufficient in avoiding fantasmatic political states. In other words, simply because democracy carries an affinity *with* traversal, it does not follow that it *is* a traversal. And in fact democracy alone does not accomplish this: it is merely a way of structuring a political body that invariably, thus far anyway, calls for extra-democratic support to give it stability and depth. Such is why radical democratic theorists are compelled to make the call for an ethos, a vague principle of intentionally encountering lack over and over again, but, given the demands of lauding antagonism, have no precise theoretical advice as to how to endure the antagonism without approaching political psychoses, or what Gramsci called organic crisis.

Thus the democratic revolution is inspiring, though it is not self-nourishing. It depends on those who shall occupy it, and they depend on their own conceptions of how it ought to be occupied. Between the two stands an open question as to what will happen next. It seems then that we have indeed encountered the fallacy of composition yet again: because Lacanian theory works on an individual level does not mean that it applies directly to a political level. There is not reversibility such that if a traversed subject looks democratic in his or her outlook, a democratic nation will therefore produce traversed subjects. The question remains open, so long as the notion of a democratic ethos is vague, as to how to achieve such a traversal on a broad scale. Radical democratic theory alone does not have the particular content to answer this universal question. But there is one primary figure within the radical democratic camp who has realized its structural failure.[48] It is with the Lacanian Act that Slavoj Žižek proposes a break from the failed repetition of democracy and capitalism. The question, as we will now see, is whether a secular sort of grace can redeem the democratic body.

4. Only an Act Can Save Us

Although Slavoj Žižek is in agreement, to a large extent, with Laclau, Mouffe, and Stavrakakis, he makes a serious break from their ranks, one paralleled only by Alain Badiou, with his concept of the Act, a Lacanian notion he utilizes to show both how radical democratic theory is essentially stuck in a Kantian rut and how to break that rut, one that mirrors all too well, in Žižek's eyes, the very conditions of the current capitalistic democratic matrix. Indeed, in *Contingency, Hegemony, Universality*, an exemplar of theoretical infighting if ever there was one, Žižek levels at Laclau and, in the case of this passage, Judith Butler, the accusation that their theories "involve a logic of 'spurious infinity': no final resolution, just the endless process of complex partial displacements."[49] The core of his argument here is one we have already examined: insofar as radical democratic theory simultaneously argues that, due to antagonism, there is no final project and, due to the nature of subjectivity, it must cling all the same to an ethos of hope and passionate attachment, a debilitating contradiction ensues: each democratic project fails to be a project in any fully realized sense of the term, rendered as it is into another 'partial displacement'. In that sense, Žižek expresses the argument made earlier concerning the nature of the political: insofar as it submits to the personification of a democracy, it can only ever function under the rubric of 'yet one more'. As such, it does not achieve a full universality of the person and must, logically speaking, always represent only a subset of personas. In his formulation of the problem, Žižek amasses a number of arguments against the democratic consensus, three of which are most relevant for our purposes here: administration, *jouissance*, and capitalism.

To begin with, Žižek views democracy in its current formation as the promise of change embalmed within the formality of administration, or procedure, allowing thereby for a constant subversion of real change: "Democracy—in the way this term is used today—concerns, above all, formal legalism: its minimal definition is the unconditional adherence to a certain set of formal rules which guarantee that antagonisms are fully absorbed into the agonistic game. 'Democracy' means that, whatever electoral manipulation takes place, every political agent will unconditionally respect the results."[50] Žižek references the 2000 U.S. elections, which he argues were democratic insofar as the rules of procedure were respected whether or not the election was soundly won. Here Žižek takes the position that Laclau and Mouffe misspeak when they talk about radical democratic theory as antagonistic: "while democracy acknowledges the irreducible plurality of interests, ideologies, narratives, and so on, it excludes those who, as we put it, reject the democratic rules of the game, liberal democrats are quite right in claiming that populism is inherently 'anti-democratic.'"[51] In other words, insofar as radical democratic theory cannot abide by any other political project than an essentially democratic one, it is really an agonistic process, a contest or battle of wills for a center that must remain the same, or empty, at all costs. Antagonism thus indicates that what is repressed is any alternative to democracy. Democracy, on the other hand, *agonistically* administers acceptable forms of contest while precluding anything beyond the democratic norm, including, therefore, a true antagonism.[52] As we alluded to earlier, democracy is radically undemocratic insofar as it cannot abide by any nondemocratic system. Of course, this does not make democracy totalitarian, even if the arguments concerning its inherent link are nonetheless true. But, democracy has its limit, and that is anything, whether totalitarian, authoritarian, or even radically socialist, that does not fall within its self-regulation.

But what is so bad about that? Here we arrive at Žižek's second and more powerful argument against Laclau, Mouffe, and even Stavrakakis; namely, their failure to deal with the distinction between democracy as a formal entity and democracy as a social contingency shot through with *objets a*. In this case, Žižek makes the argument I have about radical democratic theory; namely, that in its formal anti-utopianism it fails to actually deal with social reality. While this reference to social reality may appear ironic given the Lacanian dismissal of the very notion of reality as a true referent (as opposed to the Real of antagonism), here we mean by reality the manner in which the Real of *jouissance*, swept under the rug of fantasy, continues to motor our actions, producing as its result the fact that democracy alone always needs a nonagonistic support for desire. Žižek deals with this in a response to Stavrakakis' rejection of utopian thinking:

> [I]t fails to distinguish between, on the one hand, the contingency and impenetrability of social life, and on the other, the democratic logic of the empty place of power, with no agent who is 'naturally' entitled to it. It is easy to see how these two phenomena are independent of each other: if anything, a functioning democracy presupposes a basic ability and reliability of social life.[53]

In other words, democracy as a formal entity requires a living, breathing, contingently formed populace, a social life with its own presuppositions, fantasies, and therefore *content,* however particular, however varied, that would make democracy impossible without its existence. These various contents are what give democracy, pace Lefort, its unity, functioning simultaneous as something extraneous (because nondemocratically established) and internal because necessary for stability. And this necessity is the result of the problem of utopia as it is linked directly to *jouissance*. If there is nothing stable to invest our libidinal selves into, then we are left with only an empty center, which is less than hopeless, for it is nothing. It is precisely the lack of focus on why the body politic agonizes in the first place, on why the demos needs representations of itself, that leaves radical democratic theory arid. Between the fear of organic crisis and totalitarian obliteration, radical democratic theory cannot decide on what to do with belief. Unfortunately, as Homer pointed out, there are many who can.

Though he is surely not alone in making it, Žižek thus argues that the Left lacks what the right has in droves, however cynical—passion. While the Right, particularly in the U.S., has spent a long time creating a relatively coherent if simplified belief system that represents Truth (best expressed in the daily chum of talking points), the Left has languished in a stupefying sandpit of reactionary responses. There is no radical democratic project for the Left for at least two reasons. One, as Eric Hobsbawm and Lefort have pointed out, it has already succeeded.[54] The majority of its desires, from universal suffrage and rights to the limiting of the working day, have been met. But, more importantly, the Left has no concept of desire, of what motivates individuals. Even Lackoff's famous distinction between the liberal mothering/nurturing approach and the conservative paternal/ authoritarian approach, used in order to give the Left a new vocabulary, misses the point: the Left does not understand that an assemblage of catch- phrases, however well framed, do not amount to a vision, to a worldview, which is why an authoritarian approach will always be more immediately successful within a democratic void. In the face of no sure reference points, the body politic will always seek an Other who can, at the very least, pretend to know:

> [T]his means that the democratic empty place and the discourse of totalitarian fullness are strictly correlative, two sides of the same coin: it is meaningless to play one against the other, and advocate a 'radical' democracy which would avoid this unpleasant supplement. So when Laclau and Mouffe complain that only the Right has the requisite passion, is able to propose a new mobilizing Imaginary, while the left merely administers, what they fail to see is the structural necessity of what they perceive as mere tactical weakness of the left. No wonder

the European project which is widely debated today fails to engage, to engender enthusiasm: it is ultimately a project of administration, not of ideological passion.[55]

By being a merely administrative project, democracy as it now stands, even in its radical form, is devoid of passion (for, after all, is not the process of an ever expanded empty signifier of inclusion merely the administration of inclusion, one set up for its eventual breakdown and reemergence of equivalences on the bedrock of antagonism?). This may sound false given the revolutionary origins of many democracies, but it is descriptive of the outcome of democracy in its formal state rather than its natal inception. Once self-aware, there is nothing to believe in, for strong belief is precluded in an agonistic play of representations. Why invest utopian hope within what is essentially fleeting? Why believe in democracy with no determinate content? The mitigating relationship between drive and desire, the core motivating factor of the subject in all its split determinations, tells us that on the political level, a reassuring content, an object of fullness, will always be sought, will always be the goal. Even if democracy exhibits a formal model of political traversal, or a structural traversal accorded by its lack of a Sovereign, the empty center provides for the representation of ever more promises of democracy's demise. In essence, to the degree that democracy functions upon a representational (parliamentarian) model, its formal traversal is thereby negated by its separation of the polis from itself through representation. Here we thus encounter the reason why both Hobbes and Arendt failed to take their insights into the anxiety of the revealed person far enough: each in their own way thought the exit to be found in the persona, but such action can, at times, only provide the promise of amelioration. It does not break out of the trap of desire. The Sovereign is successful because it positioned itself, however democratically represented, as the instantiation of the Other, thereby abating the alienating displacements of the antagonism and providing a social imaginary by which to modulate desire.[56]

No less, this incessantly problematic *jouissance* leads us to the third object of critique; namely, capitalism. The argument is thus continued in the passage above with the proposition that the Left fails to take account of the "obverse, fantasmatic supplement, of democracy itself. . . ," which is in this case capitalism. Capitalism has been Žižek's *bete noir* for some time now, marking for him the truly central unspoken support of democracy. As we saw earlier in our analysis, Lacan argued that the fundamental fantasy is an underlying unconscious support for a subject, an organizing picture which gives to it a coherent way to deal with the inherent gap in the desire of the Other. As such, the goal of psychoanalysis is always to reach this support and break it apart, to help the *analysand* see and move beyond the manner in which the fantasy unconsciously and unhappily supports his or her actions. This is in essence what traversal amounts to. According to Žižek, every political entity, insofar as it affords itself some form of identity, also predicates itself on a fundamental fantasy, an unspoken support that enables the political body to think of itself as coherent, as not lacking nor antagonistic, and thus superior.[57] However, given that a fantasy is a construction that can only play at overcoming its essential lack and concomitant desire for transgression, its inability to be true to its representation expresses itself through a 'surplus *jouissance*' of various *objets a*, objects good and bad that represent indirectly this inherent lack. The truly Lacanian and, as Žižek points out, Marxist response is to find out how the 'bad object, the symptom', is operating. Thus in Žižek's first major English work, *The Sublime Object of Ideology*, he makes the following argument regarding one of the ultimate 'bad objects', the Jew:

> . . . the stake of social-ideological fantasy is to construct a vision of society which does exist, a society which is not split by an antagonistic division, a society in which the relation between its parts is organic, complementary . . . How then do we take account of the distance between this corporatist vision and the factual society split by antagonistic struggles? The answer is, of course, the Jew: an external element, a foreign body introducing corruption into the sound social fabric.[58]

Here we find the argument used by Laclau, Mouffe, Lefort, and Stavrakakis: like the sexual relationship, society does not exist, and we seek in a fantastic Other an explanation for why it does, indeed, exist and why, because it never fails to fail, there is some unfortunate and external thing blocking its proper functioning. Insofar as one identifies ideologically with one's country as beyond reproach, its inherently reproachable nature requires some sort of explanation.

The Jew, historically speaking, has been a prominent and recurring example of the fetishized bad object, the sign of a secret organization attempting mastery and *enjoying* in ways that are beyond words (thereby making their image inexplicably arousing). The fantasy of the Jew is simultaneously the fantasy of an external block to society and the manifestation of secret desire for that block, for that pleasure that the Other supposedly obtains. Such is the basis for Žižek's oft-deployed argument about official systems and their unofficial, seedy undersides. For example, the process of rendition employed by the U.S., along with its ongoing international uproar, is a case in point, merely explicating in better detail the contradictions inherent in Abu Ghraib. While the U.S. professed to follow the strict standards of the Geneva Conventions, it nonetheless sends prisoners to countries known for brutal acts of torture, such as Egypt and Syria. The U.S. government officially pleads ignorance of these acts of torture while, off the record, recognizes that the process of rendition is a necessary side route to winning the war against the 'terrorists'. It is this public disavowal of transgression which in fact indicates the secret complicity and desire for it that undergirds the process of rendition, one given verification, by necessity, 'off the record'. In fact, it could be argued that rendition is a way of abstracting the inherently unacceptable enjoyment that Abu Ghraib showed the world: as the photos made clear, the torturing of prisoners by U.S. citizens was accomplished with zeal. Though there were those who publicly supported the acts, it was clear that such activities had to take place in another scene.

The 'terrorist' is thus the U.S.'s new Jew, the object that prevents it from fully being itself, one so nefarious that we must use nefarious tactics against it, and the 'war on terror' becomes the *cause celebre* which motors the idea that the U.S. will achieve its perfected state once this one last roadblock is removed. Of course, this is merely the negative form of desire writ large on the world scene, with certain objects coming to stand-in for the impossibility of society, one after the other. It is thus no doubt appropriate that the war on terror is a *non sequitur*. One cannot, as has been pointed out repeatedly, defeat what amounts to a tactic. But such impossibility, left unanalyzed, is the type of Orwellian logic that a permanent war requires.[59] Žižek's general argument here, however, is that while the Jew, the Terrorist, the Black, and so on, function as objects that are fantasized about in terms of a lost *jouissance* and inability to achieve perfection, there is also a positive object of fantasy, an object which assumes the role of the 'good object'. In history's current configuration, this 'good object' is capitalism: ". . . insofar as we conceive of the politico-ideological resignification in the terms of the struggle for hegemony, today's Real which sets a limit to resignification is Capital: the smooth functioning of Capital is that which remains the same, that which 'always returns to its place', in the unconstrained struggle for hegemony."[60]

Capitalism, along with democracy itself, is thus the unquestioned project of the Left, either in its conservative, liberal, neoconservative, or even, to some extent, radical Leftist approach. While there is no doubt that a number of groups continue to argue vociferously against capitalism, there is also no doubt that they are rarely, if ever, listened to by the majority of the world, save for two interestingly enough; South American leftist and fundamentalist Islamic republics (which, however, have no qualms about selling vast quantities of oil on the open market). It is this assumption of the obviousness of capitalism that Žižek locates as the disturbing new Real of political society, a signifier that is 'beyond words', that structures the space of understanding and is, in itself, empty while simultaneously acting as the site of unconscionable acts of *jouissance*.[61] Indeed, Žižek makes a deft argument insofar as he links the incessant displacement of capital, its inherently antagonistic form, as Marx pointed out so long ago, to the very notion of hegemony itself: ". . . this 'generalization of the hegemonic form of politics' is itself dependent on a certain socioeconomic process: it is contemporary global capitalism with its dynamics of 'deterritorialization', which has created the conditions of the demise of 'essentialist' politics and the proliferation of new multiple political subjectivities."[62] In other words, capitalism's ability to ingest and spit out any new object for consumption is itself a process of withdrawing the essence from any object, turning it into a commodity fetish, a representation of an essence which, as Marx argued, is itself an abstracted spiritual emptiness (in other words, the fetish of Value). The ever voracious appetite of capital, as Arendt pointed out, its impossibility of ever achieving any state of repose, is thus the condition of a politics of lack. The process of hegemony qua antagonism, Žižek argues, mirrors the process of capitalism, of the attempt to dominate markets against competitors, to produce new objects of accumulation only to be dismissed in the gaining of yet some other object. Both thus exhibit a bad sort of infinity insofar as they are essentially codependent.

But why is there no strong opposition to capital? According to Žižek, beyond the fact that there is no 'critique of political economy', *jouissance* itself is increasingly subject to a bureaucratic administration. One can hear echoes here of Arendt's complaint about the rise of the social over the political, causing a sort of lobotomized demos insofar as the regulation of pleasure bypasses the process of ideals and identification. Thus, "the skeptical stance of not taking social ideals and identifications seriously is also no longer viable."[63] The ideology of today, the regulation of *jouissance* in the form of marriage, abortion, sex, guns, and of rights, bypasses the ideal and identification of fullness altogether, creating in its wake the skeptical subject. Put otherwise, insofar as the political operates as a regulator of *jouissance*, as the agonal or competitive space of various modalities of *jouissance*, or various subject positions and their desires, the concept of a full-blown political ideal is seen as unnecessary, as something too antagonistic. Partisan politics is the only politics there is—the single subject political crusade overtakes any idea of an actual fully realized and expansive movement. Such explains the impossibility of the Left ever having a coherent platform; insofar as the Left is committed to the plurality of identities, to the notion of inclusion, a truly revolutionary Left is precluded. Any such articulation would be met with instant resistance, dismissed as a fantasy or, more likely, totalitarian. The Left is thus hindered by its own *raison d'etre.*

But this does not explain the success of the right, particularly in the U.S., which does indeed provide something like a broad worldview, ingeniously concocted out of a brilliant articulation. What does explain the right is the desire of every subject, or most subjects, for an answer from the Other, for an explanation for why we are here, what we are doing, and what it all means. The Left did not provide this because it was stuck in the defense of a proliferation of identities (in this way, radical democratic theory is objectively descriptive, but of one side of the partisan divide—what it does not describe and cannot approach is *jouissance*). The right is more than successful at this because it could pull together unifying principles (of God and Country, of property, of social values), and divisive enemies (the terrorists, Massachusetts liberals, amoral Hollywood, gays, etc.). We get the picture of the whole society and the objects which prevent it,[64] a nice combo-pack of ideological fantasy that serves to placate while stoking the underlying anxiety about global capitalism and fundamentalist violence. Such was Hobbes' clear lesson; insofar as a ruling body can bring unity, its subjects will be pacified, their desire defanged, and the social body mobilized by a centralized head of state with clear and simple rules of organization. What Hobbes could not foresee was the level to which this process could take place directly out in the open. In other words, an absolute monarch is not necessary for keeping a public placated by ideological control. What is needed is a tightly scripted series of events that give the appearance of assurance. This factor has been essential to the republican edifice. In a fascinating moment of confessional hubris, a senior Bush advisor told the following to Ron Suskind:

The aide said that guys like me were "in what we call the reality-based community," which he defined as people who "believe that solutions emerge from your judicious study of discernible reality." I nodded and murmured something about enlightenment principles and empiricism. He cut me off. "That's not the way the world really works anymore," he continued. "We're an empire now, and when we act, we create our own reality. And while you're studying that reality—judiciously, as you will—we'll act again, creating other new realities, which you can study too, and that's how things will sort out. We're history's actors . . . and you, all of you, will be left to just study what we do."[65]

Reality is thus a secondary effect of the force of empire, negating the entire project of rational enlightenment principles in a thoroughly productive, if not enduring, fashion. In essence, we learn here that even social conservatives have learned all too well the lessons of postmodernity—reality is the forceful play of its mediated representation. And, in fact, the antagonisms of the Left and the sculpted imaginary of the Right merely reflect obverse sides of one another. Insofar as there are constant agonistic attempts at the empty center of democracy, no totalitarian truth is made possible. But insofar as the center is left empty by this constant tug-of-war, the desire for truth will be met by those who can best manipulate it. One has either empty ideals, ideals qua "ideals," or cynical representations of Truth. Each allows for the other and, as Žižek sees it, is based on the unquestioning acceptance of capitalism. As such, the campaign of change that deflated the hopes of a continued right expansion in 2008 was predicated on a combination of the Real of capitalism, in the form of its precipitous decline, and a message, as inspired as it is empty, of hope and change.

All of this leads to Žižek's ultimate argument concerning the act, the Lacanian moment in which the clearing provided by the fantasmic traversal affords a subject the ability to reconfigure the very parameters of reality in order to begin anew. It is thus with the notion of the act that Žižek separates from the radical democratic theorists completely, arguing that the alternatives available within agonistic anti-utopian democracy are no longer enough to break the current hold that capitalism maintains. While the idea of an act in which life is reoriented sounds distinctly similar to the idea of psychological scripting, the main difference is that in an act proper the identification that takes place is not with a new, fuller self, but with one's own lack expressed in the symptom:

[O]n the contrary, the act in its traumatic *tuche* is that which divides the subject who can never subjectivize it, assume it as 'his own', posit himself as its author-agent—the authentic act that I accomplish is always by definition a foreign body, an intruder which simultaneously attracts/fascinates and repels me, so that if and when I come too close to it, this leads to my aphanisis, self-erasure.[66]

For Žižek, an act accomplishes a full traversal of the fantasy such that the divided subject of which we spoke earlier, the subject of the signifier, suddenly comes into contact with the excluded Real, assumes its own disappearance and realizes in fact that the Other has no Other, that the Other knows not what it does. This means that the fundamental fantasy which kept everything going collapses, and the subject now identifies fully with its own manner of loss.

Žižek continues by proposing that such an act is a simultaneous moment of absolute passivity and freedom. To the extent that the subject is no longer constrained by the fantasy of the Other, the subject is let loose unto its own *jouissance*, able to accept its loss and thus no longer constrained by a need to compensate drive with fantasy. But, on the other hand, to the extent that an act is outside the limits of the knowable, beyond the clear coordinates of the signifier and its symbolic realm, an act is truly miraculous, beyond comprehension, and thus "something which unexpectedly 'just occurs.'"[67] Like Arendt's natal miracle of the self, the act is an event that could not have been planned and is not willed, that miraculously produces something unseen in the world but which, all the same, is the very sight of freedom, of the 'I can': "In an authentic choice of freedom, I choose what I know I *have* to do."[68]

According to Žižek, the act breaks through the drone of the radical democratic project without succumbing to fantasies of totalitarian completion. It is because the act occurs knowingly in the gap of the Other that it does not submit to the dream of a utopia without friction. As such, because the act releases the subject from the supporting fantasy Other who knows, it frees the subject to let go of the assumptions that had kept it docile. In other words, by giving up the fantasy, by identifying with the symptom as the outward expression of what is not there (the Jew, the terrorist, etc.), one is set loose from the stranglehold of previous assumptions, thereby opening up a truly new and radical space. Indeed, it is the very act of traversal itself that creates this space, however abnormal it appears in relation to what has occurred previoulsy. Here we can now see how Žižek's argument against capital truly functions. Global capitalism is the unspoken support/fantasy of the democratic project, and for that reason it must be traversed—our investments in it must be plundered.

Žižek's conclusion is thus provocative both for the breadth of its scope and for the sense of resignation in its conclusion. Our only alternative at this point, it seems, is to repoliticize the economy:

We should thus reassert the old Marxist critique of 'reificatin': today, emphasizing the depoliticized 'objective' economic logic against allegedly 'outdated' forms of ideological passions is the predominant ideological form, since ideology is always self-referential, that is, it always defines itself through a distance towards an Other dismissed and denounced as 'ideological'. For that precise reason—because the depoliticized economy is the disavowed 'fundamental fantasy' of postmodern politics—a properly political act would necessarily entail the repoliticization of the economy: within a given situation, a gesture counts as an act only in so far as it disturbs ('traverses') its fundamental fantasy.[69]

He continues on the next page to argue that the depolitization of the economy is what blocks the advancement of truly progressive issues because it maintains the entrenched power of the right.[70] The goal, contra Arendt, therefore is to bring the economy into the center of the political debate, to ask the question as to who owns what and why. Hence, to use Marx's term, the vampiric nature of capitalism undergirds and informs the nature of political reality, predicating both on the logic of desire and preventing the power base from being truly affected by those who are external, thus leading to a situation in which the reality for the majority is reduced to a symptom of desire that is out of their hands. Hence we arrive at a sort of absolute invisible hand of the political whereby the distribution of wealth is also the distribution of reality: "Again, does not the very absurdity of this prospect—the private control of the very public base of our communication and reproduction, the very network of our social being—impose a kind of socialization as the only solution?"[71]

One wonders, then, about the practical implications of such a revolutionary call. Indeed, what are, precisely speaking, the political conditions for an act proper? What would cause the global populace, or even one of its subsets, to truly strike at its agalma and void itself of its passionate attachment to the continued reproduction of political capital? What, indeed, would attract anyone but the odd remaining socialists to this clearly radical new step? It is at this point that Žižekian enthusiasm suddenly comes to a grinding halt, and there is no new dialectical turn or inversion to show us the real within the situation:

[O]ne cannot formulate a clear project of global change. So, contrary to the cheap "revolutionary" calls for a radical overthrow of capitalism and its democratic political form, my point is precisely that such calls, although necessary in the long run, are meaningless today. What

I am not ready to do is . . . abandon the horizon of radical change in favor of the prospect of multiple local practices of resistance, etc.— today, it is more crucial than ever to continue to question the very foundations of capitalism as a global system, to clearly articulate the limitation of the democratic political project.[72]

It appears, then, that while we cannot reduce ourselves to the service of political goods as the radical democrats would have it, there is also no true space for action. The project of the Left is to merely renounce itself as an entity, to let go of its desire to act and thus mortify itself: "The only way to lay the foundations for a true, radical change is to withdraw from the compulsion to act, to 'do nothing'—thus opening up the space for a different kind of activity."[73] There is very little left of the Left.

Internal to Žižek's argument is the thought that inaction will work as a blockage to the frenetic pace of desire, and hence the proliferation of ideal egos, once they face objects that refuse to reflect back, will abate, creating in their absence a new arena for action. The idea is not unlike Arendt's two-in-one, in which the self is able to come to terms with its division only insofar as it is not submitted to its public presentation or the private sphere of biological repetition. As such, a space of thought is opened up for subjectivity that allows the mind to explore an endless proliferation of questions whose only anchor is that one's internal division does not fracture completely: "The criterion of the mental dialogue is no longer truth, which would compel answers to the question I raise with myself. . . . The only criterion of Socratic thinking is agreement, to be consistent with oneself. . . ."[74] By withdrawing from the public realm, one is allowed the space of thought such that something new may enter perhaps, which is not submitted to the delusions of desire and, with it, the repetition compulsion of capital (in this way, one could say that Arendt dehistoricizes the symptom of the bios, formulating a compulsory effect of the economic and political space into a human faculty). While the argument for a withdrawal has much to recommend it within a temporality for which the speed of a certain kind of economic progress has no clear check other than its own excesses, it is not clear that it is productive of the conditions for an emancipatory project, for it is precisely the conditions whereby an act is made possible that we need to understand. Indeed, while an *analysand* achieves agency for her or himself through the process of analysis, what sort of agency can one derive within the political realm, particularly one that has yet to be created?

Hence the argument that an act is the Hegelian speculative fusion of opposites, a moment in which absolute freedom and complete submission take place, requires elaboration.[75] Žižek proposes that it is the moment in which I know what I must do even though I can enumerate various quite reasonable alternatives. Such a proposition produces two difficulties. To begin with, there is an express passivity to the description that is given by Žižek. But if an act is something that occurs to the subject, to what degree is it an act and not an effect? In other words, the question of political agency remains indeterminate in what is noted here as its highest expression. Furthermore, even if we bypass this question, which is perhaps the most difficult for any political system, the second issue of the necessary conditions for an act also requires elaboration. Something must happen for one to know that a given situation requires an act, but what this "something" is, politically speaking, is not elaborated by Žižek, save for a broad indication of a space of withdrawal whereby new possibilities might come to fruition. As such, it appears that we have run into the same Humean confusion between formal description and prescription that Laclau and Mouffe produced, though with this difference: while Laclau and Mouffe point to something already available, the democratic logic of the infinitely inclusive 'yet one more' necessary to antagonism, the revolutionary call for an act remains suspended within the realm of formal description.

Žižek is quite powerful in enumerating those cultural and symbolic factors that lure us into buying into sublime objects of ideology and, failing that, sublime objects of marketing. But the very strength of this analysis shows up the weakness in his emancipatory writings. An *analysand* must go through countless hours in the analyst's room. There must be, therefore, an analyst who must not only have information regarding the *analysand*, but the power to enact the cut, to actively engage in a session in order to send an *analysand* off in a certain direction that is not reductive to more of the same. Eventually, the argument goes, the *analysand* will enact her or his own freedom through a breakthrough identification with the symptom. In the political realm, however, it seems that there is a fallacy of composition if we are going to apply the analytical setting there. There is no long process of excavation and, more importantly, there is no person in a seat of power that will aid the populace in such an excavation, knowing exactly when to intervene in the contradictions of their fantasies such that they will give way to their true desire. Our fantasies drive our choices for leaders in the first place. Those who would lure us with the outright publicity of our darkest secrets will not garner our favor. If it is thus not our leaders who shall be our analysts, clearly it is ourselves or, more likely, the Real of history intruding upon our fantasies with its disconcerting materiality. Thus Žižek tends to emphasize events in which revolutionary uprisings overthrow corrupt institutions such that they negate their previous identifications. But what leads to such a state? What are the conditions in the political realm that allow for such events to occur? Does psychoanalysis, even when backed by Hegelio-Marxist readings, have anything to tell us about reaching a state of political traversal?

Within the analysis provided thus far, the answer is no. Psychoanalysis can identify the logic of the social and the modalities of identification, indicating the necessity of a hidden desire, hidden perversion, and the need to create positive and negative objects to continue a given fantasy. But until the conditions which will allow for a broad scale act to occur can be enumerated, the factor of traversal is thus not clearly located within the political. In the opening to Phillip K. Dick's *Do Androids Dream of Electric Sheep*, Rick Deckard attempts to get his depressed wife, Iran, into a more positive state by means of a device that dials in various moods. However, Iran refuses to do so, wanting to remain in a scheduled 'six-hour self-accusatory depression'. Deckard is baffled that this mood even exists:

"Dial 888," Rick said as the set warmed. "The desire to watch TV, no matter what's on it."

"I don't feel like dialing anything at all now," Iran said.

"Then dial 3," he said.

"I can't dial a setting that stimulates my cerebral cortex into wanting to dial! If I don't want to dial, I don't want to dial that most of all, because then I will want to dial, and wanting to dial is right now the most alien drive I can imagine; I just want to sit here on the bed and stare at the floor."[76]

In reverse form, we have here the very problem that Žižek and the rest cannot override in the radical Left. In a realm of manufactured feelings completely cut off from the pain of the human condition, Iran has found a way back to it. The result is a feeling of despair that leads to the impossible situation whereby the very thing that will lead her out of it, dialing 3, is that which it prevents from happening. Iran has taken a heroic stance in evading the regulated pleasure that her world so easily provides. And, in essence, Žižek is imploring us to tap into our underlying anxiety and dial in a 'six-hour self-accusatory depression'. But there is no mood organ to dial, nor any other clear way to reach said mood, the combined feeling of freedom and passivity found in the act. It is telling, unfortunately, that Iran does finally submit to Deckard, whom she allows to dial 594, or "pleased acknowledgment of husband's superior wisdom in all matters."

Notes

1 See, for instance, Carl Schmitt's early use of 'the political' to indicate an us/them formation, or the fact that there is an enemy: "The political enemy need not be morally evil or aesthetically ugly; he need not appear as an economic competitor, and it may even be advantageous to engage with him in business transactions. But he is, nevertheless, the other, the stranger; and it is insufficient for his nature that he is, in a specially intense way, existentially something different and alien, so that in the extreme case conflicts with him are possible," Carl Schmitt, *The Concept of the Political*, trans. J. Harvey Lomax (Chicago: The University of Chicago Press, 1996): 27. It ought not surprise anyone that the thinker of the state of exception would also require such an ethically vacuous political definition. On the other hand, there is no doubt that insofar as the political, when reduced to politics, is predicated on the opposition of the persona and the person, then the other qua alien and existential opposition will always have an important place, however excluded.

2 In this sense, I agree with the thesis of Horkheimer and Adorno that the Enlightenment and totalitarianism share a root whereby the logic of externality is to be eradicated. See, in particular, chapter one of their *Dialectic of Enlightenment*. However, this is predicated not on myth so much as the logic of the split of subjectivity insofar as the persona is subject to its imaginary capture.

3 See, in particular, Alain Badiou, "Against 'Political Philosophy,'" in *Metapolitics*, trans. Jason Barker (New York: Verso, 2006): 16. Here, Badiou carefully critiques Myriam Revault d'Allonnes' reading of Arendt (and thus mostly avoids direct pronouncements on Arendt) as interposing between the subject of the political event and its actual political involvement a distance of opinion that subverts any sort of true militancy. That an actual decision is required for a real politics dependent on concrete historical situations is perhaps the essence of Badiou's critique of philosophies that negate truth within the political (not to mention his three other categories of truth: love, science, and art). I will note here briefly, however, that Badiou suffers from the same obscurity of agency that Žižek does in his notion of the act. Insofar as the decision and the act are both essentially passive in their descriptions (they happen, as if from nowhere, to subjects), their force in terms of the question of political agency is at best mitigated. For instance, Badiou tells us that "[to] enter into the composition of a subject of truth can only be something that happens to you," *Ethics: An Essay on the Understanding of Evil*, trans. Peter Hallward (New York: Verso, 2001): 51. The question that hangs over Badiou and Žižek's return to political truth as one predicated on a militant involvement, in other words, is how one comes to such a choice in the first place. This produces in each an internal obscurity that would be resolved were their systems merely descriptive. However, given that both are active militants themselves, the prescriptive nature of their systems hangs in latent frustration.

4 Claude Lefort, *Democracy and Political Theory*, trans. David Macey (Minneapolis: University of Minnesota Press, 1988): 17, hereafter referred to as *Democracy*.

5 SXII, 121.

6 *Democracy*, 17.

7 Ibid., 18–19.

8 Ibid., 18.

9 Ibid., 29.

10 Ibid., 41.

11 Ibid., 37.

12 Ernesto Laclau and Chantal Mouffe, *Hegemony and Socialist Strategy: Towards a Radical Democratic Politics* (New York: Verso, 1996): 167, hereafter referred to as *Hegemony*.

13 Ibid.

14 "Once again, we find ourselves confronting the division of social space," *Hegemony*, 165.

15 Ibid., 3.

16 Ibid., 170.

17 Ibid., 111.

18 Ibid., 107.

19 Ibid., 108.

20 Ibid., 125.

21 Ibid., 129.

22 Ibid., 137–8.

23 Ibid., 142.

24 Of course, Thatcher's quote, which is extremely Lacanian in its formation, is nonetheless a support for its own fantasy of the hyper-individualism of capitalism in opposition to the welfare state.

25 Ibid., 169.

26 So we see in the *New York Times* article, 'Gay or Straight? Hard to Tell', an introductory image of Brad Pitt.

27 This integration is, of course, only partial. Gay bashing is still common, the attempt on the part of the right to deny gay, lesbian, and multi-gendered people from marriage has reached a productive constitutional hysteria, and, last but not least, it is clear that it is the gay male who has taken the privileged and somewhat accepted position within media empires. No less, the common put down for nervous heterosexual males remains the ubiquitous: "that's so gay."

28 *Hegemony*, 176.

29 Ibid., 189.

30 Ibid., 143.

31 Ibid., 188.

32 Ibid., 190.

33 Laclau and Mouffe are clear that one cannot answer by saying that the ideal would merely be the maintenance of the openness of the democratic society, which would merely be the "management of social positivity."

34 Ernesto Laclau et al., "Theory, Democracy, and the Left: An Interview with Ernesto Laclau," *Umbra: Polemos* (2001): 15.

35 Noting that Laclau and Mouffe have missed the problem of individual *jouissance* as well, Slavoj Žižek similarly argues that their project needs to be extended by taking into

account Lacan's notion of the ways in which the subject internalizes its own block—in other words, it's not the Other which blocks me from myself, but rather myself who blocks me (the Other qua block is merely the projection of my own internal impossibility). All the same, Žižek argues in the end that *Hegemony and Socialist Strategy* "articulates the contours of a political project based on an ethics of the real, of the 'going through the fantasy *(la traversée du fantasme)*', an ethics of confrontation with an impossible, traumatic kernel not covered by any *ideal.* . . ." Ernesto Laclau, *New Reflections on the Revolution of Our Time* (New York: Verso, 1990): 259. Two points: one, it is not clear that there is no ideal—rather, it seems that ideals force themselves into the picture as 'utopia', even if impossible. Two, Žižek does not in fact explicate how this traversal takes place, but rather enigmatically tells us that we shall encounter the paradox of an "enthusiastic resignation." However Kantian this enthusiasm, the reader is somewhat at a loss for its content.

36 In terms of political treatments of Lacan, Stavrakakis' text stands next only to Žižek as the most extensive. However, Žižek's texts are less structured in their presentation. Teresa Brennan, however, has made certain political formulations in her work on Lacan, though I disagree with her formulation that society has reached a state of psychosis; rather, I think that it is best expressed as subject to an extreme form of alienation. See her *History after Lacan* (New York: Routledge, 1993).

37 Yannis Stavrakakis, *Lacan and the Political* (New York: Routledge, 1999): 109, hereafter referred to as LP.

38 See LP, 49–50.

39 Ibid., 111.

40 Ibid., 112.

41 Ibid., 113.

42 Ibid., 125.

43 Ibid., 133–4.

44 Ibid., 126.

45 Indeed, it is not surprising that Bush campaigned as the CEO president in the beginning, billing himself as someone who has a keen knowledge of how to run things, thus buying into the fantasy then rampant about powerful CEOs and their ability to miraculously generate stupendous profits.

46 Butler, Judith, Ernesto Laclau, and Slavoj Žižek, *Contingency, Hegemony, Universality: Contemporary Dialogues on the Left* (London: Verso, 2000): 56, hereafter referred to as *Contingency*.

47 Even Laclau's distinction between the ontic and ontological viewpoint fails to overcome this issue: "For historical actors engaged in actual struggles, there is no cynical resignation whatsoever: their aims are all that constitute the horizon within which they live and fight," *Contingency*, 196. But this is less than forthright. Insofar as political actors are engaged in struggles within a field formally or ontologically structured by antagonism, their struggles are also constituted by the nature of antagonism, which demands that their struggles are inherently partial and are not, in and of themselves, ever achievable. Indeed, radical democratic theory tells them the following: whatever is accomplished will be simultaneously incomplete and exclusive. As such, their aims are not all that constitute the

horizon within which they live and fight—that horizon is constituted simultaneously both by counter-aims and aims which antagonistically fail to enter into the terms of the debate alongside the differences which are obliterated by any equivalence actually achieved.

48 As noted earlier, Alain Badiou's theory of the event is quite similar to Žižek's politicization of the act. However, there is not enough space in the present work to deal with Badiou's highly complicated concepts.

49 *Contingency*, 111.

50 Slavoj Žižek, *The Borrowed Kettle* (New York: Verso, 2004): 114, hereafter referred to as *Borrowed*.

51 Ibid., 92.

52 Ibid., 92.

53 Ibid., 109.

54 In Hobsbawm's words, "The Left's very success seriously weakened its program." In other words, after the 60s, it was increasingly difficult in the West to find masses of unrepresented, starving individuals being worked to the bone. Eric Hobsbawm, *On the Edge of the New Century* (New York: New Press, 2000): 100.

55 *Borrowed*, 112.

56 The success of Barack Obama has its own formulation in this regard; namely, what the Right has correctly formulated as his near messianic quality, holding the position of the Other who will deliver the demos from the failings of the previous within the vague promise of change. Of course, the denigration of the right is as content free as the promise of change, but these are battles over identification. Perhaps what is most interesting is the level to which the market crashes of 2008 functioned as a moment of the Real within the previously believed-in smooth operation of the cycles of capital—a formulation of capitalism that Marx was, as noted earlier, highly aware of. In this sense, Obama can be read as the Other that was chosen to save our imaginary selves in the face of the painful Real of job losses, wage declines, reduction in coverage, and so on.

57 In this sense, George Lakoff is quite close to Lacan when calling the nurturing/authoritarian dyad a part of a deep, inaccessible Cognitive Unconscious that must be made public if the nation is going to heal from its division. Indeed, Lakoff echoes Žižek's argument that the nation is suffering from an antagonism that is, on the one hand, defining and, on the other hand, not consciously accessible. However, Lakoff's argument that liberals need "more pride" in reframing their moral system suffers its own internal antagonism which framing alone won't help. Insofar as the liberal position is itself based on "empathetic behavior and promoting fairness," it merely replicates the democratic void: no strong, atemporal content, but rather the increasing form of 'yet one more'. See George Lakoff, *Moral Politics* (Chicago: University of Chicago Press, 2002): 417–19.

58 Slavoj Žižek, *The Sublime Object of Ideology* (New York: Verso, 1989): 126.

59 Hence the logic forces such familiar statements as the following: "I just want you to know that, when we talk about war, we're really talking about peace. We want there to be peace." President George Bush speaking at the Department of Housing and Urban Development, Washington, D.C. (June 18, 2002).

60 *Contingency*, 223. Žižek makes similar arguments in *The Borrowed Kettle* (see, for instance, 109).

61 Indeed, from the Enron and Worldcom debacles, in which massively rich men found ways to defraud large groups of people, to the global collapse of the finance markets, we see the level to which capitalism is not frictionless but structured by its own inherent transgression. Furthermore, the idea that class is dead, so to speak, has had such a strong hold that the *New York Times* felt it necessary to create a whole series of articles on why 'class matters'. Indeed, it is odd that class as an antagonistic force is so ghostlike given the increasing disparities in wealth in the U.S. While it may be the case that the proliferation of identities has made it difficult to indicate just precisely who inhabits which class, mal-distributions of income remain a fact all the same. Such a state of affairs appears to bolster Žižek's argument that the fantasy of the end of class is itself the cover for the increase in its importance.

62 *Contingency*, 319. As Marx put it in "Wage-Labour and Capital": "But it is solely these fluctuations, which, looked at more closely, bring with them the most fearful devastations and, like earthquakes, cause bourgeois society to tremble to its foundations—it is solely in the course of the these fluctuations that prices are determined by the cost of production. The total movement of this disorder is its order." Karl Marx, *Karl Marx: Selected Writings*, ed. David McLellan (New York: Oxford University Press, 2001): 279. Another way to put this is that capitalistic society is itself determined by indetermination, with its predictability similar to that of the weather. Such is the *nature* of capitalism.

63 *Borrowed*, 113.

64 Of course, the fact that the Right is not unified, that Libertarians are generally unhappy and that Christian Fundamentalists are dissatisfied with the blockage effected by old-time centrist Republicans indicates the level to which there is no real unified right.

65 "Without a Doubt," *New York Times Magazine*, October 17, 2004.

66 Slavoj Žižek, *The Ticklish Subject: The Absent Centre of Political Ontology* (New York: Verso, 1999): 374m hereafter referred to as *Ticklish*.

67 Ibid., 375.

68 Ibid., 378. For some concrete examples of acts not found in movies or books, see *Borrowed*, 87–8.

69 *Ticklish*, 355.

70 That is, by keeping economy out of the political picture, the ability of the right to maintain its economic advantage is upheld. Of course, this is a half truth. As everyone knows, the Left has amounted large sums of cash, and is not always all that eager to part ways with it. Perhaps the real secret underside of the Left is the level to which it desires to lose, not out of a psychological masochism, but out of a desire to maintain status.

71 *Ticklish*, 357.

72 Slavoj Žižek, "Ethical Socialism? No, Thanks!," *Telos* 129 (2004): 189.

73 *Borrowed*, 72.

74 LM, 185–6.

75 Similar arguments, as noted earlier, can be made about Alain Badiou and, as well, Jacques Ranciere, who, when Žižek is included, all make quite similar points regarding the

sense and nonsense of the proper political agent in contradistinction to the normal struc-tures of society. Indeed, it is arguable that these new modalities of militant truth are in some basic way reminiscent of if not derivable from Heidegger's notion of authentic resoluteness within a given historical situation. See, in particular, section II.2 of Martin Heidegger, *Being and Time*, trans. John Macquarrie and Edward Robinson (New York: Harper & Row, 1962).

76 Phillip K. Dick, *Do Androids Dream of Electric Sheep* (Ballantine Books, 1982): 4.

Conclusion: Against the Personification of Democracy

Our conclusions with regard to the possibilities of democracy thus far have been generally critical and, politically speaking, dispiriting. What is worse, they structurally contradict our earlier formulations regarding the political. This contradiction is located in the fact that insofar as the political is described as existing for the person and against the persona, most subjects are predisposed, even within a radical democratic configuration, toward mere politics. That is, the tendency of subjectivity is to abhor the vacuum of the political and seek objects of identification that will outfit them with a political fantasy, thereby necessitating as well those negative objects of explanatory disidentification, such as the Jew and the terrorist. Even when we broach a radical Left project that will break through the mold of the 'yet one more' by way of an emancipatory *act*, our hopes are dashed by an essentially passive and formal designation of what such a project would look like. In essence, then, it appears that we are stuck with either abstracted revolutionary projects of happenstance or practical yet fantasmatically driven actualities. Does such therefore constitute an irresolvable antimony of the political that results, at best, in something of a regulative ideal or, to return to Foucault again, a conditional imperative?

On the contrary, it is imperative that we stay nonetheless with Lacan and democracy, but in a fashion that is neither miraculous nor acquisitive. In other words, the Lacanian Act, much less Badiouian militancy, will not save us, nor will an intensification of the democratic addition of 'yet one more'. Therefore, we must turn to the political itself to locate an alternative to these formulations. Let me note in advance, however, that the following remarks are a deduction from the previous and thus far only formal.

Later research will have to proceed in two directions. On the one hand, analysis must describe what the practical application of the anti-sovereign political formation as a universal localization would in fact look like. What are, in other words, its conditions of operation? On the other hand, by necessity research into concrete historical instances, already pointed to by Arendt, will need to be undertaken in terms of the conditions of their causes, generation, and dissolution, directed, again, by Arendt's query as to why they are so fleeting as to be more like apparitions than modes of appearance. In essence then, a Foucaultian genealogy of disqualified moments of the political as they lay both inside and outside of various official political discourses will have to be embarked upon, one composed of a "coupling together of scholarly erudition and local memories, which allows us to constitute a historical knowledge of struggles and to make use of that knowledge in contemporary tactics."[1] We will return to Foucault at the end of this conclusion, though it is clear that the genealogy indicated here will take place within the promotion of the political as the site of a universal agency as opposed to local sites of battle, a normative point he would soundly reject. Nonetheless, I am in full agreement with Foucault when he tells us that "we should be looking for a new right that is both antidisciplinary and emancipated from the principle of sovereignty."[2]

To continue, then, it was argued earlier that a true political formation can only submit to a totalitarian description of the 'everyone already', but this can be authentically political only to the degree that it functions as an anti-sovereignty. Hence, the totalitarian nature of the political does not revert to the cult of personality in which the *agalma* of the people is presented by some individual or subset of personas (both amounting to an Other who knows). Only a formation respecting these strictures could truly enact a traversal of the political fantasy that subjectivity requires should it not fall into the traps of an imaginary productive of defiled objects. This means that rather than a militant waiting for an act to occur, like a bolt out of the blue, a restructuring of the political forum itself must take place along the lines of a universal locality. All subjects must in fact meet with one another to discuss whatever it is that is to be discussed, not in the guise of representative and not as a perfunctory appearance that fulfills the duties rubber stamped by an organization that is sovereign nonetheless. Rather, such meetings must be decisive for the persons who form them and they must concern only themselves. Their ultimate limiting principle, however, is that they cannot be productive of new personas, new representatives of a group that in some form or another is superior or sovereign in relation to them or another group. Obversely, they cannot in any way concoct new persons who are described within the rubric of the *fremde Objekt*, persons subject to liquidation rather than the subjects of political participation. We therefore agree with Hobbes: there can effectively only be one Sovereign, but it must be everybody.

Given the forgoing, universality occurs within two registers. To the degree that personas are negated, the universal person is the political actor within the meeting. On the other hand, to the degree that all persons must meet, then the totality of persons are participatory in the democratic process in a nonrepresentational (anti-persona/anti-sovereign) way. The principle of anti-sovereignty is thus structuring and protective. It is structuring insofar as it is decisive with regard to what sort of meetings must occur (meetings which are local, universal, and preclude a representative modality that would lead to the 'yet one more' or, in the worse case, a permanent subset of legitimate personas and their concomitant expendable person). It is protective to the degree that it forecloses, as does the psychotic, any principle of the Other that would come to sublimate and represent a given person against its desire.

Totalitarian and psychotic, the political does not sound obviously appealing, but these principles proceed only to the degree that they are altered by the awareness that any political formation that is predicated on the persona, what is being here called politics, leads to a logic whereby persons are created as the negative of the fantasy and thus become expendable in various ways. This negative formation has its positive element insofar as the political qua local and universal signifies the true sight of political agency due to the fact that it requires all persons to enact their own presentation in relation to others. That is, all persons must actively engage in their local political situation in order to decide what is at stake and what is to be done. To the question: what is a person?, the only answer that is possible is one who is there and who does not stand for another. In this way, a person is not the signifier of a country or a family, a race or sexuality, nor is it the possession of an identity, but a presentation of a universal one who has something to say. Obviously, to the degree that one has been identified by another, has been produced into a positive identity (say an ethnicity or a sexuality) to negative effect, then that person will present themselves as so constituted, not in order to laud the identity, but to present the issue of its formation (as, for instance, some newly valued persona or some newly devalued object). A person is thus anyone and everyone who can speak, but only insofar as they do not speak for others who are thereby made unable to speak and, similarly, others who passively submit to them their personas. A person, therefore, is the one who must come forth with others to present in a given locality what is, so to speak, on the table for that day.

No less, these localities must talk to one another, but no action can take place by means of a representative whose power is over and above the decisions of the local persons who made them. That is, there is no office of the representative, only emissaries of the presentation, which require in their correspondence with other localities a constant discussion. But such correspondence must take place on the assumption that the power is entirely directed from below (for there is no top except as a breach of the political) and discussed horizontally along the plane of localities. To reach the top is only to be back at the bottom. Hence, the political ends where it begins. In this sense, Arendt was no doubt correct in her call for a space of freedom wherein political actors could come to present themselves. However, to the degree that this political space is fleeting and representative in opposition to the social/biological drive that undergirds the entirety of the human race, Arendt's political space replicates the perilous divisions of desire insofar as there is a negative realm to be repressed, which invariably means its undesirable return. This, however, does not mean that there are not aspects of the Arendtian structure that must be maintained, just as we must submit to the fact that Hobbesian desire is descriptive of the dilemma of existence that Lacan formally lays out.[3] Indeed, it is to Arendt's great credit that not only did she locate the universality of the person, she as well edged toward its universal political formation within a framework of anti-sovereign federations that are lateral rather than hierarchical. Let us thus enumerate these moments and their tensions in order to better understand the nature of the political.

First of all, it must be the case that agency within the political requires that all persons have a space in which they can appear to one another. This appearance must be a presentation rather than a representation insofar as it is the person and not its representative that occupies the space. Hence, as Arendt shows us, our freedom as political beings has to be *enacted*, requiring a place where it can happen: "We first become aware of freedom or its opposite in our intercourse with others. . . . But the status of freedom did not follow automatically upon the act of liberation [from the necessities of life]. Freedom needed . . . a politically organized world . . . into which each of the free men could insert himself by word and deed."[4] To the degree that there must be an appearance of persons within a space that is theirs fully, the Arendtian space of appearance cannot be denied. It is no less the case, as she argued in an earlier work, that the political realm is predicated on the principle that newness ought to always be able to enter the world:

"With the creation of man, the principle of beginning came into the world itself, which, of course, is only another way of saying that the principle of freedom was created when man was created but not before."[5] As noted in Chapter 2, Arendt opposed the public realm to that of the private sphere whose concerns are entirely social, a realm that suffers a radical uncertainty appeased only by pacifying objects of consumption—the 'living room' which cashes out into a public death. The maintenance of freedom, in her formulation, therefore requires the maintenance of a public persona, one which cannot be grasped in its essence but only revealed through 'word and deed' to others who will decipher the story and what it means. This public persona, of course, rarely if ever exists for most, for these days 'public' and 'happiness' in the political realm are an oxymoronic pair.

Such public existence is our lost treasure, according to Arendt, and one cannot really argue with her on this point. All the same, metaphors of the stage and the actor can only carry us so far, nor can this space of appearance predicate itself on the assumption of liberation from necessity. It is precisely the lack of this liberation that marks the person as expendable and, as a consequence, the site of the political. As such, if the public realm is predicated on its distinction from the private, it is unclear how this private realm, given our desire, will be kept at bay such that it does not flood over, consuming it in what amounts to an essentially passive aggressive public that, in the same breath that it demands its representation, voices a frustration which is necessary to a subject that chooses its political passivity. Insofar as the public realm is filled only with the subset of those who are given to publicity, we thus increase the numbers of those who would rather submit to an Other who knows (and thereby fails) than present themselves within the unknown of an actual encounter. As we know, it is precisely the former option that will attract most. No less, insofar as the public realm precludes entrance of the unwashed masses, leaving the latter at best to mere administration, how these mere persons will end up being defined by those who choose to occupy the political space, bolstered as they are by their passively aggressive subjects, becomes a deadly political question. Put otherwise, to the degree that we eradicate the social from the public sphere, we increase the numbers of persons who are not able to enter it and with them targets of political fantasy. Multiplying the foreign objects of our disgust, the royal "we" takes its sovereignty to heart in order to purify those who do not accord with its design.

Hence, the Arendtian dismissal of the social from the political sphere of freedom creates that which spurred its very creation, the homo who is clearly not ready to present itself for judgment given its apolitical status.

Nonetheless, Arendt seems to be aware of this fact when she verges toward a universality of the local twice, though she does not tarry with the implications, a factor which may or may not be due to her supposed belief in the need for heroic men.[6] Thus when she argues that what is required is a political formation that has yet to be thought through, Arendt locates it in the fleeting manifestations of a local presentation rather than representation, such as the town-hall meeting, the commune, and the council. In contradistinction, the finally formed United States submits to the "political science" that distances itself from its people in order to stabilize desire rather than face its core conditions: "It was precisely because of the enormous weight of the Constitution and of the experiences in founding a new body politic that the failure to incorporate the townships and the town-hall meetings, the original springs of all political activity in the country, amounted to a death sentence for them."[7] The U.S. loses its *agalma*, its treasure, the moment it submits to the separation from the Other who knows in its stead, thereby achieving a base stability at the cost of giving up on its desire in the name of the proliferation of representative fantasies. The institutionalized distance of politics that thereby ensues can thus only be represented by the need for an absolute separation from one's neighbor, a distance that can be measured in the difference between what happens in a town hall and, say, a townhouse. Nonetheless, it ought to have struck Arendt that her differentiation of the social from the political is the very result of the split and alienated desire for a Sovereign, democratically representational or otherwise, the very point with which she admonished Hobbes. Thus, Arendt is only halfway to the mark in the following: "For just as there could not be much substance to neighborly love if one's neighbor should make a brief apparition once every two years, so there could not be much substance to the admonition to love one's country more than oneself unless the country was a living presence in the midst of its citizens."[8] Rather, the undesirable neighbor is the result of that rivalry of personas (a....a') enmeshed within the broad ideological apparatuses of the Symbolic, filtered and augmented as it is by the political economy that lauds competitions over encounters.

But perhaps it is just the case that one must make decisions about *which* Arendt to emphasize, for as she notes, "[t]he trouble lies in the lack of public spaces to which the people at large would have entrance and from which an elite could be selected, or rather, where it could select itself."[9] The need for public spaces rather than a public that merely needs its space thus indicates the essential failing of the American experiment, but one can note that although Arendt identifies our dependence on sovereignty as an

essential component in the failing of the political, she nonetheless
maintains a reliance on those few who would personify the public at large
nonetheless. True, Arendt understands that sovereignty is, above all else,
reducible to tyranny,[10] but tyranny applies to the agonistic realm of representation as well insofar as the reign of the Other, however pluralized,
maintains its sovereign stance from afar. Hence, at the very moment that
she edges in on the universality of the local person, she pulls away by
replacing it with the enjoyment of the few:

> [C]ouncils . . . [are] the best instruments . . . for breaking up the
> modern mass society, with its dangerous tendency toward the forma-
> tion of pseudo-political mass movements, or rather, the best, the most
> natural way for interspersing it at the grass roots with an 'elite' that is
> chosen by no one but constitutes itself. The joys of public happiness
> and the responsibilities for public business would then become the
> share of those few from all walks of life who have a taste for public
> freedom and cannot be 'happy' without it.[11]

No doubt, Arendt maintains a kind of cosmopolitan stance on the
personification of the demos insofar as "all walks of life" are given the keys
to the city. But this reduction of the universality of all persons as the total
set of those for whom the political exists to the particularity of the few,
however motley, reintroduces sovereignty into the political. Still, there is a
reason that Arendt backs away from the universal implications of the 'right
to have rights', for in her view a 'world government' could not save us
because "it is quite conceivable, and even within the realm of practical
political possibilities, that one fine day a highly organized and mechanized
humanity will conclude quite democratically—namely by majority
decision—that for humanity as a whole it would be better to liquidate
certain parts thereof."[12] This follows, of course, to the degree that the democratic plane is crossed through, like the signifier and its signified, with a
phallic *jouissance* of antagonistic democracy. In that case, it will be necessary to find those floating persons who are to explain for the failings, in this
case, of the world at large.

Hence, when the locality of the person is noted in the council where
each individual must present itself and speak, it is removed at least by one
to the smaller subset for whom speaking is enjoyable. It may be that this
politics is the result of a fear of the political that Arendt herself located in
the person, but whatever the case may be, she literally locates the answer
and, in the same moment, pulls back from it, reproducing therefore what

the later radical democratic theorists will call antagonism, though they tend to avoid notions like public happiness. Given such a starting point, Arendt is absolutely right to fear a world organization that functions under the divisions of politics. Such an organization will, no doubt, end up producing its own terrorists, for what does a persona belimed within its internal struggle do otherwise? But the political organization that is total, or universal, in its locality and its subservience to the person does not serve the same logic. Insofar as its principle is the negation of the persona, or anti-sovereignty, the liquidation of persons is precluded. Representative democracy, on the other hand, is an aggravation of anxiety/desire—it is only the personification of democracy, never its universal realization. Nonetheless, the question remains: what would a traversed political body look like? Before answering, let us explicate in full the factors according to and against which the political must be instated.

If we begin from the position that there is no Other to the Other, that all persona-based power structures contain only the semblance of a ground in fantasy while, in actual practice, submitting to the physical instruments and ideological apparatuses of power, then we can say that the Other's Other is always filled out by its maintenance of an "Other." Hence, ideological state apparatuses are employed in order to continue the maintenance of ideological state apparatuses. It is thus not arguable that nothing concrete happens within the maintenance of a fantasy. Rather, the key to the mystery of power is that it is quite concrete in the ways in which it must maintain the facticity of the fantasy that, put bluntly, it is not a fantasy (and thus the entire body of Foucault's work could be said to be an elaboration of the embodiment of ideology and the search for its remainders). For example, the so-called process of political spin, wherein it is said that truth is subjugated in the name of producing a reality that smoothes over the edges of the real is not something that one could call external to politics. It is, from the point of view of the practice of ideology, nothing other than what one does. Given that politics is inherently unstable and divided by the plurality for which it stands, any act that is not controversial is in and of itself not a function of politics (though these acts are few and far between). Hence, a so-called spin is required to make the representation appear acceptable to a wider, more generalized plural base. Subjectivity desires this on a basic level, so power gives subjectivity what it wants (or, better put, subjectivity makes sure that what it wants is maintained via the action of its everyday mode of living, thereby supporting, as we noted earlier, power in a passive manner). If subjectivity is given a power that negates its Other, that denies its semblance and avows its person in the stead of its persona, then subjectivity is given what it doesn't want insofar as desire is concerned: it is given something Real, something unadorned and raw rather than cooked.

As examples which are embedded within the logic of 'yet one more', we can note the following small set: civil rights, gay marriage, and habeous corpus. Each is a function of the giving of law, of personification, to external entities, the recognition that persons have personas. As such, they force upon historically established personas (for instance, white people, or "Americans") identification with mere persons (black people, or "Middle Easterners"). Civil Rights are thus dressed in the codification of civility and rights, as is gay marriage, while habeous corpus, the ability to reply to justice, is somewhat closer to the universality of the person (particularly in terms of its meaning, "you have the body"). These are obviously not completely unadorned, not entirely stripped or militant in their expression. More importantly, their codification and legality implies a sedimentation in the social body, a kind of hazy glamour that obfuscates the fact that they are entirely dependent on their human supports—their transcendence can only be derived from the fact that they exist, that they are something rather than nothing, but not from any transcendental or metaphysical cause. Indeed, they transcend only to the point, in reality, to which they indicate a universality of the human, to the point, in other words, that they indicate that the persona has been removed. Let me put it differently: to hand over rights to yet another group is to say, "you are yet one more—you are now one of us, and we are a closed grouping." When a political body gives, it therefore does so by means of an assumption of sovereignty insofar as it sees the person as needing protection from the Other (from others in their ensconced and destructive personas).

Politics then becomes a battle for persons in opposition to personas, but then the question becomes whether or not this political activity, so defined, is not merely a reactionary and negatively derived definition. Is politics a process of tactical rescues, a sort of guerilla warfare that will never try to set up a permanent body? Can it only ever be wary of its own instantiation while particularizing its political acts according to needful moments in time? Is it by definition anti-institutional and thus episodic, and if so, who will ever involve themselves in it save for the usual small class of militants and power brokers who are sometimes fortunate enough to be effective? These were the questions posed to radical democracy in its democratic and Lacanian formation, and in each case, the answer is only yes.

But let us begin at the presumption that the political is the formation of the polis, and thus that it is, at base, an organization of people with power residing at some point or other in terms of where and what decisions are made. In this sense, the political must express the voice, the people, whether that voice is filtered to a singular point or spread to a mass, whether it is given organization in a plurality or made momentary in a decision that can negate itself (i.e., parliamentary or representative versus direct democracy). If we invoke the person/persona distinction and with it the fact that all political formations make sense only to the extent that, as Hobbes pointed out, commodious living is their directive and not, as Thrasymachus argued, the accumulation of power for the powerful, then we arrive at the following: insofar as commodious living is denied to any member of the polis, the political has failed. Starting from the argument that the political is there to protect the person (for the person, reduced to the state of nature, is nothing but abhorrent, a pestilence and cause to desire, and therefore destroyable so long as the persona reigns), and keeping in mind that all fantasy-based politics will, by virtue of their impossible need for completion, render some portion of the populous extraneous and therefore natural (this is captured by the following: 'the state of nature' indicates the internal externality of all political formations, which thus requires its reversibility in 'the nature of state'), a political formation is authentic only to the extent that it is maintained in the name of all persons rather than a narrowly defined set of personas, even if the latter is defined by the promise of perpetual addition.

What does this mean practically? The first result of such observations is that the proper political formulation, in order to keep its 'state of nature'/'nature of state' duality conscious rather than subsumed under fantasy, will have to be a function of the voice of the people and not the people who are given a voice. In other words, representative democracy, plutocracy, monarchy, and so on are improper political formulations insofar as they define the political in terms of a refined subset of proper voices. Furthermore, in order for the person to be given a political place which is explicit, which is *express*, there will have to be direct democracy to the extent that the people will have to speak to one another, not through a narrowly defined set that exists in the name of one another. In this sense, Ranciere is incorrect to name the political as dissensus alone—dissensus, like Laclau and Mouffe's ever-expanding inclusion, is a negative formulation that can only express the bad infinity of the 'yet one more'.[13] Therein, the political act proper can only ever be a search for yet one more person/group of persons who have not been included in the equal state. Rather, the political must start from the position of the 'everyone already'—that the entirety of the grouping is already the polis, already included in commodious living. But, on the other hand, and because it cannot be the subset of a presupposed fantasy of presence and completion, what that commodious living will be cannot cash out into thoroughly explicated and preordained set of rights, economic dispersions, or legal frameworks, except for the following: The persons who are the populace will have to speak to one another, and the proper framework of the polis is to set up the conditions of these discussions such that,

1. They take place.
2. The physical conditions for their taking place exist.
3. None are excluded qua persons.
4. A framework for their local and general enactment is established such that no subset of personas is given a place.
5. Such gatherings take center stage within legal, economic, and juridical constructions.
6. No legal, economic, or judicial construction can be predicated on anything other than the protection and promotion of persons (and thus the prevention of personas).
7. Any local discussions or decisions must take place on a horizontal plane such that the emissaries of these discussions and decisions are beholden to the locality, not vice versa.

While it is true that most representative or parliamentary democracies already give a place for such local enactments, it is also true that the representative character, in conjunction with the interests and effects of capital, stand in the way of most partaking in their own political existence or, better put, allow for the passive aggression of the political body against itself as a maintenance of its desire of the Other. As such, the so-called apathy of the political body exists in democratic regimes because there is neither a framework for universal participation nor, more importantly, a systematic process whereby decisions do not tend toward the obvious continuation of current power relations and, with it, "satisfaction" of desire. In this way, it is all well and good for many to refrain from political involvement while complaining about their political conditions nonetheless—to a large degree, the system provides enough pleasure that the risks of involvement are not desirable.

Insofar as the Arendtian political can be seen as defined against the social and reduced to the pursuit of politics by those who enjoy doing so, the political is robbed of its commodious pursuit in the name of persons (it, in effect, becomes a game for elites signifying nothing). When the political is reduced to the friend/enemy distinction, as it is for Schmitt, the person/persona distinction is valorized and therefore continued, and only calamity can be its result. No less, when the political act is reduced to a passive waiting, a hope for a Heideggerian god that may or may not save us (also known as the spontaneity of the people, the act, the seizure, etc.), should it exist, then the political is voided of agency in the only terms which are important: daily existence. Similarly, when politics is reduced to a situational waiting for moments of dissensus or disavowal of the person (the stateless, the animal, the uncounted, etc.), then politics becomes a sort of watchman's game, though it is entirely unclear if there will be any who are effectively watching when the situation arises.

Alternatively, if the political is the realization that the person/persona distinction is the condition of the human, that the state of nature is also the nature of state, that internal to the political formulation is its very external-ity by definition, then the political must be an instantiation of the Real on a daily basis. It cannot be its personification, for that is the inflammation of the persona, of the fantasy projected by the person and, as is our wont, one condensed into a small cadre of personas who maintain the conditions of their own perpetuation. Rather, the political must be localized out of the voices of the everyday, voices for whom the mundane issues (the social) are always political. Arendt, no friend to current forms of representative democracy, understood this on some level, though she had no interest in laying out its implications. Her best bet was something along the lines of local councils and town-hall meetings, though, as we have seen, she reformulated these councils into personifications of democracy. Nonethe-less, she was correct in her directionality, and it is here that we must begin to think out what localizing democracy might look like, not because there are any transcendental human rights, not because there is an identifiable positive freedom there (and not because, at this point, any one has been seized by the call of an act to do so). Rather, the reason is due to the fact that only the entirety of humanity in its universal form can save itself, and it can only save itself from itself, from its own personality and in the face of the fact that there is no right to have rights. For this reason, a localized political structure that is designed around the gathering of all persons would be the true instantiation of the political qua commodious living for the universal person.

Hence all further inquiry into the subject ought to look for the concrete conditions for such an enactment of a global polis of persons. One clear result from these inquiries is that the notions of sovereignty and nation-hood ought to be done away with, at least in their current condition as supports for personas. The idea of sovereignty, as has been pointed out by many, is in many ways a cover for unbridled excess in the name of freedom and protection from the aggressions of others. But it is also a fine example of the manner in which the logic of the persona is used to intensify itself and therefore create the conditions for situations such as the Holocaust, Guantanamo, and Darfur, to name a few. To the extent that the world polis divides itself into sovereignties (and sovereignties within sovereignties), it remains entrenched in an endless dynamic that must maintain itself as a continuation of the person/persona divide. International legal bodies, including the U.N., clearly bridge this divide, and international legal treatises, such as the Geneva Conventions, are positive attempts to extricate the human mass from its self-subjugation. But as reflections on the divisions of sovereignty within current political formations, their attempts are by necessity piecemeal, and so they invariably fail, falling as they do into the 'yet one more' rather than the 'everyone already'. The only true and sovereign position is that the person cannot be made subordinate to the persona, that the 'everyone already' means the assumption that the polis is composed of everyone, already. Hence, the immigrant, the criminal, the terrorist, the homo is not in advance an externality, but is already internally a part of the definition of the polis.

There is a last conflict to be worked out here, however, which is that of desire. To the degree that subjectivity, in a very basic sense, desires its personification, or creates a personification by necessity out of its desire, the road to a universal locality of the person seems inherently daunting. While the latter is the formal result of the quandary of desire, it is also that which few will, as noted, spontaneously seek. Philosophically, of course, this is not an issue, since philosophy can take the cover of tarrying with the concept and thus dismiss the question of practical application. Nonetheless, insofar as the political is the practical, and insofar as it is the very site of an agency that has been, for the most part, submissive and docile, attempting to locate the manner in which such a presentation of the person can be made possible is, as noted earlier, the goal of future work on this subject. This, as I noted at the beginning of this conclusion, therefore requires a genealogical investigation into the historical conditions of its possibility. Of course, to the degree that the presentation thus far has been systematic and prescriptive, Foucault would no doubt find it not worth commentary. Indeed, Foucault's dismissal of sovereignty expels along with it the entirety of Hobbes' edifice, for as he says, Hobbes' theory of war is really a dismissal of war, a way of indicating that subjectivity desires Sovereignty no matter what, and hence opposing views, views that would indicate a real attack on normalized discourse, are rendered null: "It [Hobbes's discourse] is saying, war or no war, defeat or no defeat, Conquest or covenant, it all comes down to the same thing: 'It's what you wanted, it is you, the subjects, who constituted the sovereignty that represents you.' The problem of the Conquest is therefore resolved."[14] To this, however, one must ask Foucault, who, as we noted earlier, seeks an anti-disciplinary, anti-sovereign modality of right, what an emancipated politics would look like. No doubt, Foucault is correct insofar as Hobbes wished to negate all opposition so as to move on with the unary Sovereign, but what Foucault provides in its place is a theory of constant warfare that ends in what is essentially more warfare. It is thus the case, then, that Foucault's theory can only be one which submits to the accumulation of 'yet one more', that can only ever be the search for new outposts of opposition. No doubt, Hobbesian and, with it, Lacanian subjectivity wants its Sovereign, but this is the desire of the persona, not the traversed person for whom any anti-disciplinary political formation would exist.

This leaves us with a sort of beginning, at least in terms of further research. As such, the following are the primary issues to be worked out:

1. What are concrete, historical instances of the 'everyone already' or, more specifically, what historical moments exhibit a logic that allows or motivates personas of desire to exist as persons of presentation?
2. How can these concrete instances be expanded into a model for a world body of the 'everyone already'?
3. Where does Marx fit into this formulation and, therefore, in what way does the 'everyone already' replicate and, perhaps, augment the notion of communism as an actual expression of the person?
4. To what degree is the universal nature of the political a reflection of and possibility within what is called globalization (including its economic, cultural, political, and technological factor)?
5. Taking leave from Foucault's idea that universals, like personas, do not exist, save for their imaginary instantiation in concrete practices, we ask the question: what is the place of criminality within the 'everyone already'?[15] In other words, how does one create the distinction between the criminal as legitimate threat and the criminal as convenient designation for the person? One principle is already clear: any act that attempts to negate the person in the name of the persona is a criminal act with regard to the commodious life of the polis.

Whatever future research may reveal, the impasse of democracy at this point, particularly insofar as it fails repeatedly to live up to its ideals of freedom, liberty, and equality while producing countless persons upon which to drop its failings, cannot be breached save for a movement past its representational formations. As such, the nature of the political requires us to be against the personification of democracy and for the universalization of the person in and through its local presentation. Otherwise, we will be endlessly compelled by the fantastic repetitions of mere politics.

Notes

1 Michel Foucault, *"Society Must Be Defended": Lectures at the College de France, 1975–1976*, trans. David Macey (New York: Picador, 2003): 8, hereafter referred to as *Society*.

2 Ibid., 40.

3 Here we must agree and disagree with Foucault's dismissal of Hobbes as politically irrelevant. For Foucault, Hobbes' clever sleight of hand is to negate political opposition by arguing that opposition is something that we more or less cannot help. Hence, one ought to give it up in the name of the Sovereign. There is no doubt a truth in this, but once placed within the perspective of the Lacanian subject, it becomes clear that the ideological struggle that goes to define subjectivity also describes the Foucaultian struggle: for do not local power struggles with no end merely replicate the drama of the subject again and again and, no less, do they not replicate the logic of the radical democratic antagonism?

4 BPF, 148.

5 HC, 177.

6 Readings of Arendt thus often vacillate between seeing her as emphasizing a public space helmed by Heroic Men (Canovan) and one weaved together by storytellers (Benhabib). That Arendt subscribed to each view, depending on the text one is reading, is at play is perhaps best shown in Maurizio Passerin D'Entreves' *The Political Philosophy of Hannah Arendt*.

7 OR, 238–9.

8 Ibid., 253.

9 Ibid., 277.

10 OR, 153.

11 OR, 279.

12 *Origins*, 299.

13 See, for instance, Ranciere's *The Philosopher and His Poor*. For Ranciere, the authentic political moment, marked as it is by a dissensus, occurs when the normal state of consensus, which is, as he terms it, a function of the police, is broken apart by those who have been excluded from the norm, or by the 'part that has no part': "Politics only exists through the bringing off of the equality of anyone and everyone in a vacuous freedom of a part of the community that deregulates any count of parts. The equality that is the nonpolitical condition of politics does not show up here for what it is: it only appears as the figure of wrong." *Dis-agreement*, 61. As should be clear, Ranciere's view of the authentic political moment is

thus defined by a politics of a 'yet one more', whereby the disruptive addition of the excluded is found to have a place of equality within the previously smaller community. In this way, Ranciere's political approach is subject to the phallic *jouissance* of a politics of accumulation, however defined by disruption the new additions will have. Hence, his theory requires a systematic politics of exclusion so that future inclusions can take place.

14 *Society*, 98. Ranciere makes what essentially amounts to the same dismissal of Hobbes insofar as his systematic formation precludes any externality. See *Dis-Agreement*, 77.

15 "Let's suppose that universals do not exist. And then I put the question to history and historians: How can you write history if you do not accept a priori the existence of things like the state, society, the sovereign, and subjects? It was the same question in the case of madness. My question was not: Does madness exist. . . ? The method consisted in saying: Let's suppose that madness does not exist," Michel Foucault, *The Birth of Biopolitics: Lectures at the College de France, 1978–1979*, trans. Graham Burchell (New York: Palgrave Macmillan, 2008): 3.

Index

Agamben, Giorgio 3, 51, 54, 69, 112
Arendt, Hannah
  biological violence and the social 72–5,
    81, 88, 102, 106, 110–11, 153, 166,
    171, 184
  councils and critique of sovereignty 5,
    14, 50, 66, 181, 185–7, 191
  freedom and mere politics 77, 81, 183–4
  Hobbes, critique of 5, 16–17, 34–43
  natality 7, 65, 67, 77, 124, 125, 169
  persona vs. homo and universal
    human 6–7, 13, 14, 78–9, 89, 92,
    110–11, 125, 148, 156, 184
  phenomenological violence 7, 65–6, 74
  public realm and the Other 76, 184
  psychological violence 69–72
  psychology, rejection of 66, 69
  rights 52, 78, 144–5, 186
  soul and torn heart 7, 69–71, 75, 88, 95,
    102, 125
  space of appearance 144, 183–4
  state of nature 65, 67
  stateless 50, 51–2, 64, 67–9, 71–2

Badiou, Alain 13, 138, 160, 174 n. 3,
  178 n. 75, 180
Baumgold, Deborah 24
Borch-Jacobsen, Mikkel 130 n. 33
Bremer, L. Paul 41
Butler, Judith 112–13, 122, 160

democracy
  democratic consensus 17–18, 43, 91,
    138–9, 146
  fantasy of persona 181–3, 185, 189–91
  passive aggressive 190

personification 12–13, 14, 151, 187, 194
representative democracy and
  anxiety 138–41, 187
representative democracy's need for
  undemocratic actions 139–40, 157,
  161
sovereign nature of 136–7
Dick, Phillip K. 173
Dor, Joel 95, 129 n. 6

Easton, David 21–3

Fanon, Frantz 135
Fink, Bruce 96–7, 113, 130 n. 20, 130 n. 34
Foucault, Michel 22, 38, 79, 180–1, 187,
  192–3, 194 n. 3
Fraser, Nancy 44 n. 9
Freud, Sigmund 11, 18, 27, 28, 90, 97–8,
  102–3, 107, 109, 117
Friedman, Milton 20–1, 49

Gramsci, Antonio 11, 17, 19, 146, 149, 159
Gray, John 20

Hardin, Russell 5, 6–7, 12, 22, 23–4, 35,
  43 n. 5, 153
Heidegger, Martin 130 n. 20, 137, 142,
  178–9 n. 75
Hersh, Seymor M. 86 n. 66
Herzog, Werner 129 n. 11
Hobbes, Thomas
  against bourgeois individualism 5–6,
    37–8
  desire and anxiety 10, 16–24, 27–32
  ideology and interpellation 6, 16–17, 19,
    35–8, 40

Hobbes, Thomas (*Cont'd*)
  language and meaning 25–6
  motion 8, 25, 27–8, 30, 50, 57, 76, 88,
       102, 124
  passions, imaginary form of 27–30
  persona 77–8
  power 27–9
  reason and irrationality 24–5, 30–3, 40
  sovereign 27, 32–3, 35–9, 76
  summum bonum, lack of 9, 42, 57
  thief and the contract (state of
       nature) 56–7, 82–3 n. 11, 98, 100
Hobsbawm, Eric 162

Kristeva, Julia 64
Kymlicka, Will 44 n. 11

Lacan, Jacques
  alienation 96–9, 107–8
  application to political realm,
       problems with 11, 115–19, 126–8
  Arendtian subject, explanation of 9, 106,
       110–11, 124–6
  death drive 28, 90, 103, 104–6
  desire and anxiety 8, 97–8, 115
  desire and persona 103–4
  fantasy and ideology 107
  fragmented body 92–3
  fundamental fantasy 11, 116–17, 119,
       124–5, 126, 139, 140, 163–4, 169–70
  imaginary 19, 28, 89, 90, 91, 93–5,
       99–100, 103–4, 107, 108, 111,
       115–17, 122, 125, 127, 128, 129 n. 5,
       129 n. 11, 132 n. 58, 134–5 n. 93,
       154, 181
  jouissance 8, 10–11, 90, 99, 106, 107,
       113, 114, 118–19, 121–4, 125–7,
       134 n. 93, 138–40, 151–3, 154, 186,
       194–5 n. 13
  mirror stage 92–5
  myth of motherhood 95–6
  objet a 3, 46 n. 35, 64
  Other, m(O)ther, and
       Sovereignty 99–100
  paternal metaphor and primary
       repression 21, 85, 108–10

phallus and its misreading 89, 112–15
  primary signifier as desire of other 97,
       108–10
  real 2, 3–5, 107, 111, 120, 125, 131
       n. 48, 134–5 n. 93
  separation 116–17
  sexuation 104–5, 122–4
  signifier 97, 100–3
  symbolic 8, 90, 105, 108, 109, 114–16,
       118–19, 122, 125, 129 n. 5,
       132 n. 58, 169, 185
  traversing the fantasy 118–22
Laclou, Ernesto 152, 158, 176 n. 47
Laclou, Ernesto and Chantalle Mouffe 10,
       137, 145–52, 154, 155, 156, 157,
       160, 161, 162–3, 164, 172, 175 n. 33,
       189
Lakoff, George 177 n. 57
Lefort, Claude 10, 53, 87, 137, 142–5, 146,
       148, 149, 151, 154, 162, 164
Locke, John
  anxiety and desire 57–8
  desire of the demos, problem of 10–11,
       59–61
  freedom and property 20, 21, 55–6
  monarchy 18, 62
  reason as successful 21
  thief and the contract (state of
       nature) 56–7
  summum bonum, lack of 54

Macpherson, C. B. 5, 16–17, 33, 34,
       49–50
Martinich, A. P. 43 n. 1
Marx, Karl 20, 55, 146, 164, 166, 170,
       178 n. 62, 193
Mehta, Uday 60, 83 n. 25

Pasquino, Pasquale 43–4 n. 5
Passerin D'Entreves, Maurizio 194 n. 6
person
  anti-representational nature of 13
  negative effects on desire/negative object
       of ideology 5, 8–9, 18–19, 50–4,
       60–1, 76–82, 89–91, 98, 104–7,
       117–19, 124–8

presentation
  universal human/center of the
      political 4, 13–14, 136–7,
      see conclusion 180–94
persona
  creation of object of revulsion 88–9, 91,
      126–8, 180–2
  function of politics 145
  imaginary/sovereign structure of 3–5,
      9–10, 43, 50–4, 55, 60, 68–9, 76–82,
      105–6, 117–19, 124–8, 138–41,
      see conclusion 180–2
  representative democracy 13–14
  'yet one more' 188
Plato 5, 15 n. 4
political
  anti-representational space of the
      person 4–6, 13–14, 17–18, 80–2,
      136–8, 180–94
  empty center 142
  state of nature and the person 42–3,
      49–54, 62–4, 80–2
  symptom of politics 103–4
  universal presentation of 'everyone
      already' 13–14, 18–19, 41, 181,
      189–90, 192–4
politics
  creation of the person 53, 79, 89–90,
      103–4, 138–9, 174 n. 1, 180, 182,
      186, 194
  Lacanian phallus 89
  representative and imaginary form of
      'yet one more' 13–14, 41, 81, 124,
      127–8, 139–41, 185–9, 194–5 n. 13

radical democracy
  intensification of anxiety 10–11, 140–1
  requirement of an excluded body 11–12

tension between descriptive and
      prescriptive claims 187–8
Ranciere, Jacques 10, 15 n. 4, 178 n. 75,
      189, 194–5 n. 13
rights 52–3, 80–1, 190–1
Rousseau, Jean-Jacques 2, 20, 56, 61–2

Safouan, Mustafa 133 n. 68
Sandel, Michael J. 20
Schmitt, Carl 4, 5, 51, 53, 80, 81, 86 n. 67,
      136, 174 n. 1, 190–1
Smith, Adam 123, 134 n. 90
state of nature
  internal externality 54, 61, 78, 80–1, 87,
      145
  nature of state 3, 6, 63, 91, 149, 189, 191
  ontological reality 6
Stavrakakis, Yannis 10, 11, 137, 154–9,
      161, 164, 176 n. 36
Strauss, Leo 18, 31

Tuck, Richard 29

Verhaeghe, Paul 94, 103, 104, 121, 131 n. 35

Wittgenstein, Ludwig 26–7, 147

Žižek, Slavoj
  capitalism, critique of 163–7
  democracy as administration 160–3
  identification with symptom 156
  political act 12, 141, 159–60, 168–71,
      174 n. 3
  political act, problems with 12–13, 171–3
  radical democracy, critique of 11, 137,
      140
  reality as secondary effect of fantasy and
      jouissance 161–3, 167–8